Working People
of Philadelphia
1800–1850

TEMPLE
UNIVERSITY
PRESS
Philadelphia

BRUCE LAURIE

Working People of Philadelphia, 1800-1850

Library of Congress Cataloging in Publication Data

Laurie, Bruce.
Working People of Philadelphia, 1800–1850.

Bibliography: p.
Includes index.
1. Labor and laboring classes—Pennsylvania—
Philadelphia—History.   I. Title.
HD8085.P53L38   305.5′6   79-28679
ISBN 0-87722-168-5

Temple University Press, Philadelphia 19122
© 1980 by Temple University. All rights reserved
Published 1980
Printed in the United States of America

To the memory of my father
Phillip Laurie

Contents

Acknowledgments

This book would not have seen the light of day without the assistance of several institutions and numerous friends and colleagues. John Platt and Tony Roth of the Historical Society of Pennsylvania and Lillian Tonkin of the Library Company gave generously of their time and expertise, and graciously complied with my excessive requests. The staffs of the Presbyterian Historical Society and Old St. George's Methodist Episcopal Church directed me to a treasure-trove of primary and secondary material that greatly enriched this manuscript. The research performed at these repositories was supported in part by a grant from the National Endowment for the Humanities.

It is difficult to imagine a more cooperative group of colleagues than my fellow historians at the University of Massachusetts at Amherst. They are a reservoir of inspiration and dialogue. Stephen Nissenbaum, Paul Boyer, Ronald Story, Leonard Richards, and Robert Griffith helped me think through perplexing issues, and I am richer for their rigor and spirit of collegiality.

Theodore Hershberg, Director of the Philadelphia Social History Project at the University of Pennsylvania, deserves special mention. He awakened me to the possibilities of quantitative methods and although we disagreed over the nature of the historical process and relative value of statistical techniques in revealing its secrets, he never wavered in his personal generosity or support for my scholarship. He accorded me free access to the files and records of the P.S.H.P., sharpened my understanding of the antebellum city, and made my stays in Philadelphia intellectually rewarding and socially enjoyable.

I am deeply indebted to two distinguished scholars and dear friends. Milton Cantor, my colleague at the University of Massachusetts, read the entire manuscript and offered invaluable editorial advice. This book is much improved for his efforts and I am profoundly grateful for his unselfish dedication to my work. Those who have had the privilege of working with David Montgomery, formerly at the University of Pittsburgh and now at Yale University, know of his contagious enthusiasm and extraordinary intellectual powers. He has been a constant source of scholarly and political inspiration, a rare individual whose contribution to my own maturation and that of untold members of the profession is hard to capture in prose and impossible to repay. He has read and criticized more drafts of this work than either of us cares to remember and my fondest hope is that the final product is worthy of the time and effort he has invested in me.

My greatest debt is to my spouse, Leslie Tarr Laurie. Her quiet persuasion prodded me along; her love and companionship sustained me in moments of doubt. She is the invisible shepherd of this work.

Introduction

This book explores the contours of working-class cultures in antebellum Philadelphia. It is a contribution to what has been called the "new labor history," and like previous works in this genre, it leans heavily on the concepts of class and culture.[1] Such terms have evoked some confusion and it is helpful at the start to define how they are used in this context.

The most basic and for years the prevailing definition of class in Marxian terms implied a set of structural or objective relationships. Classes thus consist of individuals sharing a common relationship to the means of production, and typically are designated as workers, on the one hand, and employers, on the other. Most practitioners of the new labor history employ this Marxian notion and it informs this study as well. More to the point, this analysis assumes that, in purely structural terms, recognizably modern classes of workers and employers took shape with the emergence of industrial capitalism in the opening decades of the nineteenth century, although, as we shall see, wage earners performed their jobs in vastly different settings and their employers were differentiated according to the scale of their enterprises.

The key word here is structural. In this sense, class refers strictly to the objective conditions in which individuals found themselves and it is to be distinguished from the subjective dimension of class, or class consciousness. Class, or class consciousness, is the way human actors interpret and give meaning to their own experiences and circumstances, and as E. P. Thompson argues, it may be understood as a "social and cultural formulation." Or, in Thompson's unforgettable

contention, "Class consciousness is the way in which these experiences are handled in cultural terms," and culture itself is reflected
"traditions, value-systems, ideas, and institutional forms."[2]

In applying this conceptual frame to early nineteenth-century
England, Thompson uncovered a single cultural expression which
was self-consciously radical. His *Making of the English Working
Class* set off a flurry of scholarship in America and countless efforts
to reproduce his magisterial work.[3] Among the most successful of
these were Paul Faler and Alan Dawley's studies of the shoeworkers
of Lynn, Massachusetts; and their work reveals a more complex
cultural landscape. They uncovered not one but three forms of
working-class culture—loyalists, rebels, and traditionalists—with
unique organizational matrices, recreational interests, and values.[4]

My debt to Faler and Dawley should be obvious to anyone
casually familiar with their seminal work. This study also posits the
existence of distinctive worker cultures, but differs from their
treatment in several respects. First, having been influenced by recent
investigations of the ethnocultural basis of voter loyalty, it identifies
religion as a major component of worker culture.[5] Rationalism,
evangelical Protestantism and, to a lesser extent, orthodox Protestantism and Catholicism are seen as critical forces in the shaping of
worker values and practice. Second, it seeks to disclose the backgrounds and urban experiences, both cultural and material, of the
workers comprising each cultural category. Third, it examines how
such cultures changed over time under the impact of demographic
and industrial change.

A few caveats are in order before we begin. I had the option of
treating the cultures under analysis in terms of tendencies or as ideal
types. There are advantages and liabilities to each approach, and
after weighing the alternatives, I chose the latter—in part for reasons
of convenience and in part because it permits rendering each culture
in more vivid form. History, of course, is not always so neat. It does
not come wrapped in tiny bundles, and scholars who package the
data in this way run the dual risk of distorting the record and of
ignoring individuals and groups that do not conform to the
categories. My response to the first peril is that I have done my best
not to reduce the cultures to caricatures. As for the second, I can only
plead that one cannot do everything, even in a concerted effort to be

thorough. At least two groups—women and Blacks—do not figure *systematically* in what follows. Their omission stems not from bias but from the limitations of the record. Documentary evidence on the cultural lives of women and Blacks is painfully thin. Smatterings of what is available suggest that both groups may be subsumed under one or more of the categories used in this study, but, alas, the record is insufficiently compelling. Consequently, the exploration of the cultural lives of antebellum Philadelphia's working-class women and Blacks has been left to other scholars.

Bruce Laurie
Amherst, Massachusetts

Part One:
The Work Setting
1800-1850

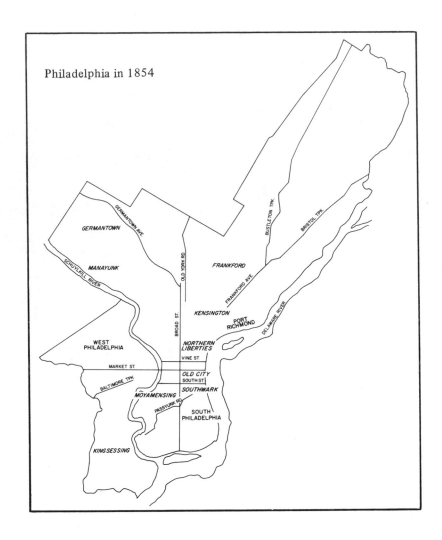

Philadelphia in 1854

GERMANTOWN

GERMANTOWN AVE

MANAYUNK

SCHUYLKILL RIVER

OLD YORK RD

FRANKFORD

BUSTLETON TPK.

BRISTOL TPK.

FRANKFORD AVE.

KENSINGTON

BROAD ST

PORT
RICHMOND

DELAWARE RIVER

WEST
PHILADELPHIA

NORTHERN
LIBERTIES

VINE ST

MARKET ST

BALTIMORE TPK.

OLD CITY

SOUTH ST

MOYAMENSING

SOUTHWARK

PASSYUNK RD

SOUTH
PHILADELPHIA

KINGSESSING

Reproduced from Allen F. Davis and Mark H. Haller, eds., *The Peoples of Philadelphia: A History of Ethnic Groups and Lower-Class Life, 1790-1940* (Philadelphia: Temple University Press, 1973).

The Sources of
Industrial Diversity

1

On July 4, 1788, Philadelphians commemorated the ratification of the federal Constitution. The jubilant occasion came as a welcome respite from years of war weariness and recession that followed the signing of the Treaty of Paris and, buoyed by the promise of the new government, Quaker City residents turned out in droves. Nearly 17,000 of them, or just about a fourth of the population, deserted counting house and workshop to take part in an unprecedented display of patriotic fervor and national élan. The form of the celebration, a procession of leading citizens and occupational groups, testified to the importance of handicrafts in Philadelphia's economy. Representatives of the wide variety of trades outfitted in the dress of their vocations—robust German brewers, craft-proud printers, lowly seamen and hand loom weavers—drew colorful floats and bore banners emblazoned with mottoes expressing hope in the new nation. "May the federal government revive our trade," proclaimed the

Material on work environments has been adapted from an article I wrote with Prof. Mark Schmitz entitled "Manufacture and Productivity: The Making of an Industrial Base, 1850–1880," in *Towards an Interdisciplinary History of the City: Work, Space, Family and Group Experience in Nineteenth-century Philadelphia,* ed. Theodore Hershberg (New York: Oxford University Press, forthcoming).

bakers' flag; "May industry ever be encouraged," declared the porters' masthead.[1]

It was thoroughly appropriate that artisans figured prominently. Tradesmen made up nearly half the work force, even though Philadelphia was still a commercial port vending commodities produced in other locales. No single calling dominated. Carpenters, bricklayers, and other building tradesmen accounted for one-fifth of the artisans, followed by tailors and clothing workers (17 to 19 percent), leather workers (13 to 15 percent), and so on.[2]

These men found employment, as David Montgomery observes, partly because of the social division of labor enforced by urban living. Unlike rural homesteaders, city dwellers were unable to produce basic necessities, and had to turn to the exchange economy for goods and services. This demand kept artisans busy supplying food, clothing, and housing, as well as books, newspapers, and other commodities that were so much a part of city life. The social structure itself also created a market for locally made products. Philadelphia's fashion-conscious merchants and professionals, aping their European counterparts, had a flair for expensive clothing and for fine household furnishings. Artisans who were capable of replicating Continental styles did a brisk business.[3]

The vast majority of such craftsmen were independent producers who owned a set of tools, worked alone or with an apprentice or two, and would hire a journeyman when markets picked up. Home and workshop were one and the same, or at least in close proximity. Masters would set aside a room or floor of their dwellings or set up shop in an adjoining edifice. The ambience of these workshops was casual. Master and helper worked at their own pace, fashioning goods to order or occasionally building up small inventories for sale to browsing shoppers.[4] John Fanning Watson, an early chronicler of the Quaker City with vivid memories of his adolescent years, captured the tone and texture of handicraft production. In his youth, he reminisced,

> No masters were seen exempted from personal labour in any branch of business—living on the profits derived from many hired journeymen; and no places were sought out at much expense, and display of signs and decorated windows, to allure custom. Then almost every apprentice, when of age, ran his equal chance for his share of business in his

neighborhood, by setting up for himself, and, with an apprentice or two, getting into a cheap location, and by dint of application and good work, recommending himself to his neighborhood. Thus, every shoemaker or taylor was a man for himself. . . . In those days, if they did not aspire to much, they were more sure of the end—a decent competency in an old age.[5]

Other accounts indicate that Watson's memory was selective. He described only one side of the world of production and ignored a small minority of proprietors who broke out of this traditional mold. More enterprising and ambitious than the neighborhood master remembered by Watson, they are best described as entrepreneurs eager to expand by exploiting wider markets. Concentrated in light consumer goods, they turned out shoes, clothing, furniture, and other commodities in quantity and retailed a portion of their wares to local customers but reserved the bulk for Philadelphia merchants and general store owners in the surrounding countryside. Because they dealt in volume and tied up large sums of capital in raw materials, entrepreneurs were forced to pay more attention to costs and labor costs in particular.[6]

Such imperatives goaded entrepreneurs into altering habitual trade practice. As a study of apprentice indentures shows, relations between employer and apprentice turned increasingly on market-place considerations at the expense of tradition. Late eighteenth-century masters gradually refrained from honoring filial obligations to apprentices, whether this meant commemorating promotions to journeyman status with gifts or teaching apprentices to read and write. They offered cash payments in lieu of the customary suit of clothes or set of tools and limited educational responsibilities to teaching the "art and mystery" of their craft.[7]

The harmony between employer and journeyman also showed signs of strain. Evidence of stress, if not outright conflict, can be gleaned from the groupings of the Federal Procession. Masters and journeymen representing at least two trades marched in separate cadres, and while they mingled in every other craft, the euphoria of the moment did not carry over into workplaces.[8] Journeymen printers and cordwainers formed combinations and struck for rate increases in the 1790s, and during the following two decades masters and journeymen in a dozen callings organized distinct trade societies, indication enough that each side recognized peculiar class interests.[9]

These early incidents of class conflict are instructive. They indicate that contrary to view put forth by John R. Commons and his associates, class antagonism erupted long before employers reached out for national or even regional markets. Philadelphia employers who collided with journeymen over wages were retailers linked to local and metropolitan sales. Yet it is clear that most businesses were still quite small at the turn of the century and class lines remained fluid. The average journeyman could look forward to setting up his own shop, earning a modest income as an independent producer, and perhaps accumulating a sufficient surplus to tide him through his declining years.

Several forces conspired to keep down growth and the scale of enterprise. Capital was dear and quite scarce for entrepreneurs. Bankers and merchants regarded production as too risky to merit much capital, and preferred to invest in the orthodox channels of land and shipping and in the growing areas of marine insurance and transportation.[10] Import merchants in need of capital easily outbid entrepreneurs in money markets and deterred industrial growth with their mass importation of foreign manufactures. British-made goods, for example, had a competetive advantage in American markets and such imports daunted the development of many industries, cotton textiles being one example.

If the experience of John Bedford indicates anything, it is that the locus of the market also impeded growth. Philadelphia's largest boot and shoe manufacturer around 1800, Bedford hired twenty to twenty-four workmen at home and at his shop, and built up a thriving business on custom and retail trade. His footwear enjoyed a good reputation among upper-class Philadelphians, owing to his accomplished journeymen, who turned out current European styles and added the Continental touch of inscribing the customer's name on the inside lining of boots and shoes. Bedford's fortunes took a turn for the worse, however, when, in 1800, local markets contracted and inventories piled up. His capital "tied up in stock" and faced with impending ruin, Bedford was struck with "the idea of going southward" in order "to force a sale" and boarded a vessel bound for Charleston, where he contracted with two customers and made bargains with others in the countryside.[11] He returned home prepared to fill orders in excess of $4,000, but was confronted with irate journeymen; they demanded a wage advance and laid down their tools when Bedford invoked the iron law of contractual obligations and stood firm. The strike interrupted production and forced him to default on some orders.[12]

Bedford's travail is as revealing to historians as it was frustrating to him. It indicates that local markets were large enough to bear relatively large scale enterprise, but they were easily saturated and insufficiently flexible to sustain growth. Entrepreneurs like Bedford realized as much in seeking southern customers, and the city's renowned merchant princes joined together with them in an effort to expand commercial outlets. Led by Thomas Pym Cope and Samuel Breck, Philadelphia's men of commerce grew uneasy over the city's commercial prospects and competetive position, as Congress debated building a National Road to the south and New Yorkers discussed digging the Erie Canal. Both developments and alarming rumors that New Yorkers were also about to inaugurate packets and thus corner the coastal and European trade, galvanized Philadelphia's business-men and boosters, including the journalist and political economist Matthew Carey. They formed an impressive lobby to perfect oceanic transport and develop inland facilities.[13]

Pooling resources, these promoters invested heavily in trans-Atlantic and coastal shipping after 1810. By 1821 a group headed by Cope launched the city's first transatlantic packet line and merchants with interests in the South followed suit in the coastal trade. Packets proved something of a sensation. They were more reliable than regular traders and transients and quickly displaced both carriers, hauling more than half of Philadelphia's coastal trade by the late 1820s.[14] Construction of the Erie Canal set off a panic in commercial circles and stimulated merchants and entrepreneurs to new levels of activity. Determined to keep pace with their New York rivals, they poured surplus capital into canal and navigation companies, and constructed a network of waterways radiating outward from the city. They also turned their attention to the state legislature and mounted a feverish lobbying effort to extract appropriations for a system that would compete with the Erie. This ambitious project became the obsession of the Pennsylvania Society for the Promotion of Internal Improvements, a Philadelphia group that eventually branched out to nearly every county in the Keystone state. Hoping to marshall support for the east-west connection, Philadelphia leaders called a convention at Harrisburg in 1825, but it attracted scores of back-country delegates, each of whom had a pet project and a voice that mattered in the legislature. This merger of urban and rural interests made a powerful impact. Lawmakers incorporated the designs of both groups in planning and funding the state canal system.[15]

Beginning in the late twenties the state of Pennsylvania commenced what one writer aptly describes as a "building craze," which left behind nearly 900 miles of canal beds by the 1840s. The heart of the system, the Main Line, connected Philadelphia with Pittsburgh through a series of waterways and a mechanized portage railway that scaled the eastern slope of the Alleghenies. Branch canals linked both cities (and Harrisburg) to their hinterlands.[16] The railroad mania occurred during the midst of canal fever. Trunk lines criss-crossed the eastern anthracite fields by the late twenties and they were followed by intrastate lines financed by private interests and public funds. The state-sponsored Philadelphia and Columbia Railroad provided an alternative to the canal route to Harrisburg in 1834, the same year in which the Philadelphia and Trenton had its maiden run. Four years later the last spike was driven into the track of the Philadelphia, Wilmington, and Baltimore; and in the mid-forties workmen began constructing the Pennsylvania Railroad which carried its first freight in 1852.[17] By the time it was completed, the state boasted 900 miles of track, virtually all of which had been built in the previous decade.[18]

The modernization of transportation proved to be one of the most far-reaching innovations of the age. Few Pennsylvanians, whether they lived in congested Philadelphia or in the state's rural areas, evaded these tentacles of commerce. Both "blacklanders" and yeoman who raised crops for exchange and produced necessities for use were forced into a new relationship to the market. The rural invasion of canals delivered commodities to their front porches, and brought about a price revolution, as water carriers gradually displaced waggoners and other slower and more expensive modes of transport. Costs per ton mile plummeted on canals between 1820 and 1850, and merchants and manufacturers, in passing the saving on to consumers, lured rural homesteaders into commodity markets. Farmers began to consume items traditionally produced at home: or as a keen observer noted in the late 1830s, "Formerly no man thought of going to a tailor for a shirt. Now everybody goes to one even for a handkerchief."[19]

The transportation revolution also helped transform the structure of opportunities in the countryside. Farmers were already on the threshold of a crisis by the last third of the eighteenth century, when the best farm land was cleared and settled and minimum-sized holdings were reached. Population pressure was so great in some areas that families shifted to impartible inheritance in order to ensure at least one son a workable farm. Second and third sons, deprived of rights to family holdings, were forced to seek alternatives. Some moved to central and western Pennsylvania or to remoter areas in the Ohio Valley. Others left farming altogether and apprenticed themselves to tradesmen in nearby towns and villages. Still others postponed moving by renting or mortgaging land and turning to tenancy. Tenants continued to have relatively large families and their sons reached maturity by the second decade of the nineteenth century, which placed additional strains on the population-to-land ratio.[20]

The coming of canals exacerbated the predicament of poor farmers, small tradesmen, and their sons. Land adjacent to inland water routes skyrocketed in value, which induced owners to raise rents beyond the means of lessees and expel tenants, and the influx of urban commodities undermined many independent tradesmen. An unknown number of displaced Pennsylvanians, especially the young, followed in the footsteps of previous migrants and went westward in search of farm land. Others, and perhaps a growing majority, went eastward to the Quaker City in hopes of finding a better life.[21]

The flight to the city is largely responsible for the urban population explosion in the antebellum period. Between 1800 and 1850, Philadelphia grew from 81,000 residents to over 408,000, and, as John Modell has shown, rural-urban migration and natural increase far outstripped immigration as the principal generators of growth prior to the 1840s. Immigrants were no more than 10 percent of the population in 1830 and did not arrive in appreciable numbers until the forties. As late as 1840, then, native-born Americans pre-dominated and many of them were rural-urban migrants forced off the land or drawn to the city by the promise of advancement.[22]

The forging of the transportation network and massive migration from the countryside, in connection with the expansion of credit and imposition of erratic but protective tariffs, solved major problems for urban entrepreneurs. In combination such developments supplied access to regional and distant markets, provided a relatively cheap, if still inadequate, labor pool, and offered more credit. Endowed with these factors of production, entrepreneurs changed Philadelphia from a commercial port with a broad but shallow industrial base to a major center of commodity production, whose industrial output reached $140 million and was second only to New York on the eve of the Civil War.[23]

Such industrial growth necessarily altered the landscape of Philadelphia. Colonial patterns of land use and spatial relations, which mixed together rich and poor, home and workplace, persisted well into the nineteenth-century, but were beginning to yield to more familiar patterns of segregation and specialization. The gradual industrialization of the core chased some of the rich and well-born to the greener pastures of the western fringe, where they built elegant mansions on tree-lined streets and verdant squares.[24] It also pushed working people and the poor into cheaper housing in the newly emerging suburban districts that formed a semicircular ring around the old port. Kensington and the Northern Liberties in the north, and Southwark and Kensington in the south, increasingly became the refuge of native and foreign-born wage earners.[25]

The core itself, though still highly commercial and residential, assumed a more industrial quality with the passage of time. Following the war of 1812, factories specializing in light consumer goods began to concentrate east of Seventh Street; textile mills, brickyards, and other industries dependent upon water power appeared to the west, along the banks of the Schuylkill.[26] During the next four decades, such trends proceeded rather uniformly in the city but unevenly in the suburbs. Farther up the Schuylkill, a few miles from the downtown, was Manayunk, an area that was agricultural in 1820 but which became the heart of the county textile industry by the early thirties. Huge fieldstone mills, with water-powered spinning and weaving machinery, and tenements housing scores of operatives were built there overnight.[27] Textile factories and artisan's shops were found adjacent to weavers' sheds in Kensington and Moyamensing, but the distinguishing feature of these areas was outwork. In the shadow of the mills were thousands of weavers who turned out cotton cloth on hand frames in tiny red-brick cottages lined up in monotonous rows on grid-like streets. Southwark and the Northern Liberties, older boroughs settled in Colonial times, retained vestiges of their preindustrial character. Small shops offering all manner of goods and commodities abounded as late as 1850, but more advanced forms of production were very much in evidence. Both districts became the home of tradesmen who, separating home and workplace, found employment either in the large workshops that crowded the core or in Southwark's modern machine foundries.[28]

From the perspective of this study, however, two changes stand out. The first has to do with the redistribution of wealth that occurred between the signing of the Declaration of Independence and the onset of the Civil War. Late Colonial Philadelphia was hardly an egalitarian paradise. A large proportion of the population owned no property, and an underclass of casual laborers, seamen, and tradesmen lived in poverty. Yet the distribution of real property, skewed though it was, looks equitable in comparison to later periods. At the close of the 1790s, the top 10 percent owned about half the wealth, which left a relatively large share for the smaller merchants, petty professionals, and master craftsmen who comprised the middling order.[29] The ensuing seventy years witnessed a wholesale redistribution toward the top, so that by 1860 the leading 10 percent owned 90 percent of the wealth while the privileged 1 percent owned a substantial 50 percent.[30]

A recent analysis of this antebellum elite indicates that few of them claimed humble origins or were self-made men. The typical member bore the venerable surname of Biddle, Ridgeway, or Pennypacker, and could trace his family fortune to the eighteenth century. Like the Colonial elite, moreover, most of these men, or six in ten, engaged in commerce; another 15 percent practiced a profession or were in finance. Manufacturers made up only 5 percent of the upper crust and they alone can be described as self-made.[31]

The early stages of industrial capitalism, in a word, did not give rise to an upper class with fortunes grounded in production alone. The wealthiest Jacksonian Philadelphians were merchants and financers, just as they had been in Colonial times. The difference was that the Jacksonians sold commodities produced in their own backyard as well as European-made goods. They also boasted more diversified investment portfolios, for such elites lent some surplus capital to manufacturers.

The solidification of this upper class had its counterpart in the mass of men and women dependent exclusively on wage labor for sustenance. The condition of wage earners is still in dispute. Early studies of the standard of living pressed the case that real earnings rose between the 1820s and 1840s, and declined in the 1850s, which brought a net gain of from 10 to 13 percent.[32] The absence of adequate data and additional research prohibits resolving this issue one way or another, but a few points deserve attention. Even if one concedes that real earnings rose in these years, the distribution of the increase remains an open question. Artisans in the better trades seem to have been the chief beneficiaries; the majority of skilled and unskilled workers, conversely, probably saw their incomes decline. A budget computed in 1851 by English immigrant John Campbell shows that even the modest rise in real earnings left the typical wage earner without enough resources to support his family at minimal comfort on his earnings alone. Campbell's budget, which included allowances for food, rent, clothing, and candles but excluded medical care and recreation, came to $10.37 a week, or $518.35 a year, based on fifty weeks, at a time when the average yearly income of male workers in fourteen major industries was only $288.[33] Printers and compositors, who were among the best paid of all journeymen, averaged only $370, or about $150 less than the minimum.[34]

This glaring shortfall caused workers to make adjustments. Most cut back on consumption, limiting their intake of meat and other expensive foodstuffs, conserving fuel costs by scavenging the countryside for wood, and partronizing the many second-hand shops in the city and suburbs. They also relied on multiple incomes, although it is impossible to know how many depended upon the earnings of wives and children or to identify the occupations of all secondary breadwinners. The employment of wives evidently varied according to the availability of work, the occupations and earnings of husbands, and the willingness of husbands to allow wives to work outside the home.[35] Wives of textile hands, for example, probably had the highest labor force participation rate (outside the home) for three reasons: male earnings were low, work was readily available, and women's occupations were seen as women's work and posed no serious threat to men. Wives of outworkers in the shoe, needle, and weaving trades helped husbands bind shoes, sew slop clothing, and wind yarn.[36] Spouses of better paid craftsmen, however, worked inside or outside the home only in hard times. A large proportion of older working-class women probably contributed to the family coffer by taking in boarders. Children were more likely than wives to enter the work force and were found in a spectrum of jobs. Sons had a wider range of choice than daughters and followed every trade and calling from printing to textiles. Daughters were typically restricted to the needle trades, textiles, and domestic service.[37]

The second salient change of this period has to do with the nature of work. The small craftsman of Watson's youth, who served local customers on casual work schedules, was gradually eclipsed by the entrepreneur in many trades. Evidence of modernity, barely perceptible in Watson's boyhood, was everywhere apparent by mid-century. Large multistoried industrial structures that occupied entire city blocks in the downtown and bunched along waterways competed with church steeples for domination of the city skyline. Oliver Evans' Mars Foundry, Philadelphia's largest business in 1815 and the envy of every aspiring entrepreneur, seemed modest by mid-century standards. Whereas Evans employed some thirty-five workmen during the War of 1812, thirty-five years later, over ninety firms hired in excess of one hundred workers each, and slightly more than 40 percent of the labor force worked in establishments with over fifty employees each. (See Table 1.)[38]

The rise of large units of production geared to mass markets announced the beginning of the end of artisanship and artisanal practice. The lax pace of work, the skill and autonomy of journeyman and master, and other handicraft characteristics eroded under the drive for economy and productivity carried on by highly competetive entrepreneurs. Most tradesmen felt the impact of early entrepreneurship. But while they shared common experiences on the shop floor, the fact remains that the new order did not bear down evenly on all of

Table 1
Percentage of Workforce by Size of Firm, 1850

Industry	Firm Size (no. of workers)				Avg. Firm Size (no. of workers)
	1-5	6-25	26-50	51+	
Iron	2.6	16.1	14.8	66.5	34.5
Machine tools	11.5	23.0	12.8	52.7	16.1
Textiles	2.6	12.0	13.8	71.6	37.0
Printing	3.6	26.1	28.6	41.7	22.5
Building construction	9.4	34.7	29.0	26.8	14.3
Clothing	3.1	26.4	14.6	55.8	25.7
Hats and caps	15.6	41.0	15.8	27.5	10.5
Shoes	17.5	35.3	11.3	35.8	10.0
Furniture	19.4	38.7	21.6	20.3	9.3
Leather	9.0	37.3	30.9	22.7	12.1
Food	65.5	25.6	8.9	0	2.8
Tobacco	33.2	59.1	0	7.6	4.2
Blacksmiths	70.1	29.9	0	0	3.4
Traditional metals	42.2	25.9	17.2	14.7	0
All industries	12.4	28.4	16.1	43.1	12.9

Source: United States Census Office, *Census of the United States, Industrial Schedule, Philadelphia County, 1850* (microfilm, MSS, National Archives, Washington, D.C.). The proportion of workers and employers in shops with fewer than six employees is underestimated because census marshalls recorded firms doing business in excess of $500, and thus ignored myriads of small producers in the old crafts.

them, partly because industrial change was spectacularly uneven, and partly because newer methods of production did not completely displace older ones. Preindustrial and transitional forms, such as small shops and outwork, showed striking resiliency in some trades. Thousands of hand loom weavers, shoemakers, tailors, other tradesmen, and women worked in shabby cottages in the suburban districts, while textile operatives and metallurgical workers toiled in large factories, and operated some of the most modern equipment in the world. Moreover, as the coexistence of hand loom weaving cottages and textile mills suggests, there were important variations within trades as well as between them.

Work Settings

A comprehensive view of the unfolding of early industrialism thus requires a conceptual frame of reference that takes account of uneven development and sorts out work environments. A helpful model posits the coexistence of five discrete but overlapping work settings—factories, manufactories, sweatshops, artisan shops, and outwork—distinguished by scale and mechanization as the first order of differentiation and market orientation as the second.

Factories. Factories refer to workplaces equipped with steam engines, water wheels, or both. The *sine qua non* of industrialization in the minds of most historians and economists, factories have received more than their share of attention from scholars probing industrial capitalism in England and New England. Philadelphia, however, was not similar to New England. Her factories employed less than a third of the labor force at mid-century and were limited to a few industries, the most important being textiles and heavy industry. Most artisans worked in nonmechanized settings. (See Tables 2 and 3.)

The importance of factories in these industries is easily explained. Offspring of the industrial revolution, heavy industry, and, to some extent, textiles, had no real tradition of craft organization. The absence of craft traditions, coupled with the rapid development of machine technology and the inherent need for large scale enterprise, at least in metallurgy, account for the shape of this production. Heavy industry thus short-circuited the customary path of development, in which manufacture moves from home and small shop to factory; iron, steel, and heavy equipment were produced in large, mechanized workplaces from the beginning. Cloth manufacture varied slightly, owing to the mixed history of the steps involved in making cottons and woolens, and to the demographic peculiarities of Philadelphia. Spinning and carding flourished in the countryside but not in the city, and both procedures, along with dying and printing, were centralized when factories proliferated in the late 1820s.[39] Weaving, on the other hand, had a long history as a cottage industry in the country and city, and, at first, early factory owners were content to farm out loom work to outworkers or to contract with merchants who hired frame tenders. Many owners eventually purchased or rented looms and brought weaving under the same roof

Table 2
Percentage of Firms Using Steam or Water Power,
and Percentage of Workers in Mechanized Firms, 1850

Industry	Percentage of Firms	Percentage of Workers
Iron	58.8	85.5
Machine tools	30.7	62.5
Textiles	38.6	54.0
Printing	15.1	30.5
Building construction	6.2	19.8
Clothing	3.3	10.3
Hats and caps	1.7	3.3
Shoes	0	0.8
Furniture	4.8	6.9
Leather	4.2	10.2
Food	0.8	6.7
Tobacco	2.7	12.1
Blacksmiths	0	0
Traditional metals	9.5	37.2
All industries	10.8	27.7

Source: United States Census Office, *Census of the United States, Industrial Schedule, Philadelphia County, 1850* (microfilm, MSS, National Archives, Washington, D.C.).

with other operations. Yet the number of hand loom weavers still increased, earning Philadelphia a reputation as a haven for this old-fashioned craft. Thousands of impoverished Irish frame tenders, making at least a stand against industrialism, lived cheek by jowl in Moyamensing and Kensington, and this abundant source of cheap labor kept industry alive.[40]

Philadelphia's early textile manufacturers are anonymous. None achieved the status of the heralded Boston Associates, and thus failed to raise the interest of contemporary biographers, hagiographers, and industrial promoters. We know them only through scattered bits of evidence, but such sources provide some helpful observations. Most textile manufacturers were not former merchants and financiers. Local merchants invested in New England mills and supplied capital for regional ventures, but as a rule, Philadelphia's textile bosses were men of humble origins. Former journeymen and small businessmen, they ran comparatively modest businesses, and few of them accumulated competencies. At Manayunk, Philadelphia's answer to Lowell, only two of over thirty owners had any real property in 1850, and most were such marginal producers that they rented space and machinery.[41] The majority of them remained small, and many succumbed to the erratic economy. Failure was so common at Manayunk that thirty-four individuals operated twenty separate businesses between the early twenties and mid-forties.[42]

Table 3

Distribution of Workers by Work Environments, 1850

Industry	Artisan		Sweatshop		Manufactory		Factory	
	No.	%	No.	%	No.	%	No.	%
Iron and steel	21	1.7	54	4.5	100	8.3	2178	85.5
Machine tools	395	10.1	416	10.6	660	16.8	2449	62.5
Textiles*	178	1.7	826	7.9	3790	36.4	5628	54.0
Printing	76	3.6	515	24.6	866	41.3	639	30.5
Building construction	355	9.1	1151	29.6	1611	41.5	767	19.8
Clothing†	324	3.1	2635	25.0	6483	61.6	1090	10.3
Hats and caps†	284	15.4	734	40.0	759	41.3	60	3.3
Boots and shoes†	1091	17.5	2207	35.3	2946	47.1	5	0.1
Furniture	225	19.9	399	35.3	427	37.8	79	6.9
Leather	251	11.9	643	30.6	995	47.3	215	10.2
Food	867	80.2	142	13.1	0	0	72	6.7
Tobacco	291	40.3	343	47.6	0	0	87	12.1
Blacksmiths	399	70.1	1158	27.8	12	2.1	0	0
Traditional metal	218	40.2	98	17.9	26	4.7	203	37.2
All industries	6779	11.7	13586	23.4	21581	37.2	16072	27.7

*About half to three-fourths of those in manufactories and factories were actually outworkers.

†About half of those listed in manufactories and factories were actually outworkers.

Source: United States Census Office. *Census of the United States, Industrial Schedule, Philadelphia County, 1850* (microfilm, MSS, National Archives, Washington, D.C.).

The most successful of the lot was Austrian-born Joseph Ripka, and even he failed to avoid the whim of the volatile market. Ripka started out as a weaver, presumably a journeyman, and accumulated enough capital and knowledge of the "management of the loom" to strike out on his own. Migrating to Lyon in 1814, he opened a cotton and silk mill, but the political chaos of Restoration France drove him to the brink of ruin and also from the Old World to the New—and then to Philadelphia, where he promptly reentered the textile business. He opened a small hand loom weaving firm in Kensington in 1817, and four years later added another mill and a warehouse to his holdings. The mid-twenties was a pivotal time for him. He took over a power loom factory on the Pennypack, constructed a weaving and spinning mill at Manayunk, and garnered the capital from these to expand sharply in the coming years. At the beginning of the forties the sixty-year-old immigrant owned a minor textile empire that embraced a string of warehouses and at least eight mills, and was numbered among the wealthiest Philadelphians. But success eluded him. The panic of 1857 left him with large inventories, few customers, and many debtors whose defaults mounted and drove him to ruin. A casualty of hard times, Ripka died a poor man in 1862.[43]

Ripka's mills and those of his competitors were the most advanced businesses in the region. Powered by steam engines or water wheels and equipped with batteries of machines, these monuments of rising industrialism were the equivalents of early automobile assembly plants. Production rhythms were maddeningly syncopated, fluctuating between periods of intense activity and slack times. Owners would operate part time or cut employment rolls when chronic overproduction glutted markets, and would shut down entirely when steam engines malfunctioned, waterways froze or dried up, or canal companies dredged silted trenches.[44] But in prosperous times no work environment demanded as much discipline or exhausting physical labor as did textile factories. (This distinguished textile operatives from metallurgical workers who were located in factories. The work life of first-generation machinists, iron puddlers, rollers, and kindred wage earners was qualitatively different from that of the operatives. They were highly skilled factory workers who commanded exceptionally high wages and exercised control over the conditions and instruments of production. Metal tradesmen were numerically significant in antebellum Philadelphia, but deficient data on their early experiences precludes incorporating them into the following analysis.)[45]

Operatives put in one of the longest workdays of all wage earners. They toiled up to fourteen hours daily at the end of the twenties, and in 1835, when craftsmen throughout the city struck successfully for a ten-hour day, textile hands had to settle for a compromise of eleven hours. The eleven-hour standard held throughout the depression of 1837; owners, however, reimposed longer hours following recovery in the middle of the forties. Textile employees had come full circle and worked a thirteen-hour day once again.[46]

The shop experience of millhands differed from artisans in other ways as well. Unlike the great majority of wage earners who worked by hand or with the aid of simple tools, they operated power-driven machines and adjusted to a work pace over which they had no control. And while all artisans worked harder and more intensively as time wore on, mill workers faced the most gruelling regime of all. In 1833, for example, a mule spinner estimated that a competent practitioner turned out about 4,000 hanks of a standard thread a week.[47] Fifteen years later a popular manufacturers' manual recommended a weekly output of twice that rate.[48] Supervision was strict and overbearing. Operatives toiled under the direction of overseers and room bosses who detected the slightest "falling off" and, did not shy away from exercising their authority to discipline the guilty.[49] Owners specified what constituted laxity, posting written rules and regulations that one of their number described as "chiefly indispensable for . . . good management."[50] Ripka levied fines for "neglect of work," carelessness, mistreatment of machinery, and poor performance or work "badly done." He encouraged promptness by docking "every hand coming to work a quarter of an hour after the mill started" a quarter of a day['s wage.]"[51] Small wonder that Manayunk operatives considered textile manufacture a "clock-work system."[52]

The tight surveillance on the shop floor occasionally spilled over into housing. The leading firms imitated Rhode Island manufacturers and boarded families in company-owned tenements. These dull, gray buildings, built from the same material as the mills, were governed by principles similar to production itself. Tenants were carefully screened, barred from "sinful" behavior, and subjected to a curfew.[53]

Workers bound to the authoritarianism of textile manufacturers were among the most impoverished of all wage earners. Owners initially lured them into the mills with relatively good wages, but having attracted a sufficient corps of workers after the early thirties, drove down the rates. Average yearly earnings varied with the job; male mule spinners commanded two to three times the scale of women power weavers. But males still earned pitifully low wages. In 1850 they averaged slightly more than $210 a year, which placed them near the bottom of the occupational pyramid.[54]

Manufactories. Early nineteenth-century Americans used the term *manufactory* interchangeably with *factory* to refer to any large industrial establishment. In this context, however, *manufactory* identifies plants with more than twenty-five workers (whether employed inside or outside the premises) but without power sources. Or, phrased another way, manufactories are nonmechanized factories. These establishments grew at the expense of small shops and outwork and by mid-century absorbed one-third to one-half of the printers, saddlers and harnessmakers, shoemakers, tailors, cabinetmakers, and, if one wishes to include nonproduction craftsmen, building tradesmen as well. (See Table 3.) That firms in this stage of development grew large without mechanizing is shown in Tables 1 and 2. The first table discloses that one-half to three-fourths of the craftsmen concentrated in shops with more than twenty-five fellow workers; the second demonstrates that mechanization hardly made a dent in these pursuits. Printers and publishers headed the rank order, and only 15 percent of them used steam engines or water wheels, which is another way of observing that by 1850 it was quite common to find upward of fifty craftsmen in a single plant working exclusively by hand.

Owners of manufactories derived from two sources. There was the "insider" or former artisan who was "brought up to the trade" and would become the revered Jacksonian entrepreneur and expectant capitalist. Then there was the "outsider" who entered manufacture by way of commerce. Insiders dominated most trades, but it was not unusual for a representative of each group to become partners, insiders providing the expertise in production, outsiders supplying the capital. The pattern in shoe and clothing manufacture diverged somewhat. Evidence gathered from other locales indicates that the pioneer manufacturers were outsiders operating through the putting-out system and then through central shops. Some of them transformed such shops into factories by mid-century, but most withdrew from production in the late 1830s, leaving the trade to the insiders.[55] Such may have been Philadelphia's mobility pattern. Of the city's forty largest shoe manufacturers in 1850, thirty-two (and possibly as many as thirty-six) rose within the trade from the ranks of masters and journeymen. The remainder were merchants who put together partnerships with insiders instead of going it alone.[56]

Whatever their background or calling, craft entrepreneurs ran their businesses in similar ways and, in some respects, in concert with textile manufacturers. Confronted with the dual need to increase output and tighten work discipline, they hired more workers and manipulated piece rates. Shoe manufacturers were singularly aggressive in the area of wages. Between the late 1820s and early 1830s, they slashed the standard on fancy boots by 150 percent and cheap work by a third. The reduction of cheap work forced journeymen to "turn out triple the quantity . . . to obtain a living," and to extend their workdays.[57] The general strike of 1835 brought a ten-hour day, but frequent wage cuts in the following decade erased its fruits for many journeymen. A mechanic writing in the late forties protested that "every pursuit of labor has, within ten or fifteen years, been shorn of from one-third to one-half of its former gains; or where the rates remain nominally the same, instability of employment and superseding expedients has [sic] produced the same effects; though perhaps in a majority of cases, an actual reduction in rates is the active cause."[58] During the 1840s, journeymen shoemakers and tailors were putting in up to sixteen hours a day in the busy season.[59]

The resemblance between factories and manufactories extended to managerial practice. As in factories, the scale of operations in manufactories induced the delegation of authority to overseers and foremen, who by the 1830s and 1840s constituted a thin but growing stratum of middle-level managers. The specific responsibilities of foremen are obscure. It is unknown if they enforced rules and regulations like textile overseers, but one can infer that they ruled over a broad jurisdiction. They probably hired and fired and, clearly, supervised the labor process, substituting their standards of workmanship for those of the workers. A clothing manufacturer parlayed his managerial arrangement into a sales ploy. His advertisements in the local press wooed customers with the assurance that employees made up the garments "on the premises under the more immediate, personal, careful, rigid supervision than is customary."[60]

Here the similarities between manufactories and factories diminished. The prodigious technological advances that eased the transition to factory production in textiles were unavailable, prohibitively expensive, or both, for entrepreneurs in the crafts. Deprived of machines, aspiring manufacturers turned to the division of labor, and in varying degrees broke down skills into specialized tasks. Judging from the rush of protest on the part of shoemakers and tailors, it appears that their employers led the way in dividing up the work. Indeed, no single group of large manufacturers assaulted skills as quickly or as thoroughly.[61] By the late 1830s, shoe bosses effectively detached cutting the leather from lasting and bottoming, and carved up the remaining procedures into menial occupations. At the other end of the spectrum were book and newspaper publishers. They simply separated operating the press from setting the type, and, like shoe and clothing manufacturers, stationed workers in rooms or departments dedicated to specific jobs.[62]

The debasing of skill and other features attendant upon the modernization of the crafts have long been matters of record and bear no repeating here.[63] It is appropriate, however, to draw attention to several points that historians have slighted or ignored. First, the division of labor did not uniformly reduce craft work to semiskilled jobs, as is commonly believed. Instead, it created a new hierarchy of occupations whose components required some training and considerable expertise, modest amounts of both, or very little of either. At the top were such jobs as leather and garment cutting, shoe lasting, typesetting, and others that were not mastered without years of experience; at the bottom were shoe binding, cloth stitching, and other menial tasks that could be picked up in a matter of weeks. The former continued to be dominated by men, and the latter were assigned to youths, "half-trained" men, and women. Second, though most craftsmen worked in manufactories by the 1840s, those whose bosses installed power-driven equipment were not necessarily converted into machine operatives. The few manufacturers of light consumer goods who did deploy steam engines harnessed power to a few tasks, so that mixes of hand and machine work existed in the same firm. To take but one example, publishers who exchanged screw devices for power-driven presses, and recruited young men and women to run them, left setting the type to skilled males who worked by hand.[64] Third, specialized workers employed in manufactories experienced a more exacting work regimen, but were somewhat more autonomous than textile operatives. Since they worked by hand or with the aid of hand tools and rented independently owned homes (or at least homes not owned by their employers), they had more latitude and social space in which to act out their lives.

Finally, the evolution of handicraft production was such that some entrepreneurs reshaped the nature of work outside the walls of their own establishments. Shoe and clothing manufactories, for example, originated as small shops where the cloth and leather were cut and footwear and garments were packaged and prepared for shipment. Outworkers performed the intermediary steps in their homes, which left the bulk of the labor force outside capital's immediate supervision. This awkward arrangement was the source of inefficiency and loss, and was an incentive for the herding of labor under one roof. But the typical shoe and clothing manufacturer never did shed his dependence on outworkers and "sweaters." It was he, in fact, who fostered the sweating system and resurrected the putting-out system.

Sweatshops. It is virtually impossible to distinguish garrets or sweatshops from neighborhood or artisan shops. Both were small and unmechanized, usually hiring under twenty-five workers, but evidence suggests that sweatshops were the larger of the two. These businesses will thus be treated as firms with six to twenty-five employees.[65]

Sweatshops emerged in three ways. Merchants would buy in volume from small producers; they would advance capital or raw material to producers and demand shipment of finished goods by fixed deadlines; or, as implied above, merchants and manufacturers would contract with producers to perform limited tasks.[66] The first and third types were common in footwear and apparel; the second enmeshed many trades. Proprietors selling directly to merchants, or the first type, usually owned raw materials and produced the entire commodity in the shop, as did the second type. The third and second were supplied with raw materials and were responsible for a few tasks in a larger production process.

Most "sweaters" were former journeymen who took advantage of the low capital costs and easy access to employer status. Staying in business, however, was no mean accomplishment, because of the traditional fragility of small enterprise and the unique market position of "sweaters." Forced to meet rigid production schedules and hounded by competitors, they were pressed to speed up production and trim costs at every turn. They hired cheap labor, scrupulously directed production, and, in order to hold down costs, even toiled alongside journeymen. The tempo itself was wildly irregular. The production season necessitated long and wearying toil with the men rushing to fill orders; dull times brought long periods of unemployment in which bosses and journeymen alike eked out an existence doing repair work.[67]

It is difficult to gauge the proportion of sweatshop workers in the various trades during this period. An educated guess would place one-half of the shoemakers and tailors in garrets in the 1830s, and about a third of them there twenty years later. Slightly higher percentages of furniture workers and traditional metal tradesmen worked in such shops in both periods.

Outwork. In antebellum Philadelphia, the putting-out system was restricted to shoemaking, tailoring, weaving, and a few marginal industries. For these trades, it is impossible to compute the ratio of such outworkers to shopmen with any precision. One can only assume that the share of male tailors and shoemakers declined as production gravitated to manufactories during the thirties and forties. By mid-century outworkers probably numbered in the neighborhood of a fifth of both trades. Hand loom weaving, on the other hand, obstinately persevered as a cottage industry despite the spread of the power loom and of textile mills. The number of frame tenders working at home or in small sheds grew from about 4,500 in the late twenties to nearly 6,000 by the fifties, when they accounted for more than half of the weavers in the county.[68]

Outworkers were the lowliest of all artisans. They stood on the fringes of the sweated trades or practiced occupations that were so easily learned that there was no apprenticeship or formal training. Hand loom weaving was passed on through a kind of on-the-job training and was probably learned in a matter of months. Shoe binding and stitching ready-made clothing, two mainstays of outwork, required even less time. Outworkers inevitably earned low wages, far lower than shop workers, and if hand loom weavers are a reliable guide, only slightly better than unskilled laborers.[69] They were a casual labor force employed by either merchants or manufacturers, depending on the trade and period of time. Boss hand loom weavers, for example, were usually merchant capitalists who maintained warehouses and controlled large stocks of raw materials but did not own the machinery. They simply gave out yarn to weavers who worked at home on their own frames. Some of them, it is true, flirted with modernization by renting small shops, purchasing looms, and centralizing the weavers, but most clung to old ways and continued to employ cottagers well into the 1850s.[70] Boss shoemakers and tailors, on the other hand, were increasingly likely to be manufacturers who employed shopmen as well as outworkers.

Whatever their trade, outworkers lived in a world of their own. A contemporary Philadelphian observed that hand loom weavers (and by extension outworkers in general) "have no practical concern with the ten-hour system, or the factory system, or even the solar system. They work at such hours as they choose in their own homes, and their industry is mainly regulated by the state of the larder."[71] This derisive view was only partly correct. Cottagers were in the thick of the general strike for a ten-hour day in 1835, and none completely dodged industrial discipline. Even their employers resorted to negative incentives and penalties for turning in faulty work or failing to return cloth to warehouses by prescribed deadlines.[72] These practices notwithstanding, cottagers still exercised far more control over their work than any other journeymen. Toiling at home far from the watchful eye of boss and overseer, they worked pretty much at their own pace.

Artisan or Neighborhood Shops. Small shops that employed fewer than six workers and were neither garrets nor sweatshops fared unevenly after 1800. They were nearly eclipsed in some trades, and persisted as the prevailing form in others. As late as 1850, one-half to three-fourths of the traditional metal tradesmen (coppersmiths and tinsmiths), blacksmiths, butchers, and bakers, among others, and about one-fifth of the shoemakers and furniture makers worked in these shops. (See Table 3.) It should be emphasized, however, that while such establishments hired a declining share of the labor force (only 12.8 percent by 1850), they comprised the vast majority of the employers, or just about 60 percent in 1850. (See Table 4.)

Owners closely resembled the small craftsmen of Federalist Philadelphia. A combination of worker, foreman, and merchant in one, they set their hands to manual labor, directed the work of those in their employ, and marketed their own wares and services directly to consumers. Such artisans either supplied Philadelphians of all classes with food, tobacco, household utensils, and other commodities, or fashioned fine goods for the city's upper crust, whose taste for custom work persisted in spite, and perhaps because, of the advent of mass production. Journeymen were among the most skilled and accomplished in the city. Working by hand, they made the entire product from beginning to end and, except in baking where a punishing routine was endemic, enjoyed relatively relaxed work schedules. They also earned the best wages, and along with garret workers, had a comparatively easy entrée to ownership. He who accumulated $500 to $1000 could open his own shop. Thus, class lines were still fluid, and social relations between master and journeymen comparatively harmonious at this level of production.[73]

No analysis of antebellum wage earners would be complete without some recognition of the unskilled. Such laborers fall outside the categories outlined above, for most of them were involved in commerce and construction rather than manufacturing. They were

Table 4
Distribution of Firms by Size Category, 1850

Size Category (no. of workers)							
1–5		*6–25*		*26–50*		*51+*	
No.	*%*	*No.*	*%*	*No.*	*%*	*No.*	*%*
2621	57.7	1458	32.2	257	5.7	206	4.5

Source: United States Census Office, *Census of the United States, Industrial Schedule, Philadelphia County, 1850* (microfilm, MSS, National Archives, Washington, D.C.).

found on the docks, in the streets, and at construction sites, among other nonindustrial settings, doing the arduous tasks of loading and unloading barges and riggers, and transporting materials in and around the city.

The term *unskilled* is essentially generic. It subsumes an array of jobs whose common denominator is the absence of skills, such as "laborer," "hod carrier," "stevedore," "carter," "draymen," and so on. Taken together, these categories accounted for about 16 percent of the labor force in 1850.[74] The working conditions of the unskilled varied widely, but may be grouped into two categories. The smaller of these, which might be described as "individual" or "entrepreneurial," encompasses workers with either the capital to purchase a horse and cart or the ingenuity to construct human-powered vehicles. They toiled alone or as individuals, carting refuse and raw materials for municipalities and businessmen. The larger group, or "collective," consisted of coal heavers, stevedores, and others who owned no equipment and usually worked in teams or groups under their own direction.

Worker and Workplace: Who Worked Where?

A major theme of the new labor history is that working-class culture and consciousness do not simply happen or develop in a vacuum. Instead, culture and consciousness are made and remade by the interplay of living and working conditions and what individuals bring to communities and workshops from prior experiences. A complex process in itself, it is confounded in antebellum Philadelphia not only by the disparate environments of workers but also by their varied backgrounds. We know from other studies, for example, that native-born and foreign-born workers unacquainted with urban ways and industrial exigencies brought with them into urban labor markets expectations and assumptions of a different order from those artisans familiar with insurgent politics. The cultural baggage of each group shaped behavior inside and outside the workplace, and was itself metamorphosed under the impact of changing conditions on the job and in the community.[75] Given the central importance of work in this formulation and the range of industrial environments in early nineteenth-century Philadelphia, the link between worker and workplace must be established. The difficulty of this task should not be underestimated. Since no single source provides the necessary information, the mosaic must be pieced together from scattered bits of evidence and at times from inference.

The chore can be lightened somewhat by distinguishing the 1820s and 1830s from the 1840s. Prior to the cataclysmic panic of 1837, most manual workers were native-born Americans who were evenly divided between small shops and outwork, on the one hand, and factories, manufactories, and sweat shops, on the other. They were found in all descriptions of skilled and unskilled labor, but there was an important difference between the urban born and bred, who had served regular apprenticeships, and the recently-arrived rural-urban migrant, who entered the city without craft knowledge. Male and female migrants fulfilled the same role in Philadelphia as the Irish in Boston and New England farm women in Lowell. Being a pool of cheap and untrained labor, they paved the way for the mass production of cloth and light consumer goods, and supplied the muscle of the army of unskilled labor. Some of the men worked as casual laborers and staffed the sweatshops, and members of both sexes drifted into factories and manufactories or worked at home under the putting-out system. Urban-born artisans and those reared in the city were the seasoned workers who cornered custom and retail work, and who concentrated in artisan shops, or at least worked there as long as employment was available. The frequent lulls in trade forced them to double as outworkers and perhaps seek occasional employment from garret bosses and large manufacturers.

Other custom workers simply lost the freedom to choose their place of employment. The continued consolidation of production into larger units drove scores of small employers out of business and left masters and journeymen without work and with little alternative but to file into sweatshops and manufactories. Few took kindly to this. A group of cordwainers faced with this prospect complained that manufacturers "have embarked on our business, and realized large fortunes, by reducing wages, making large quantities of work, and selling at reduced prices, while those of us who have served time to the trade, and have been anxious to foster its interests, have had to abandon the business or enter the system of manufacturing."[76]

Immigrants comprised about 10 percent of the work force in this period. The Irish, the great majority of the foreign-born, were former peasants and crofters or artisans who had learned the basics of hand loom weaving, shoemaking, tailoring, and other skills in their native land or in the west of England. The first group, clearly the majority, concentrated in casual labor and in unskilled work of all types. Some of them moved into the semiskilled ends of the declining crafts and into weaving, but they and their skilled countrymen did not necessarily find their way into factories and manufactorics. Displaying an aversion to modern work disciplines, they preferred outwork in Philadelphia just as they had in the Old World. English immigrants, having emigrated in the early stages of the industrial revolution, came to Philadelphia as craftsmen and skilled textile workers. Many of them were recruited by textile bosses in need of skilled workers, and most spread themselves across the occupational spectrum and across most work settings as well.

The decade and a half following the panic witnessed the continued massing of workers into factories and manufactories and the concommitant, if variable, decline of garrets, artisan shops, and the putting-out system. The protracted depression expedited this process, and no one realized this more than small businessmen. A former garret boss who lost his shop in hard times counted two thousand fellow owners who were "reduced . . . to journeymen . . . working for large [manu]factories."[77] Such a winnowing out of small producers decreased the number of traditional settings, as well as the garrets, without completely destroying either or both in many trades. In 1850, select groups of craftsmen still earned their living working for small proprietors.

The continuity in industrial development contrasts sharply with the striking shift in the composition of the labor force during the forties. Two waves of immigrants from western Europe at the beginning and end of the decade inflated the proportion of foreign-born Philadelphians from 10 to nearly 40 percent of the male labor force. Two-thirds of these newcomers were Irish peasants in flight from the horrors of the Great Famine. About four in ten of them worked as hod carriers, carters, stevedores, draymen, and casual laborers. Another 40 percent can be identified as skilled workers, but most of them were involved in hand loom weaving and in bastardized segments of the sweated trades. Germans accounted for another 20 percent of the foreign-born, but they hardly fit the stereotype of the unskilled immigrant. Having come from small towns with artisan economies, they were the most skilled immigrants ever to enter America, and used this background to good advantage in Philadelphia. Fully two-thirds of them assumed skilled jobs, and while shoemaking, tailoring, furniture making, and butchering had special appeal, they worked at every craft. The occupational profile of the native-born whites, who fell from about 90 to less than sixty percent of the male manual labor force during the decade, closely mirrored that of the Germans. The difference lay in their distribution among the trades. They were largely displaced by women and immigrants in the semiskilled jobs of the declining crafts and by Irish immigrants in casual labor during the forties. At the close of the decade native whites were dominant only in the more prestigious crafts of printing, carpentry, and the like and in the better jobs within the sweated trades, such as leather and garment cutting and shoe lasting.[78]

The combination of this demographic shift and ongoing industrial change redistributed Philadelphia's wage earners within work settings. Most workers of all national origins and backgrounds were found in the modern (factories) and the modernizing (manufactories and sweatshops) workplaces as the forties drew to a close. The only exceptions to this were large numbers of Irish males, small but substantial groups of native white and German males who staffed the small shops, and women of all nationalities who continued to work under the putting-out system.

Seen from this perspective, industrializing Philadelphia is a fascinating blend of the old, the new, and the transitional.[79] Such uneven development, though noteworthy in its own right, also had an important influence on class relations, the social basis of politics, the configuration of political coalitions, and other matters that are explored below. For the moment we turn our attention to uneven development as a component in the forging of working-class culture. Specifically, we shall examine how the interaction of the backgrounds and work experiences of Philadelphia's wage earners produced three discrete subcultures in the years preceding the panic of 1837.

Part Two:
The Forging of Working-Class Cultures 1820-1837

Revivalists:
The Militias of Christ

2

On a muggy summer day in August 1828 Kensington's hand loom weavers announced a holiday from their daily toil. News of the affair circulated throughout the district and by mid-afternoon the hard-living frame tenders and their comrades turned the neighborhood avenues of commerce into a playground. Knots of lounging workers joked and exchanged gossip, and sought relief from the suffocating heat with generous helpings of liquor and beer. The more athletic challenged one another to foot races and games, but, like their fellows, also quenched their thirst with frequent drams. The spree was a classic celebration of St. Monday.[1]

Spirits were more somber in the adjoining borough, the Northern Liberties. There workingmen's wives went door-to-door, bible in hand, preaching the gospel to the unregenerate. They were emissaries of the Reverend James Patterson of the district's First Presbyterian church and were carrying out their minister's charge to "go out into 'the streets and lanes of the city,' according to Christ's command, and 'compel' the impenitent to come" into his house of God. And come they did. Persuaded by Patterson's zealots, hundreds of men joined their wives and daughters at church, and sat in nervous expectation of the evangelist's fiery words. Few of them made it through one of Patterson's intimidating sermons without breaking down into tears or flailing their arms about in fits of uncontrolled emotion—and then opening their troubled hearts to Jesus.[2]

As these residents of Kensington and Northern Liberties worshipped their respective saints, still another gathering of wage earners took place in the lower end of the city, at Commissioners' Hall in Southwark. William Heighton, an English-born and Philadelphia-bred shoemaker, rose to the rostrum and delivered a prepared speech on "The Principles of Aristocratic Legislation." Neither the gathering nor the role was strange to the humble but articulate journeyman. Twice in 1827 Heighton had come before the same audience with a radical polemic and the outline of a plan to unite workingmen into a city central union around a program of social reconstruction. His listeners had heeded the clarion, and in 1827 joined forces in the Mechanics' Union of Trade Associations, the nation's first city-wide organization of journeymen. They now gave an attentive ear to their leader's analysis of the causes of inequality and the need for its antidote in the form of a unified and enlightened working class.[3]

These vignettes each resonate with one of the working-class cultures forged in the two decades preceding the panic of 1837. Such cultures can be formalized in the following way: the St. Monday celebration of the Kensington weavers may be called *traditionalism*; the evangelical meeting of the Northern Liberties men and women may be called *revivalism*; and the conclave of Southwark journeymen may be called (*rationalist*) *radicalism*.[4] These cultures were the lens through which wage earners imagined one another and their social superiors both inside and outside the workplace. None of these was wholly new or completely old. Much like the industrial base of the city, each contained elements of the past and the present, and none can be easily understood without some grasp of its antecedents. Revivalism is a case in point.

Philadelphia revivalism took shape in the first quarter of the nineteenth century within the contexts of religious apathy in the larger society and rancor in the Protestant denominations. The apathy was a carryover of late eighteenth-century rationalistic humanism, and manifested itself in low church attendance and a falling rate of baptisms.[5] Most Philadelphians remained shamelessly unchurched and some were openly hostile to mainstream religion. The dissension within denominations pitted factions of revivalist

Arminians against orthodox Calvinists in bitter squabble deriving from the painful process of industrialism.

Orthodoxy was synonymous with the Presbyterian in Philadelphia. No Protestant denomination had a larger following in the Early National period and no clergy was as self-consciously conservative. Stodgy and aristocratic to begin with, older Presbyterian divines closed ranks around the Westminster Confession when they were confronted with mounting attacks from New England liberal Calvinists and local revisionists. They invoked the doctrine of human depravity and appealed to the arbitrary God of John Calvin in answer to those who bent their energies toward improving public morality, doing good works, and saving souls. Some, to be sure, were concerned about the moral climate, but all of them insisted that salvation was independent of personal conduct and human will. Theirs was an inscrutible God who conferred grace as He saw fit.

Orthodox Presbyterians thus spoke for the old order. Their case-hardened Calvinism was thoroughly consonant with hierarchical social arrangements in which each man knew his place and opportunities for rapid advancement were limited. They gave their blessing to static social forms and offered no comfort to laymen who claimed superior social or religious status on the basis of worldly success or moral rectitude. In the elusive search for salvation, the merchant prince enjoyed no inherent advantage over the drawer of water, and here lay the central dilemma of orthodoxy.[6]

Religious reformers in rural and urban areas undergoing economic change discarded old-style Protestantism. Led by Charles Finney, they adjusted doctrine to the market economy and spread out across the nation in the 1820s. Finney's protégés won over throngs of converts in rural America before bringing their message to the city in the late 1820s. Philadelphia was fertile ground for their "new measurers."[7]

Finney's chief counterpart in the Quaker City was Albert Barnes. Born in small-town New Jersey in 1798, Barnes graduated from Princeton Seminary in 1824, and a year later was called to the pulpit in his native village of Morristown. As spiritual leader of the First Church, Barnes pushed the moderate liberalism he learned at Princeton to Arminian extremes. Rejecting limited atonement, the cornerstone of orthodoxy, he affirmed that salvation was more a matter of human will than divine whim. "I stand as a messenger of God," the flamboyant rebel told his communicants in 1829, "with the assurance, that all that *will* may be saved; that the atonement was full and free; and that if any will perish, it will be because they chose to die, and not because they are straitened by God."[8]

An outspoken Arminian, a spellbinding revivalist, and a tireless temperance advocate who singlehandedly closed down the local liquor business, Barnes quickly gained regional eminence. His reputation stretched to Philadelphia, where the members of the prestigious First Church called him to their pulpit. Never one to avoid a challenge, Barnes accepted the invitation and promptly set off a storm of controversy in the capital of orthodoxy. The Old Guard wasted no time in registering their feelings, and twice charged him with heresy. Yet through all the turmoil of the trials, Barnes commanded the unyielding loyalty of his wealthy parishoners; they saw him not as a heretic but as a prophet of the new order.[9]

Barnes' sermons and lectures can be read as celebrations of industrialism and acquisitive man. Lecturing on the "Choice of a Profession," he characteristically summoned the metaphors of economic advancement. He exhorted his listeners to employ their talents wisely lest they "wear out the system like a machine without a balance wheel or governor," and likened the professional's contribution to society to "the movement of each part of a well structured machine."[10] Those who achieved success, Barnes assured, need not suffer the guilt and psychic anguish that tormented the orthodox, for as with religion, so with individual achievement. Men were responsible for their own destiny before both God and society, and success in one's calling was a sign of regeneration rather than disgrace. Or, as Barnes maintained, "By their fruits they shall be known."[11]

Like most antebellum Arminians, however, Barnes stopped short of condoning wordly success per se. He shared the current suspicion of inherited fortunes and the accumulation of "sudden wealth" and counseled "stability of purpose and settled intention," and "honest and sober industry."[12] In keeping with these strictures and with his labors in New Jersey, he held communicants to total abstinence from drink, and became a leading crusader against liquor in Philadelphia. His temperance pronouncements bore the same homiletic imprint as his sermons, and pressed the same themes. Singing the praises of temperance in a July Fourth speech in 1835, Barnes linked total abstinence with success, drink with failure and ruin, warning that the consumption of spirits "produces idleness and loss of property." To underscore the point, he draped the temperance cause in the mantle of patriotism and left his listeners with this thought: "Our freedom rests on securing the avails of honest industry. The man who will not work, I repeat, is the enemy of this country."[13]

The growing popularity of Arminianism and moral reformism, or what Paul Faler aptly terms "industrial morality," on the one hand, and the hardening of orthodoxy, on the other, opened an unbridgable gap within Presbyterianism.[14] Furious debates between New and Old Schoolers reduced the sedate General Assembly to the chaos of a Democratic party convention. The climax came in 1837 when, after years of raging battle, the factions split into separate churches.[15]

The Presbyterians were not the only Protestant sect to become embroiled over moral issues. Methodists went through a similar, if less publicized, debate in this period. Early church records belie the image of the ascetic Methodist damning sin and evil, and reveal that the behavior of the typical Revolutionary Methodist would have scandalized his offspring. Circuit riders supplemented paltry incomes by peddling spirits; merchants kept kegs of liquor on hand for the enjoyment of leisurely shoppers; and congregations paid a portion of tradesmen's wages in liquor, as did the communicants of Southwark's Ebenezer Church.[16] An entry in the church record during the 1790s thus reads: "Cash—rum and sugar for work men at the fence."[17] Such practices explain why the General Conference repealed Joseph Wesley's ban on the buying and selling of ardent spirits in 1791.[18]

Some early nineteenth-century church officials took offense at these violations of the Wesleyan spirit. Inspired by reigning American Bishop Francis Asbury, they campaigned for tighter mortality on the local and national level. They were repeatedly thwarted, however, and usually resorted to weak pronouncements and anemic amendments to the discipline. Philadelphia Methodists who chafed at church-sponsored "fancy" fairs and pressed for their prohibition had to settle for a mild 1834 resolution describing such events as "improper" and "inexpedient."[19] Two years later the Philadelphia Conference passed an equally moderate motion vowing "more energetic administration of the Discipline, particularly in excluding

. . . immoral persons."[20] And restoring Wesley's restriction on drink caused no end of frustration. Local congregations made some progress under the leadership of forceful ministers who preached temperance, but their numbers did not amount to much in regional and national conferences. As late as 1828 the General Conference went no further than advising members to discontinue the manufacture and sale of drink, and urging employers to cease giving grog to their employees.[21] Not until 1848 did Methodism succeed in reestablishing the founder's prohibition on drinking.[22]

As in the Presbyterian church, this adoption of a strict code of conduct was part of a larger process in which evangelicals conformed to the exigencies of economic change. Methodist ministers who condemned popular amusements and advocated total abstinence, sexual continence, and other injunctions of the new morality also welcomed the advent of the industrial age. The Reverend J. Kennady is typical. A dynamic lecturer and rabid revivalist, Kennady at once interpreted the transportation revolution and "steam power" as evidence of "man's elevation" and urged an audience of Sunday School teachers to do their part for industrialism by impressing children with the value of celerity and promptitude. "Be *punctual* and *prompt* in your attendance and doings," he enjoined them.[23] One of his colleagues put the issue even more directly by exhorting teachers to instill "habits of industry" and "love of employment" in their young pupils.[24]

It is difficult to measure accurately the strength of new Protestantism prior to the panic of 1837. Figures on church membership are often unreliable and can be misleading because they do not separate communicants and constituents (those who attended church but were not formal members). More difficult, perhaps, is distinguishing evangelical-Arminian congregations from orthodox and traditional churches. Membership figures, therefore, should be used with caution and regarded as no more than a rough gauge of general trends. The figures show a steady but modest growth in Presbyterian and Methodist strength between the War of 1812 and the Great Panic. These churches added 240 and 265 members annually which gave them an aggregate following of about 14,000 (6,000 Presbyterians and 7,340 Methodists) in this period.[25] Even if the minions of smaller sects are included, it is hard to escape the conclusion that in spite of the accretion, organized religion had a small following. And if we can generalize from the schism in the Presbyterian church, it appears that only about half the members were new Protestants.

Formal church membership, however, is rarely a reliable index of the popularity of religion and religious values. This is especially true in an age of reformist zeal that saw Arminian divines exercise influence beyond their pews and pulpits by means of a crusade designed to foist the new morality on the unchurched. New School Presbyterians were in the forefront of this effort.[26] Their theological guide was Samuel Hopkins (1721–1803), the influential New Englander who had argued that true Christian endeavor and Christian love required the exercise of "disinterested benevolence."[27] Early application of this principle led to the famous Plan of Union (1801) and to Presbyterian-Congregationalist cosponsorship of the bible and tract societies, Sunday school unions, missions, temperance groups, and other components of the "benevolent empire" that stretched from city to frontier by the 1820s.[28]

This crusade was a major point of contention between Old and New School Presbyterians. It had the moral and financial backing of New School laymen, as well as the clergy, and, as Robert Doherty has shown, this is easily understood. Doherty's study of Old and New School congregations in the downtown area discloses that each faction appealed to different social strata. Old Schoolers tended to have the support of artisans and unskilled workers. New Schoolers, conversely, were likely to be merchants and large manufacturers, to own more real and personal property, and to invest heavily in industry and transportation. Rising entrepreneurs like locomotive builder Matthias Baldwin were a natural constituency for New School Presbyterianism, whose Arminian theology justified their own worldly strivings and whose Arminian morality, as expressed through the benevolent empire, promised to create a sober and tractable working class.[29]

New School ministers and their lay advocates lashed out at all manner of sin and urban measures that, in their view, abetted idleness and profligacy. One of their favorite targets was social welfare. They attacked outdoor relief as a subsidy to dependence, and condemned gathering the needy into the poorhouse because it reduced the "sense of shame, by creating a community of paupers, protected from the gaze of all who are not in their class."[30] They fought for free public schools, not because poor children needed instruction, but because schools reached a portion of the community—"the ignorant, the degraded, the grossly sensual, the idle, the worthless—the refuse of society"—who could not be reached through revivals. Their classrooms were the agents of social control providing "self-denying instruction" for the children of the needy.[31]

Of all the causes advocated by moral reformers none consumed more energy than the battle against demon rum. The temperance movement in the Quaker City surfaced in 1827 when the communicants of the Second Presbyterian church joined forces with like-minded clergy and laymen in the Pennsylvania Society for Discouraging the Use of Ardent Spirits. An ecumenical group, the Pennsylvania Society included Quakers, some Old School Presbyterians, and even Universalists, but was dominated by New School Presbyterians and the wealthy, regardless of religious preference. Its roster included Matthew Newkirk, wealthy merchant and inspirational force behind the Pennsylvania Railroad; Alexander Henry, retired merchant turned industrial investor; and locomotive builder Matthias Baldwin. The Pennsylvania Society affiliated with the American Temperance Society, but quickly took an advanced position within the national organization, rejecting temperance for total abstinence from all intoxicants. (So did the Pennsylvania Temperance Society which succeeded it in 1834.) Like most branches of the American Society, the Pennsylvania held lectures and distributed tracts that blended homilies with the latest "scientific" data on the harms of drink. It also gave rise to local groups variously known as the Union Temperance Society, the Young Men's Temperance Society, and similar organizations.[32]

How successful were these agencies of social control? There is no simple measure of this, but there is reason to doubt that moral reformers had much impact on worker behavior and morality in this period. Reformers compiled a mixed record in seeking to mold municipal institutions to their interests. They condemned the laxity of the police and the rowdyism of the firemen, but never did achieve their goals of replacing these volunteers with paid professionals. Both services remained in the hands of workers, the very people the reformers wished to control. Even when the forces of order and morality had their way, the results were not always gratifying. Barnes and his supporters, for example, were largely responsible for establishing the public school system in 1834, and for designing the curriculum, but it is doubtful that classrooms exerted much influence on working-class children in the thirties, both because the system was so new and because parents did not immediately take advantage of it. Parents seemed to be more interested in teaching their children a trade than in educating them, which helps account for the low and erratic attendance in early classrooms.[33]

I he temperance crusade evoked a similar reaction. The movement was suspect among wage earners because it promoted total abstinence and was closely identified with the Presbyterian clergy. Presbyterian domination of the antiliquor movement prompted the enmity of freethinking and unchurched workingmen, who dismissed it as a vehicle of "creeping priestcraft."[34] They were also offended by the Presbyterians' upper-class pretentiousness. Even Thomas Hunt, a Presbyterian minister himself, thought as much, and accused his colleagues of being "too conservative" and of casting "a look of suspicion upon all workingmen."[35] The most sympathetic wage earners, as Hunt understood, supported temperance in the thirties, but looked upon advocates of total abstinence as "fanatics." For example, Benjamin Sewell, a journeymen tanner and local labor leader, in recalling his days as a wage earner, said that his comrades had "no objection" to moderate drinking. "My company all drank a little," he observed, "'but nothing to hurt' we used to say."[36] Men like Sewell were so accustomed to drink that they could not break the habit, even if so inclined, simply by signing a temperance or total abstinence pledge (which the Pennsylvania Society naively considered "essential to the support and prosperity" of the cause).[37] They needed the encouragement of their peers, but most workers were unprepared to lend such support. Sewell thus remembered the tragedy of a young friend who signed a total abstinence pledge against the advice of comrades who recommended that he simply "cut down." Branded as a teetotaler and chided by shopmates, he relapsed into heavy drinking and lost his job. He then left for West Philadelphia in order to "hunt work and reform," but was told by an employer acquainted with his drinking problem, "we have no work for *you*." Distraught and demoralized, he wandered aimlessly for a few days and then hanged himself.[38]

Such factors dampened the popularity of the early temperance

movement and restricted memberships in mainstream societies to
respectable Philadelphians. The Pennsylvania Society, for example,
counted only 4,500 temperance advocates in the county by the middle
of the thirties, despite years of energetic campaigning, and most of
these partisans were probably middle class.[39] Even temperance
groups that advertised themselves as workingmen's societies had
heavy middle-class memberships. One such group, the Mechanics'
and Workingmen's Temperance Society, was not working-class at
all. Its list of leaders was crowded with the names of prominent
merchants, large manufacturers, and master craftsmen, and included
the wealthy entrepreneurs Baldwin and (shipbuilder) John Vaughan.
The social composition of the Society, in fact, closely resembled that
of the New School Presbyterian church.[40]

This is not to suggest journeymen were immune to evangelical
Protestantism or the new morality. To the contrary, there is
compelling evidence of a small and growing group of working-class
evangelicals in the late 1820s and 1830s,[41] but to attribute their
conversion to the persuasion and manipulation of upper-class
Philadelphians and their clergy is to inflate the power and influence
exercised by the elite. Some wage earners joined the evangelical fold
because the new morality filled their needs and because humble New
School Presbyterian and Methodist clergymen related to them more
effectively than did the prominent divines.

These obscure ministers had much in common. With the notable
exception of James Patterson (1779–1837), they were born around
the end of the eighteenth century and most attended, but were not
graduated from, Princeton Seminary.[42] They abandoned bucolic but
dull Princeton for the challenge of saving souls in the city, finding
Presbyterian Philadelphia, however, no more hospitable than did
Barnes. The "Doctors" or "Reverend Fathers," as they referred to
their superiors in the Presbytery, conveyed an intimidating air of
"coldness and formality," and, on top of this, often withheld
preaching licenses from novitiates suspected of Arminian inclinations.[43] Most of them, in fact, were drawn to Philadelphia and
subsidized by lay groups and not the Presbytery.[44] As urban
missionaries stationed at store-front churches and leading fledgling
congregations in the working-class suburbs, they considered themselves to be a group apart from the clerical establishment, so much so

that they formed their own organization, the Pastors' Association, in the late 1820s. Monthly meetings of the Association brought Patterson together with William Ramsey, Anson Rood, Robert Adair, William Carroll, and others, and featured discourse on the "best plan of doing good to the immense population in the suburbs."[45]

Theirs was a monumental task. The moral state of the outlying districts was so appalling that established clergymen—Old School and New School alike—considered them lost and confined their ministrations to the city. Patterson and his clique of zealous neophytes were no less horrified. A. O. Halsey described the southern suburbs as the "very charnal house of this ungodly city . . . a 'fac simile' of the very portals of the regions of all moral filth and blasphemy."[46] William Ramsey, one of Halsey's associates fresh from seminary in the mid-twenties, patiently recorded his thoughts in a voluminous diary. Awe-struck by Southwark's libertine street life, he intoned "Lord have mercy on *Southwark*."[47] The northern suburbs, bailiwick of Robert Adair, were not much better. There one found a "mass of neglected population who went nowhere to hear the gospel." Instead, "they desecrated the Sabbath by collecting in groups round the dram shops . . . spending. . . [the] holy hours in rioting and drunkenness."[48]

The very conditions that repelled downtown clerics proved an incentive to the young pastors. In their crusade against sin, James Patterson, minister of the First Church in Northern Liberties and one of the most imaginative evangelicals of his time, was the guiding light. Employing Finneyite measures long before Finney himself deserted the bar for the pulpit, Patterson staged protracted meetings as early as 1816. One of them extended for seventy-six consecutive evenings and nearly cost the indefatigable divine his voice. Patterson preached from the soap box in vacant lots and the district square, visited private homes and workshops, and pioneered methods of lay participation worthy of a skilled community organizer. Women were divided into committees of two, assigned a specific neighborhood, and then charged with proselytizing the impenitent wherever they were found. The "anxious" were encouraged to attend church, where they occupied special pews and were subjected to peer pressure to mend their ways. Those unmoved by exuberant laymen and women might be inspired by accounts of Patterson's revivals in local newspapers. He was one of the first of his profession to advertise church events in the press and, by all accounts, was Philadelphia's premier evangelist.[49]

Patterson's admirers borrowed some of his methods. None came close to duplicating their mentor's achievement, but they did make enough converts to elevate their missions and shabby store fronts into settled congregations. By the early thirties they went a step further and, joining with sympathetic downtown ministers, formed a separate Presbytery.[50] A center of pro-Finney sentiment and revivalist fervor, this Presbytery rallied to the defense of fellow member Barnes in his ongoing battle with the Old Guard, and became the nucleus of New School élan in the impending schism.

Members of the Pastors' Association sided with downtown New School ministers, but did not necessarily impart the same message to their flock. A major class difference existed between the communicants of each cluster of churches, and ministers tailored their style and sermons accordingly. Ramsey had several sobering encounters with the evangelicalism of the wealthy. One of these occurred in 1824, when he paid a visit to Thomas Skinner's finely appointed church in the downtown. "What splendor!" he wrote in amazement. "The church is beautiful . . . *a mahogeny pulpit, sloping pews—a descending floor—and a hollow-toned organ*," he continued and added with more than a tinge of sarcasm that such opulence "constitute[s] the ornaments of the house of God."[51] Four years later he discovered that the tastes of class extended beyond aesthetics to what was expected of ministers. Ramsey was asked to deliver a guest sermon in another elite church and evidently gave considerable thought to his presentation. He wrestled with the idea of recognizing the genteel sensibilities of his listeners and sparing them his disposition for fire and brimstone, but decided to treat them as he would his plebian parishoners in Southwark. The young pastor preached "the law," speaking "very plainly" . . . [on] the importance of doing Something for the Lord Speedily," but was received coldly. "I expect my message was unwelcome," he lamented, but then buoyed himself, musing, "God forbid that I should ever preach to please those who are dosing away . . . and rock the cradle while they Sleep. I told them what they must do if they desired the blessings of God to rest upon them." His lofty mission in the service of Christ required him to "preach the truth" whether "I preach before beggars or Kings."[52]

Ramsey's sloppy social categories may be challenged, but he deserves to be credited for identifying a major dimension of antebellum religion, nonetheless. Religion, he implied, was not class-neutral or beyond the leaven of social distinctions. What suited Southwark's plebian churches was inappropriate in fasionable places of worship, notwithstanding the fact that both were Presbyterian (and New School). As Ramsey learned, class mediated religious practice and the differences alluded to by the young minister manifested themselves in a number of ways.

The style of delivery New School ministers used for working-class congregations was more appropriate to the firebrand Methodist than to the Presbyterian, Old or New School. Much like new Methodists but unlike lettered Presbyterians, such ministers eschewed written sermons and "splendid specimens of rhetoric," as one of them put it, for extemporaneous speaking.[53] As a result, none of their sermons survive, but diary entries and cryptic notes indicate that they had the Methodist penchant for what E. P. Thompson calls "religious terrorism." Patterson, wrote an observer, "attacked and exposed the peculiar vices of his hearers" and "Against these crimes . . . arrayed the terrors of the Lord, passed on them an unsparing condemnation, and pointed out the tremendous punishment which God would inflict on their finally impertinent perpetrators."[54] Ramsey employed the same tactic of dangling frightening images in front of communicants. "No soul gets into heaven without being scared," he asserted. "If sinners were only dipped into hell a few times & were right well schorched [sic] . . . there would be fewer of them in hell."[55]

These ministers resembled new Methodists in another respect. They enforced strict standards of behavior and resorted to remedial measures that were simply unacceptable in upper-class congregations. Patterson was an especially severe disciplinarian. He was one of the first Presbyterians in Philadelphia to subject prospective communicants and members charged with moral turpitude to the scrutiny of the church. The accused were ordered to appear before the church session and those found guilty were suspended or expelled, if they were members, and denied admission, if they were new converts.[56] Patterson's youthful followers disciplined members for such sins as "playing cards," "using profanity," "fornication," an act for which women alone were castigated, and, of course, "drinking."[57]

Observers insist that such ministerial labors produced two closely related results. First, it is claimed, these efforts ushered in a fundamental change in the morality and social personality of suburban dwellers. This population, exulted Reverend Robert Adair, "seemed to start into a new social, intellectual and moral life. Habits of sobriety, industry, economy, peace, and friendship were formed." Second, "many" communicants were said to have acquired a "competency, and enjoyed domestic comforts to which they had been strangers."[58] The first contention is excessive. As we shall see, a large segment, and perhaps a majority, of suburbanites stood outside the moral force of the church, and some converts found it impossible to negotiate between the moral rigidity of evangelicalism and the surveillance of fellow Christians. These backsliders were expelled, banished, as it were, from the community of Christ. The dutiful Christian, however, unquestionably experienced the kind of personality transformation described by Adair. Evangelical ministers would have it no other way.

The second assessment is tested in Tables 5 through 7, which list the occupations and property holdings, and trace the careers of the members of the Ebenezer Methodist Episcopal and the First Presbyterian Churches in Southwark. The data on property suffer from the shortcomings of the 1850 census, the sole catalogue of property holders, which fails to record many members of the sample. Moreover, there is no way of determining holdings prior to 1850; consequently, we do not know whether an individual lost wealth, although this is unlikely since many were of humble origins. The data, therefore, are imperfect, but good enough to construct a reasonably accurate picture of the congregations.

The findings tend to support the relationship that ministers perceived between evangelicalism and modest property accumulation. (See Table 7.) About one-third of each church owned real property at mid-century, with the average holding falling between $3,800 and $4,280, not a princely sum but more than enough for a well-furnished house on a good-sized lot. Such a finding takes on added significance when one recalls that only 10 percent of Philadelphia's adult male population owned any property at all in 1850. These evangelicals were uncommonly successful.

Table 5
Occupational Profile of Revivalists, 1830s

Occupation	Methodist		New School Presbyterian	
	No.	*%*	*No.*	*%*
Gentlemen	0	0	0	0
Professional	3	2.9	9	18.8
Merchant and Retailer	16	15.5	2	4.2
Manufacturer	1	0.9	0	0
Lower white-collar*	4	3.9	2	4.2
Master Craftsman	10	9.7	4	8.3
Journeyman	64	62.1	27	56.2
Unskilled labor and street trade	5	4.9	4	8.3
Total‡	103		48	

*Includes clerks and public officials.

†Craftsmen with two addresses listed in the directories, one for residence and one for place of business, are treated as masters. Those with a single address are treated as journeymen. Admittedly, this is an imperfect method of distinguishing masters from journeymen since some masters ran their businesses from their homes. It would have been preferable to differentiate these groups on the basis of property holding, but the necessary sources, local tax lists, have not survived.

‡The original Presbyterian sample contained 77 names; the original Methodist sample contained 119 names. Forty-eight or 62.3 percent of the former and 103, or 86.5 percent of the latter, were located in the directories. The disparity is probably explained by two factors: the Methodist sample is drawn from a published source, which is not as complete as the Presbyterian church manuscripts, and the Methodists lived closer to the city and thus are more fully covered in the city directories.

Source: First Presbyterian Church in Southwark, Minutes, 1830–1840, Presbyterian Historical Society, Philadelphia: First Presbyterian Church of Southwark, Trustees Minutes, 1818–1832, Presbyterian Historical Society, Philadelphia; and Centennial Publishing Committee, *History of Ebenezer Methodist Church, Southwark* (Philadelphia: J. B. Lippincott, 1892); and city directories, 1830–1835.

Table 6
Career Mobility of Journeymen, 1830–1850

Occupation		Methodist		New School Presbyterian	
1830	*1850*	*No.*	*%*	*No.*	*%*
Journeyman	Nonmanual	9	18.3	1	6.6
Journeyman	Master	18	36.7	7	46.6
Journeyman	Journeyman	21	42.8	6	40.0
Journeyman	Unskilled	1	2.1	1	6.6
Total		49*		15+	

*Represents 76.5 percent of the journeymen in the linked sample.
†Represents 55.5 percent of the journeymen in the linked sample.

Source: First Presbyterian Church in Southwark, Minutes, 1830–1840, Presbyterian Historical Society, Philadelphia; First Presbyterian Church of Southwark, Trustee Minutes, 1818–1832, Presbyterian Historical Society, Philadelphia; and Centennial Publishing Committee, *History of Ebenezer Methodist Church, Southwark* (Philadelphia: J. R. Lippincott, 1892); and city directories, 1830–1835.

An analysis of their occupational careers shows the same pattern. The great majority of both chuches were journeymen in the late 1820s, but not typical wage earners. (See Table 5.) As Stuart Blumin has shown, opportunities for advancement narrowed in the four decades preceding the Civil War and artisans were more likely to experience downward rather than upward mobility.[59] Evangelical journeymen were glaring exceptions to this rule. Over half of the Presbyterians and the Methodists who started out as journeymen in early thirties wound up as master craftsmen or small retailers by 1850.[60] (See Table 6.)

We gain further insight into the status of these evangelicals by comparing them with their downtown coreligionists. According to Doherty, downtown evangelicals were rising industrialists who lacked the pedigree and wealth to be considered "proper Philadelphians" but did "lay the base for eventual acceptance into the city's upper class."[61] Suburban evangelicals were a cut below Doherty's nascent elite. Only a third of them owned real property, compared with 90 percent of the downtowners, and average holdings were modest by comparison. (See Table 7.) The employers among them, moreover, hardly measured up to the likes of Matthias Baldwin and other center-city entrepreneurs. Methodist iron founder Thomas Tasker was the largest of the group and his work force of 200 employees was a third of Baldwin's. Most of Tasker's entrepreneurial colleagues employed fewer than twelve workers, and were neighborhood artisans and garret bosses.[62] If Doherty's New Schoolers constituted an emergent upper class, these evangelicals were a rising middle class of former journeymen who had scratched their way to employer status and middling respectability.

Several forces propelled these Philadelphians into evangelicalism. Chance cannot be discounted. The accidents of personal loss or tragedy—debilitating illness, the death of a friend or loved one, or even extended unemployment—could move the depressed into seeking consolation in religious emotionalism.[63] Dynamic ministers also swelled revivalist ranks. Their charisma could capture the most hardened doubter, regardless of his health or state of mind. Nor should one discount the influence of evangelical women. Widows,

Table 7
Property Holding

	No.	% with Real Property	Average Holding	% with $3000+	% with $9000+
Presbyterians (Southwark)	22†	27.3	$3,800	insig.	0
Methodists	80*	30.0	4,280	30	2.5
Presbyterians (Doherty sample)	NA	88.0	NA	50	11

*Represents 77.7 percent of the linked sample.
†Represents 45.8 percent of the linked sample.

Source: Robert M. Doherty, "Social Basis of the Presbyterian Schism, 1837–1839: The Philadelphia Case," *Journal of Social History 2* (Fall, 1968): 74–75; and United States Census Office, *Census of the United States, Population Schedule, Philadelphia County (Southwark), 1850* (microfilm, MSS, National Archives, Washington, D.C.)

wives, and daughters comprised the vast majority of evangelical parishioners, and they diffused the revivalist spirit in public and in the privacy of their homes. Cadres of female home visitors coaxed men into James Patterson's pews, and evangelized wives often passed on their religion to husbands. Mrs. F. V. Bussier, for example, worshipped at William Ramsey's church, but her husband was a former Quaker converted to Unitarianism and a "remarkably worldly" man. Bussier had some toleration for his wife's religious instincts but precious little for her minister and even less for his social calls and evangelical dissertations at the dinner table. Ramsey's visits aggravated the family's denominational differences and so upset Bussier that he scribbled a note to Ramsey complaining that he disturbed domestic harmony and warning him against setting foot in his house again. Peace reigned in the Bussier household thereafter, but not because of Ramsey's absence. Instead, Mrs. Bussier's piety infected her husband and he jettisoned the cold formality of Unitarianism for the enthusiasm of revivalism.[64] The Mrs. Bussiers of Philadelphia proved effective agents of revivalism and temperance.[65] Their crusading spirit and quiet advocacy recruited untold numbers into both causes and gave revivalist organizations a unique cast of sexual integration. But three factors, each of which reflect deeper social experiences, bear more weight.

The first is social background. Church records show that congregations were rather volatile, losing members due to apostasy and out-migration, and replenishing themselves through revivals and "transfers."[66] Transfers typically were rural-urban migrants whose backgrounds and reasons for migrating predisposed them to evangelicalism. Most of them, and possibly many converts as well, were church members out of rustic New Jersey and Pennsylvania who came to Philadelphia in search of opportunity and simply reestablished church ties or were "quickened" during the revivals of the late 1820s and early 1830s.[67]

The quality of the urban milieu and of the work settings in which these newcomers found themselves also reinforced the evangelical urge. Strangers in the impersonal city, they discovered the consolation of community and fraternity in the church. Bonds of friendship that grew out of the collective experience of conversion imparted a sense of belonging in the anonymity of the burgeoning metropolis. Moreover, since these migrants were without skills, they entered the most advanced work settings, which relied more on brawn and dexterity than craft knowledge, and which enforced a rigorous work routine. The regimen of the factories, manufactories, and sweatshops that absorbed newcomers, in turn, conditioned worker behavior along the lines expressed by the new Protestantism. We get a hint of this process in a letter by Manayunk's Methodist textile hands, who swore off drink and came together in a temperance society in the mid-thirties. As if assuring readers that they had not been manipulated by employers, they boasted that their society was gotten up "without the aid or countenance of the talented and influential members of the community!" Work conditions, not employer machinations, impelled them to forsake spirits, for intoxicants tended to "confuse the brain, cloud the mind, and warp the judgment, thereby rendering those who indulge in them, totally unfit to superintend the movements of complicated machinery."[68] Their religious counterparts working in Southwark and other suburban districts outside the textile mills admittedly did not operate power-driven equipment or confront so taxing a work pace, but the incentive to endorse the new morality was the same for all in-migrants employed in modernizing plants: the need for greater self-discipline wrought by the unfolding of industrial capitalism.[69]

Finally, the career patterns discussed above helped sustain working-class evangelicalism. For these workers, at least, the promise of social mobility that was rapidly becoming a national faith, thanks in large part to the efforts of their own ministry, was no pipedream. Highly mobile men, they had careers that coincided with, and might have hinged on, the Protestant work ethic conveyed by the new morality. Worldly success and evangelical morality reinforced one another, and the mobile journeyman became a model to emulate, living proof of the promise inherent in evangelicalism.[70]

Thus revivalist workers represented a distinct culture with its own values, institutions, and standards of right and wrong. Social activity and moral conduct outside the workplace were governed by the strictures of the new Protestantism and by peer pressure, which together ruled out traditional working-class pastimes and radical politics. Life revolved around hearth, home, and the church. When not acting the part of the dutiful father, husband, and responsible breadwinner, the revivalist filled his social calender with church activities, such as entertaining the pastor, holding evening Bible class, attending frequent meetings on congregational governance, and volunteering assistance for special events.[71]

The new morality imbued revivalists with a unique social identity and cultural perspective. Unlike long-time artisans of urban birth and urban upbringing, who identified as workingmen or as practitioners of a specific craft, revivalists saw themselves in ethnocultural terms and identified themselves as Protestant Americans. Fortified by the heavy-handed morality and effusive spirit of evangelicalism, they were intolerant of nonevangelicals and reserved special hostility for Catholics, who were considered carriers of moral decay and religious corruption. This nativist bias, when coupled to the cultural causes championed by leading ministers, not only set them against other workers, but also cemented political ties between revivalist workers and moral reformers, through the agency of the Whig party.

The relationship between revivalist workers and their employers at the point of production was complicated. No group of workers was so consumed by the drive for material improvement, and this preoccupation could turn them against employers who arbitrarily reduced wages or lengthened the workday. But such moments were rare. In the main revivalists were the most individualistic and deferential of all wage earners. An evangelical who had "nothing to boast of, in regard to this world's wealth or its honors, and who looks for none save the attainment (by honest industry and the use of his right arm) of a competency for himself and family" still attacked trade unionism as subversive.[72] He attributed poverty to individual shortcomings, flawed character, and the inability to overcome "habit's power." His advice to those who shared his dream for a competency was disciplined effort at the workbench.

Traditionalists:
"The Boys of Pleasure"

3

Presbyterian minister James W. Alexander often shuttled back and forth between his home in Princeton and Philadelphia. His route took him through the thinly populated countryside of eastern Pennsylvania and southern New Jersey, with its small towns surrounded by patches of piney forest and expanses of fertile farmland. The subtle beauty of the landscape paled with each trip and the garrulous preacher welcomed the opportunity to relieve the boredom by exchanging a word with passers-by and local folk. One of his more memorable dialogues took place during the dawn of the Great Depression in the late thirties, when he came across an elderly tailor and a young companion reclining in a field. Evangelists instinctively reacted with hostility to the spectacle of idle workers. It was particularly galling to Alexander, a leading exponent of the new morality with a keen interest in the morals and manners of workingmen. He assumed that the loungers were unemployed because of the recent panic, but was corrected by the salty tailor, who snapped, "Not at all, we are only enjoying the *Tailor's Vacation*." And he continued, "Pressure is well enough, as I can testify when the last dollar is about to be pressed out of me, but *Vacation* is capital. It tickles one's fancy with the notion of choice. 'Nothing on compulsion' is my motto."[1]

The journeyman's retort to the good reverend is more than a humorous anecdote. It represents the gist of working-class traditionalism, an indefatigably autonomous culture whose adherents outraged revivalists and respectable Philadelphians alike. Their behavior inside and outside the workplace recalled an earlier era in which society made no hard and fast distinction between work and play, nor defamed certain amusements as sinful. They were bearers of older ways, whose blend of leisure and work furnished a bountiful market for local vice industries.

Declaring vacations from work was hardly unique to tailors or to traditionalists. Hand loom weavers and workers of all trades had their versions of the "tailor's vacation" and passed holidays in relaxation. They took off from work in celebration of national heroes and patriotic events, on "red letter days," on their own birthdays, or on any occasion that suited their whim.[2] Nor did traditionalists monopolize all forms of leisure. To whatever extent all wage earners appreciated respites from toil and overwork. One did not have to be a traditionalist to enjoy fishing the sleepy Schuylkill for its prodigious supply of shad or hunting small game in nearby fields and forests. An observer tells us that the "fair" days of early spring raised worker interest in both sports.[3] The warmer months also brought circuses and road shows, balloon launchings, tramping athletes, and other popular attractions that drew crowds of curious and fun-loving workers from home and shop.[4]

Some activities were the exclusive preserve of traditionalists, none more so than drinking and the social rituals surrounding it. Unlike the emerging industrial elite, the evangelical middle and working classes, and, as we shall see, the radical workingmen, traditionalists clung tenaciously to customary notions about the value of spirits. They prized liquor for its own sake and for medicinal purposes; they used it to combat fatigue, warm the body in winter, cool it in summer, and lighten moods in any season.[5] The focal point of social drinking was the neighborhood tavern or a less respectable tippling house. Grog shops and tippling houses, being unlicensed, were concealed in cellars and garrets; pubs and taverns, on the other hand, could not be overlooked. Amusing signs above their doors distinguished them from the sedate houses catering to the middle class and at times boldly proclaimed their class nature. "The Four Alls," a popular pub in Moyamensing, owed its title to the following apothegm:

1. *King.* I govern all.
2. *General.* I fight for all.
3. *Minister.* I pray for all.
4. *Laborer.* And I pay for all.[6]

Neighboring Southwark housed a good number of these venerable drinking places. One of them sported a placard depicting a dog barking at a full moon and the questions:

Ye foolish dogs! Why bark ye so?
While I'm so high and you're so low?[7]

Pubs and taverns offered an assortment of entertainment, legal and otherwise. Cock-fighting, a popular spectator sport in Colonial Philadelphia but thereafter shunned by men of social standing, prospered in the working-class pubs of Jacksonian Philadelphia and usually played to as many spectators as the facility could handle. William Cook ran one of the larger cockpits. Encircled by an amphitheater with a seating capacity of seventy-five, his pit lured many enthusiasts, who bet on their favorite birds.[8] Working-class gamblers not excited by the gory sport could try their hand in gambling halls. Policy houses, furtively located in the back alleys of poorer neighborhoods, waited fortune seekers looking to turn modest investments of "3 cents to half a dollar" into windfalls.[9] Taverns featured games closely resembling "menagerie" in which participants sat around a circular board divided into pie-shaped units, each of which bore the picture of an animal. Each player placed a coin on his choice and waited for a spinning pinwheel to designate the winner.[10]

Despite these attractions, traditionalists probably visited pubs for the sake of camaraderie. At the end of the workday homeward-bound artisans went to their favorite taverns to meet friends and discuss the events of the day over drams of malt liquor or spirits. Tavern traffic picked up noticeably on Sunday night, most observers agreed, and in the winter months, when trade slowed.[11]

Traditionalist workers, however, did not adjust their love for liquor to the rhythms of the economy. To the surprise of many observers, they carried on the eighteenth-century tradition of drinking in the shop. Sylvester Graham, the noted Presbyterian minister and temperance advocate who would become a leading dietary reformer, was astonished to find journeymen looking forward to the late afternoon, when "treating time" signalled the occasion to lay down tools and pass around the communal jug.[12] Graham's testimony is supported by Benjamin T. Sewell, whose memoirs recollected the worker practice of sipping grog from flasks, right in the shop. When flasks ran dry an apprentice was delegated to get them refilled at the local pub, which gave many youngsters a taste for hard liquor, since as reward for his trouble, he "robs the mail . . . takes a drink before he gets back."[13]

The persistence of such casual work habits in an age of advancing industrialism and evangelical fervor may be attributed to the backgrounds and laboring experiences of traditionalist wage earners. Most Philadelphia workers, it should be recalled, were drawn from the American and European countrysides. These in-migrants and immigrants came from vastly different social and economic settings, but subgroups within each population had more in common that has been thought. Most of the Irish, the city's leading immigrant group, arrived in Philadelphia directly from rural Eire, and they were the farthest removed from advanced production techniques or even from the discipline of the market economy. Nominally Catholic at the start, or at least more peasant than Catholic, they were imbued with the gloomy pessimism of the peasantry—rich in folk custom and sorely deficient in the attitudes of the productive worker. Survival, not occupational improvement or income accumulation, was uppermost in their minds. Americans of rural birth and most of those reared in the city were as accustomed to hard work as the Irish, but not to the rhythms and exigencies of industrial pursuits. The nonevangelicals among them were either orthodox Protestants or unchurched, but whatever the case, their outlook on work conformed closely to that of the Irish.[14]

The extent to which Irish immigrants and native-born Americans honored older concepts of work and productivity hinged mainly on their occupational locations in the city. Those who performed casual labor or worked at home under the putting-out system had little incentive to cast off traditional ways. They were the poorest of all wage earners and enjoyed the autonomy and independence that nurtures tradition.

Old-World customs that repeatedly interfered with work thus remained intact among Irish outworkers and unskilled workers. These immigrants deserted workplaces for days at a time to celebrate a wedding, console at a wake, or demonstrate athletic prowess in the Donneybrook Fair, the Irish national games held in August[15] None of these occasions was complete without liquor, and every Irish community had its pubs and taverns, the nerve centers of local life. Irish and American outworkers, however, did not need the formal excuse of a wake, wedding, or national holiday to avoid work. Cottagers and laborers of both nationalities took off days whenever they saw fit. They often repaired to the country for picnics and celebrated St. Monday with frolicing in the city streets.[16] "All work and no play," said one of them, "makes Jack a dull boy."[17]

Artisans employed in neighborhood shops, though not as independent as outworkers and casual laborers, still had considerable self-determination and, thus, casual work habits. They were rarely sweated or driven by employers, either because markets were slow at this level of production or because masters were former journeymen steeped in preindustrial shop customs. The casual and easy-going manner of such masters caught the attention of many contemporaries. Temperance reformer Thomas Hunt knew a journeyman who was fired on account of "idleness and neglect of business, but not for drinking; for they all [masters] drank themselves."[18] These employers, said another Philadelphian, "expected" journeymen to lose time because of excessive drinking and holidays—official and unofficial—and endured them as long as they showed up "tolerably regularly" and avoided getting "absolutely drunk" as a matter of habit—all of which explains why some workers unconcernedly drank in their small shops.[19]

All expressions of traditionalist behavior, however, were not survivals of custom nourished by the "holes and pores" in production. Some facets of traditionalism took shape in the city itself and were local to the urban milieu. Nothing illustrates this better or offers more insight into the consciousness of traditionalist workers than the history of Philadelphia's volunteer fire department.

The volunteer fire department of Colonial Philadelphia was perfectly reputable. Founded by the energetic Dr. Franklin, it recruited public-spirited residents of all classes, but relied chiefly on the commercial elite and mechanics who looked upon public service as an obligation of republican citizenship. As befits this social composition, companies closely resembled respectable dinner clubs. They met in rented halls and public houses, and operated on an ad hoc basis, mobilizing bucket brigades of citizens in emergencies. Such outfits left something to be desired as effective firefighters, but most clearly took their mission seriously.[20]

Population growth and the coming of industrialism drastically altered the fire department. The increase and dispersal of population in the second half of the nineteenth century multiplied the demand for firefighting services, and led to a marked proliferation of member companies. Nearly two per year were organized in the second quarter of the century and by the early fifties there were some seventy units in the city and surrounding districts.[21] These were equally divided between hose companies, which carried lengths of leather hose on spindle-like carriages, and engine companies, which manned mobile pumps. Although local law limited the former to twenty-five members and the latter to fifty, personnel mushroomed along with the number of companies, sometimes reaching into the hundreds. Companies used the dues of their large memberships, the contributions of neighborhood businessmen, and public subsidies to construct fire houses, which ended the era of meetings in rented quarters.

The most important change was in the membership. As upper-class Philadelphians turned their attention to entrepreneurship, they withdrew from the companies, leaving them to the newly formed working class, or to some segments of it.[22] One of the most striking aspects of the companies was their relative absence in areas where advanced production prevailed. In Manayunk, for example, the textile elite created the fire department, controlled its apparatus, and screened its members, thus depriving it of an independent and autonomous existence.[23] In areas dominated by outwork and small shops, however, the companies thrived and were free from elite control. Southwark and Moyamensing in the south, Kensington in the north, and the western hem of the old city, with their large concentrations of artisan shops, outworkers, and unskilled workers, had the greatest number of companies and the most active ones as well.[24]

The hallmark of these lusty volunteers was competitiveness. The first companies to arrive at a fire controlled the best hose and hydrant connections and earned a reputation for speed and efficiency. This was no small honor and some volunteers showed great ingenuity in jockeying for an edge. Aptly known as "bunkers," they spent the night in the firehouse and took turns at the tower watching for traces of smoke. The more ambitious among them, it was said, even "delighted in a day watch."[25] Fire alarms occasioned races between rivals pulling their gaudy tenders and carriages through narrow streets, and fires became the scene of comical scuffles between engine companies hurrying to hydrants and hose companies battling for their favorite tenders. Getting to a blaze often required repelling combatants who jammed spanners into spokes and cut tow ropes, but fighting off assaults brought great joy. One volunteer attached such importance to winning that he confessed to being able to "work better after a long sun and race with the P—and had beaten her, but if his company was 'waxed' he could'nt [sic] work at all and had to lose a day."[26]

Such antics and blasé attitudes toward work failed to amuse local entrepreneurs. These businessmen envisioned the volunteers not only as firefighters but also as employees and had nothing good to say about their performance in either capacity. They condemned the worker-firemen's rowdiness and cursed their deserting workshops at the sound of an alarm and wasting precious time loafing in fire houses.

To them, the volunteer system was a nuisance and, as they put it, a "relic" of a "primitive state of society" that distracted workers and interfered with the production process.[27] Those who could afford it purchased their own equipment and many more joined together with merchants, land speculators, and insurance salesmen in a vigorous but fruitless movement to replace the volunteers with paid professionals.[28]

As the critics knew so well, fire companies were not merely feckless agencies of public safety. Rather, they were vital social organizations deeply embedded in traditionalist communities that fulfilled the cultural needs of their members. Fraternal-clubs-*cum*-athletic-teams, they offered outlets for recreation and centers of camaraderie. They also conferred upon their impoverished followers the status and recognition denied them by the larger society. Membership in a company was a sign of social acceptance, for new recruits were not admitted without the sponsorship of a member and a majority vote of the entire body.

Executive offices were open to all and fellow firemen bestowed no greater honor than electing one of their number to a directorship. Directors loosely supervised the actual firefighting or at least tried to bring a semblance of order to the chronic chaos and confusion. This office seems to have been the "summit of the hopes" of the typical volunteer, and with good reason. Directors were fully outfitted with "a trumpet in one hand, a spanner in the other, and a lantern affixed to a leathern belt around his waist" and reveled in the paraphernalia of rank.[29]

This was exclusively a man's world. Women were barred from fire companies and, as far as one can tell, rarely frequented the pubs and tippling houses that dotted traditionalist neighborhoods.[30] Manly values governed the behavior of firemen at all times. The more daring and assertive the volunteer, the more respect he commanded from his comrades and from youths, who took to "running with" or escourting companies to and from fires. Firemen and "runners" venerated the company "tough" and followed him with "awe and reverence."[31] The ethic of manliness implied in such behavior is unmistakable in the following swaggering song written by a Philadelphia fireman:

> We are the Ancient Rams,
> Who never fear our foes,
> And at the corner of Second and Wharton we stand,
> And run with the Wecca hose.
>
> Then arouse ye gallant Rams,
> And by the Wecca stand,
> And show our friends and foes,
> That we're a sporting band.

Our foes are called the Scroungers,
A name we never fear,
For when they see us ancient boys they soon
will disappear.

On the first of September,
Upon a Wednesday night,
They stood at Wharton and Rye Streets,
To show the Rams the fight.

They stood a single minute,
Then found it was no go,
They ran away from us ancient boys,
With steps not very slow,

We fear no equal party,
To meet us on the ground,
For we're the Ancient Rams,
No braver can be found.

Then come ye boys of pleasure,
Wherever you may be,
Come join the sporting Rams,
The boys of fun and glee.[32]

. . . .

A decade later this ethic would touch off brutal clashes between warring white traditionalists. In the 1830s, however, intercompany rivalries were still relatively benign. Skirmishes rarely pitted native-born American against immigrant, because most companies were integrated along national lines, and infrequently claimed lives. In probing the meaning of these scuffles one historian draws a distinction between expressive and instrumental violence. Expressive violence, he argues, seldom has a specific purpose and is less controlled and goal-oriented than instrumental violence, which is purposive and limited.[33] Most firemen's struggles in the 1820s and early 1830s were expressive if not necessarily bloody. More often than not they stemmed from the volunteers' love of fight and desire to avenge insults and threats to manliness. Others were unquestionably instrumental, if not always controlled or limited, and they consisted of two distinct but overlapping types: territorial riots and job riots. Instrumental riots would become the principal mode in the forties, but they were already evident in the early thirties. Such brawls usually arrayed white traditionalists against Blacks.

Interracial violence flared up sporadically during the first third of the nineteenth century, but the first major race riot in Philadelphia took place in the hot summer of 1834.[34] The setting was a carnival near Seventh and South Streets that included a kind of merry-go-round known as "flying horses." It attracted a rough clientele of street-wise whites and Blacks, who shoved and quarreled in the competition for seats. Patience was thin on both sides the evening of August 12, when a shouting match developed into a fight in which the Blacks bested their foes or humiliated them enough to provoke severe retaliation. Later that night a crowd of vengeful whites armed with brickbats and paving stones, assembled in a field opposite Pennsylvania hospital, and went on a rampage through the Afro-American community. The mob first trashed a tavern owned by the proprietor of the "flying horses" and then turned on Black residents and their property. Club-wielding whites mercilessly beat their adversaries in the street and fought their way into homes. They pilfered at will and systematically destroyed furniture, sometimes ceremoniously smashing furnishings in the streets. The area was littered with the splintered remains of dresses and bedsteds and broken bits of pottery and china by the time the police arrived, at 11 p.m. In hopes of preventing further incidents, they arrested eighteen alleged ring leaders, but the tactic failed to quell white rage.

Although stripped of their leaders, the whites reconstituted their forces near the hospital the following evening. Roving bands again invaded the ghetto and went about their work with "renewed . . . fury." One group assaulted "The Diving Bell," an interracial tavern and lodging house; another sacked the First African Presbyterian Church; and still another marauded through the adjacent streets and alleys. At least twenty Black homes were pillaged, and scores of their occupants savagely abused. In one ugly episode a mob broke into a home, took a corpse from a coffin, and hurled it into the street; in another a dead or sleeping infant was snatched from bed and thrown on the floor, and the terrorized mother was "barbarously treated."

Once again the authorities arrived as the violence subsided. They made twenty arrests and then took precautionary measures. The mayor mustered a posse of 300, ordered the First City Calvary Troop fully equipped, and put the Washington Greys under arms. The next evening he marched the posse to the mob's staging ground near the hospital, only to find that it had already wrought havoc—this time across the city line into Southwark. It had stolen to the southern end of the district and destroyed a Black church by sawing through its support beams and pulling it down with guy ropes. By the time a contingent of the posse reached the scene, the building was reduced to a pile of smoking rubble, and the mob was terrorizing and looting neighborhood Blacks. The only bright spot in this nightmarish evening occurred when the mayor got word of a confrontation brewing at a house in which sixty Blacks sought refuge from a menacing mob. He stationed his men between the mob and the edifice, and calmed tempers while his assistants slipped inside and allowed the frightened Blacks to escape out the back.

Minor street fights between whites and Blacks broke out in other districts over the next few nights, but the worst of the rioting ended on Thursday evening. Miraculously, only two Blacks lost their lives, or only two deaths were reported, although two churches and upward of thirty black homes were destroyed.

These incidents command our attention for a number of reasons. First, the participants were not the "gentlemen of property and standing" who were known to lead or participate in anti-Black and antiabolitionist rioting.[35] On the contrary, respectable Philadelphians were cast in the role of curiosity-seekers, and observers characterized the rioters as a mixture of men and "apprentices and half-grown boys" and "very young men" of the "lowest social classes."[36] It is impossible to confirm their age composition, but some evidence supports those who perceived the assailants as lower class: the most common occupations of the apprehended were "laborer" and "weaver."[37] Second, the raids were planned and carried out with community support. On each night rioters congregated in a vacant lot on the city line adjacent to the southern districts and plotted the evening's events. Smaller bands were probably ordered to specific streets or commanded to assault certain buildings. The destroyers of Wharton Street Church, for example, had gathered in the early part of the evening with the deliberate intention of tearing down the building. "No one was to be seen [when the posse arrived] except the neighbors, who stated that the destruction had been affected with much deliberation, and . . . those engaged in it, after effecting their purpose, walked cooly away."[38] Rioters also used code words, such as "Gunner," "Punch," and "Big Gun," probably to coordinate activities or warn of the authorities. Or such terms might refer to firemen. The southern districts, after all, were firemen centers and the location of the riots, coupled with the remarkable efficiency of the participants, suggests a pre-existing organization base.

Third, objects of mob wrath were selected with some discrimination and betray the underlying cause of the riots. Whites who could not bring themselves to beat Blacks or destroy their homes expressed sympathy with the mob by placing lighted candles in their windows. Their homes escaped destruction. Other whites did not escape; namely those who consorted with Blacks, cohabited with Black men or women, or operated businesses catering to Afro-Americans.[39] Attacks on them as well as on the Blacks themselves, underscored the bald racism of the mob. Such assaults may be likened to the territorial riots, in that the violence was partly contrived to intimidate both Blacks and white sympathizers into leaving the area. But there was another dimension to the rioting that indicates that it was rooted in job competition between white and Black workers.

Black workmen in this period did not constitute the usual underclass of casually employed day laborers and a vast army of the unemployed. Instead, they included a small group of artisans and many unskilled, but employed, laborers toiling at construction sites and on the docks as hod carriers and stevedores. The artisans, however, were skilled workers in name only. Unable to practice their trades because of the pervasive racism and absence of a substantial group of Black masters, they were forced into unskilled jobs. The ironic result of this was both that Blacks came to monopolize several categories of unskilled work and that some Black workers, as the looting and destruction of the whites showed, earned good incomes and accumulated some worldly possessions.[40] (Indeed, this was one of the few, and perhaps only, race riots in the city in which white mobs destroyed and looted the personal property of Blacks!) At the same time the influx of unskilled rural-born whites and Irish immigrants exacerbated competition for jobs at the bottom of the occupational ladder. Thirsting for such work, the white newcomers could not gain access to employment without dislodging the Blacks and intimidating their employers.

Evidence abounds that whites attacked Blacks (and some employers) in order to muscle their way into jobs on the waterfront and elsewhere. Mobs sacked the homes of a white shoemaker and chimney sweep believed to have hired Black labor, and at the end of the August riot, it was reported, "colored persons, when engaged in their usual occupations, were repeatedly assailed and maltreated, usually on the Schuylkill front of the city. Parties of white men have *insisted* that no blacks shall be employed in certain departments of labor."[41] An investigation of the riot conducted by local patricians drew the same conclusion. Singling out job competition between the races, the report reads:

> An opinion prevails, especially among white laborers, that certain portions of our community prefer to employ colored people, whenever they can be had, to the employing of white people, and that, in consequence of this preference, many whites, who are able and willing to work, are left without employment, while colored people are provided with work, and enabled comfortably to maintain their families, and thus many white laborers, anxious for employment, are kept idle and indigent. Whoever mixed in the crowds and groups, at the late riots, must so often have heard those complaints, so as to convince them, that the feelings from which they sprung, stimulated many of the most active among the rioters.[42]

Whether they participated in riots against Blacks or merely sympathized with the rioters, traditionalist workers shared a common style of life and social perspective. The tavern, street corner, and fire company were to them what the church, Sunday school, and temperance society were to revivalists. Where revivalists internalized the Protestant work ethic with all that it implies, traditionalists honored casual work practices and, by extension, cared less for social mobility and self-improvement than for survival and group solidarity.

Traditionalists identified three enemies or threats to their well being: Blacks and especially Black dockers who dominated unskilled work, civil authorities who hindered their efforts to intimidate the

Blacks, and moral reformers and evangelicals who would undermine their neighborhood institutions and leisure-time activities. They waged concurrent struggles against all three groups, but in different arenas and with different weapons. When confronting Blacks, they resorted to direct action and collective violence, which in turn drew them into conflict with the civil authorities. Their continual defiance of the police showed that they were anything but deferential or obsequious in the face of authority. Indeed, no group of workers was as inclined to use violence to solve problems or as disrespectful of state power. Yet traditionalists used violence selectively. There is no evidence at all of their employing collective force against moral reformers or evangelicals in this period. Rather than fight these groups in the streets, they did battle with both in the realm of politics. Here they found a worthly ally in the emerging Democratic party, whose ideology of cultural pluralism and freedom from state intervention protected traditional culture from the meliorative policies of Whigs and evangelicals.

Traditionalists thus evinced a peculiar form of class consciousness. Theirs was an "us-them, we-they" mentality that imparted intense feelings over race, on the one hand, and an abiding hatred of upper-class reformers, on the other. They did not, as yet, transfer their suspicions about moral reformers to employers, but were not averse to contesting for their rights at the workplace under certain circumstances. Nor were they inherently conservative or resistant to radicalism. They would follow the lead of radical activists whose program promised to deliver both material security and insulation from the designs of moralists.

Radicals:
Thomas Paine's Progeny

4

Philadelphians received unsettling news in the spring of 1832. For months they had nervously followed reports of the cholera epidemic sweeping westward across Europe. They now learned that the disease had attacked England and threatened to cross the Atlantic. In June the inevitable happened. The pestilence struck east coast cities and towns, sparing only Boston and Charleston, before beginning its death march inland. It took a heavy toll in Philadelphia's poorest enclaves and set off a panic. Thousands retreated to the safety of the countryside. Thousands more, many of them impoverished and infirm, remained stranded, and crowded into churches in search of solace and reassurance.[1]

Denominational rivalries dissolved as God's agents pulled together in the crisis. In late June, leading Protestant clergymen called a meeting to consider remedial action, and the gathering, attended by over 250 preachers of various sects, was one of the largest church-sponsored ecumenical events ever held in Philadelphia. Speakers described the epidemic as divine retribution for man's depravity and called for a day of fasting and prayer "as means of averting the scourge and inducing the Lord to be gracious."[2] The resolutions passed overwhelmingly, with only two dissenters being recorded.

The lone dissidents, Zelotes Fuller and Abel Thomas, were Universalist ministers. Thomas examined the proposals point by point, and rebutted each one with impeccable logic. He scoffed at the idea of fasting, which he saw as debilitating and likely to reduce one's resistance, and discouraged large prayer meetings that risked spreading the epidemic. The act of praying implied that the disease was a "visitation from God, in consequence of the sins of the people, a "judgment," or even a "malady of the soul," in spite of the scientific evidence that cholera had a "natural cause" and was not amenable to spiritual remedy. But he convinced no one, and the hostile audience applauded a disparager who denounced him an an infidel.[3]

This disagreement was part of a deeper division between casts of mind and cultures. One of these, or evangelicalism, is already familiar. The other, a prime example of rationalist radicalism, has either received surprisingly short shrift from historians of the period or has been dismissed as unimportant. A recent scholar of early radicalism tells us, for example, that "In England, anticlerical rationalism was a major component of radical thought throughout the nineteenth century; in America, far more critics of society spoke the language of revivalist Protestantism and of Christian perfectionism than of deist rationalism."[4] This assessment applied to New England, where radicalism and evangelicalism blended together easily in the minds of prominent working-class leaders, such as Seth Luther, and to post-depression radicals in Philadelphia, where there was no contradiction at all between these strains of thought. Predepression radicals in the Philadelphia region were different.

They wedded rationalism to radicalism and the consonance between these formulations emerges in bold relief in Anthony F. C. Wallace's masterful study of Rockdale, a small textile hamlet just south of Philadelphia. There, anticapitalist rationalism constituted a major cultural force that waged a heady battle with evangelical capitalism, or "Christian capitalism," as Wallace would have it, during the second quarter of the nineteenth century. Wallace is rationalism's best historian to date. To his credit, he places rationalism at the center of the cultural paroxysm generated by the early industrial revolution, but his rendition of it is slightly distorted. He relies mainly on elite sources and the social identities of his antievangelicals mirror the bias of such materials. Wallace finds only one "son of the Enlightenment" in Rockdale, an eccentric mill owner who still managed to socialize with the evangelistic members of his class. This discouraging fact forces him to look outside the village for a rationalist consituency. Turning to Philadelphia and its environs, he uncovers a large following, but chooses to focus on its intellectuals, most of whom leaned toward utopian socialism. Thus he ignores working-class rationalists in Rockdale, if indeed there were any, and mentions their Philadelphia counterparts in passing.[5] Their rationalism and the interior life of their culture remain mysterious to us, but it is they who occupy our attention here.

Universalism and Free Thought, the two most important rationalist currents, were products of the liberal humanism of the Enlightenment. Late eighteenth-century Universalists and Free Thinkers, to be sure, had their differences with regard to church policy and the fine points of doctrine. Universalists were closer to conventional religion. They attended formal churches, consulted the bible for inspiration and moral guidance, and sponsored a ministry, although their ministry's training hardly measured up to that of established denominations. Free Thinkers resembled debating clubs more than congregations. They did without a clergy and dismissed the bible as a bundle of contradictions providing no evidence of a benevolent deity. Both groups, however, shared a common view of God and man wholly at variance with orthodoxy and reformed Protestantism. They deprecated orthodoxy's miserly deity for conferring grace on an anonymous few, and attacked Arminianism's more democratic but discriminating God for dispensing salvation as reward for good works and worldly success. Their deity promised salvation to all, regardless of moral character or social station. He was a moral instructor and a mechanic whose handiwork was revealed through scientific inquiry. His children were inherently virtuous and accountable to one another in this life; they understood that benevolence was both its own reward and inextricably bound to the pursuit of happiness.[6] "To be good," proclaimed a leading deist, "was to be happy."[7]

Neither group survived the eighteenth century in quite this form. Universalists were rent by discord between unitarians and trinitarians, and underwent several schisms following the War of 1812.[8] Some of them, unable to resist current religious styles, even adopted evangelical ways. Free Thinkers, whose forebearers resisted the stigma of atheist or infidel, gave up all pretense to being Christians and took some pride in the label "infidel" by the 1820s.[9] But the broad outlines of both movements, particularly their emphasis on reason, scientific inquiry, and moral integrity, remained substantially intact by the time Andrew Jackson assumed the Presidency for the first time.

Partly in reaction to revivalism, both groups enjoyed a rebirth in the twenties and thirties. The First Universalist Church, founded in the 1780s and located near the southern line of the city close to the artisan stronghold of Southwark, was the lone Universalist institution in Philadelphia in 1815. Within twenty years there were two additional congregations in the Northern Liberties and Kensington, and a third in the city.[10] Unlike Universalist organizations, deist groups failed to span the eighteenth and nineteenth centuries. Societies gotten up in the late eighteenth century atrophied or died off shortly thereafter, leaving the city without any Free Thought clubs until the mid-twenties and early thirties, when at least two, and possibly as many as four, organizations and a newspaper suddenly appeared.[11] Neither group had a great following in terms of formal members. Taken together there were about two thousand Universalists and Free Thinkers (or as they preferred Free Enquirers) on the rolls of churches and societies by the beginning of the thirties, about four-fifths of which were Universalists.[12] But such rationalists included the most active and vocal trade-union radicals in Philadelphia, such as the cordwainers William Heighton, Solomon Demars, John Caney, William English, and Israel Young; the carpenters Thomas Wise and William Thompson; and the hand loom weaver John Ferral. They also had a hefty constituency whose numerical strength cannot be gauged, but if traditionalists were the largest working-class subculture and revivalists the smallest, it is probable that radicals fell somewhere in between.

The organizational base of radicalism was two-tiered. One of these, to be treated in the next chapter, consisted of trade unions and their auxiliaries, and embraced workers of other subcultures. The other, which concerns us here, represented a network of debating clubs, lyceums, and discussion groups, and was more restrictive, though not by design. The curious were always welcome, and some did attend, but they catered to the committed. Topics of interest ranged from religion, political economy, and science to contemporary poetry and prose, and these were aired at several forums. Universalist communicants formed scientific study groups independent of churches, while congregations spawned libraries and reading rooms, as well as institutes for adults and adolescents that held lectures and discussion on holy scripture, politics, self-improvement, and other matters that appealed to rationalist sensibilities.[13]

Deist intellectuals belonged to the Society of Free Enquirers. Founded in the early 1830s, it sponsored debates as well as annual dinners in commemoration of patriotic events and the birthdays of Revolutionary heroes. On January 29, for example, the Society celebrated the birthday of Thomas Paine with a light meal followed by guest speakers and toasts in which members showed their respect for the written word and their intellectual versatility. One celebrant raised his glass to "Godwin and Shelley—posterity will appreciate their merits." Another honored "the writings of Byron and Shelley." Still another paid tribute to Paine himself and with a twinkle in his eye, offered the toast, "Thomas Paine has proved to the patriots of '76 and their posterity that he was no sham Paine."[14] Those interested in nature and technology, or what passed for "useful knowledge," studied science and medicine and discussed the latest technological literature. Phrenology commanded special interest because of its inherent fascination and because it suited polemical needs: deists, ever attentive to the practical application of knowledge, used it to disprove the existence of the soul and hence of the afterlife![15] Followers of both groups, wishing to own personal copies of political tracts, literary classics, and scientific brochures but unable to afford them, organized early-day versions of book clubs that supplied cheap editions.[16]

Such intellectual endeavors flowed logically from the ethical code of radical artisans, who carried on the Enlightenment's tradition of critical inquiry and its penchant for self-education. They were autodidacts who, like William English, "never . . . entered a school by the light of day," and taught themselves to read and write or were instructed by friends and parents.[17] English's will to improve himself is paralled by his predictable opinions on drink and recreation. Radicals decried total abstinence as the extremism of punitive evangelicals, but practised and counseled temperance because the latest medical intelligence frowned upon excessive drinking and because over-indulgence interfered with individual enrichment. Honor and dignity were also at stake: drunkenness was disgraceful. Radicals dedicated their leisure hours to cultivating themselves by reading and reflecting and to challenging one another in debate and discourse. Such intellectuals stood clear of revivalist and traditionalist gathering places.[18]

Subtle status differences also set radicals apart from revivalists. We get a sense of this in Table 8, which presents occupational profiles of the members of the Society of Free Enquires and the First and Second Universalist Churches, and, for the sake of comparison, the communicants of Ebenezer Methodist Church in Southwark. The data show that artisans dominated all groups. The Universalists

Table 8

Social Profile of Free Thinkers, Universalists, and Methodists, Late 1820s

Occupation	Free Thinkers		Universalists		Methodists	
	No.	%	No.	%	No.	%
Gentleman	0	0	6	5.6	0	0
Professional	1	3.3	0	0	3	2.9
Merchant and retailer	0	0	1	0.9	16	15.5
Farmer	0	0	2	1.9	0	0
Manufacturer	0	0	7	6.6	1	0.9
Lower white collar	2	6.6	14	13.3	4	3.9
Artisan (master)	4	13.3	17	16.0	10	9.7
Artisan (journeyman)	23	76.7	53	50.0	64	62.1
Unskilled worker	0	0	6	5.7	5	4.9
Total	30		106		103	

Source: First Universalist Church, Minute Book, 1820–1842, Historical Society of Pennsylvania, Philadelphia; Second Universalist Church. Minute Book, 1820–1854, Pennsylvania Historical Society, Philadelphia; *Temple of Reason,* Feb. 6, 1837, and Feb. 8, 1838; Thompson, *Oration, on the Ninety-Eight Anniversary of the Birthday of Thomas Paine, at the Military Hall, before the Society of Free Enquirers* (Philadelphia: Thomas Clark, 1834); Centennial Publishing Committee, *History of Ebenezer Methodist Church, Southwark* (Philadelphia: J. B. Lippincott, 1892); and city directories, 1824–1834.

appear to be more prestigious than the Methodists since a fourth of them were nonmanual workers and gentlemen. On closer examination, however, this impression is blurred. The public officials among them were not rich and powerful politicians, but appointed public servants who earned low salaries and exercised virtually no authority. The manufacturers were also something less than their title indicates. They were small producers of light consumer goods such as buttons, tobacco, lamps, suspenders, ornaments, and stoves—hardly the stuff out of which industrial revolutions are made—and thus resembled master craftsmen more than manufacturers. By lumping them together with the masters in the Universalist sample, we inflate the proportion of master craftsmen to over 20 percent, or about twice the size of the Methodists.

During the early thirties, then, the Universalists were more established in politics and in small businesses than the Methodists. The reason is clear. Like most evangelicals, Methodists drew disproportionately from those in their teens or twenties, while Universalists recruited older folk. The evidence supporting this contention is twofold. First, a goodly number of the names on the roll of the First Universalist Church at the end of the twenties appear on the church's charter of incorporation of 1802.[19] Assuming that these members were in their twenties at the time of incorporation, they were evidently in their forties or fifties by the 1820s. Both churches attracted younger followers in this period, but the continued presence of the founding members inflated the average age of the Universalist sample. This age dimension in turn helps explain the occupational superiority of the Universalists during the late twenties and early thirties. Because many of them were middle-aged, they were at the pinnacle of their careers and slightly better off than the younger Methodists who were just entering their most productive years. It is hardly surprising, therefore, that the journeymen in the Universalist sample did not achieve the success of their Methodist counterparts in the ensuing two decades. Indeed nearly 60 percent of them, as against 45 percent of the Methodists, remained wage earners throughout their lives. (See Table 9.)

There were narrow but significant differences in the occupational preferences of each group as well. As we have seen, revivalists tended to come from vocations (and segments of them) undergoing the

Table 9
Occupational Mobility of Universalists and Methodists,
1830–1850

Occupation		Universalists		Methodists	
1830	*1850*	*No.*	*%*	*No.*	*%*
Journeyman	Nonmanual	0	0	9	18.3
Journeyman	Master	13	41.9	18	36.7
Journeyman	Journeyman	18	59.6	21	42.8
Journeyman	Unskilled	0	0	1	2.1
Total		31*		49†	

*Represents 58.4% in the linked sample.
†Represents 76.5% in the linked sample.

Source: First Universalist Church, Minute Book, 1820–1842, Historical Society of Pennsylvania, Philadelphia; Second Universalist Church, Minute Book, 1820–1854, Historical Society of Pennsylvania, Philadelphia; Centennial Publishing Committee, *History of Ebenezer Methodist Church, Southwark* (Philadelphia: J. B. Lippincott, 1892); and city directories, 1830–1850.

division of labor, and performed in factories, manufactories, and sweatshops. Rationalists were divided between tradesmen in honorable pursuits practiced in small shops or at home—including clock and watchmaking, comb- and brush-making, and hand loom weaving—and tradesmen in the sweated crafts being debased through the division of labor and increasingly carried on in manufactories and sweatshops—including shoemaking and tailoring. The background of these artisans is unknown, but their cosmopolitan perspective and defense of artisanship suggests that they were long-time urban residents rather than recent in-migrants from the countryside, and had served regular apprenticeships in Philadelphia or other urban areas. Their national origins are difficult to pin down. John Ferral and William Heighton were Irish and English immigrants, respectively, but to imagine radicalism as a foreign import is to accept at face value the stigma attached to it by conservative critics. Most radicals appear to have been native-born Americans.[20]

This portrait strengthens our grasp of early radicalism's social basis. As scholars of European socialists and radicals have observed, these dissenters were not neophytic factory hands or proletarians, but veteran artisans who shaped an independent culture in the autonomy accompanying handicraft production.[21] Nor were they upwardly mobile workers or "expectant capitalists" clamoring for greater opportunity in the name of radicalism. Comparatively few of them ascended the occupational ladder or expressed much concern for mobility. They aimed for a competency, and seemed less riled over narrowing opportunities than over growing inequality and the steady decrement of artisanship and independence. Yet radical hostility toward industralism did not depend on material self-interest alone. As rationalists and practitioners of a discrete way of life, they recognized the cultural side of industrialism and distinguished between, but did not separate, the cultural and the material. Their touchstones were economic and cultural, and they employed both in putting forth a holistic critique of emerging industrial society.

The labor theory of value was at the core of radical thought. This formulation was not the invention of militant Philadelphians, for it informed the work of John Locke, Adam Smith, David Ricardo, and other classical political economists, and versions of it enjoyed wide currency in antebellum America. No Philadelphian read such economists with a more critical eye than William Heighton. Born in Oundle, Northamptonshire in 1800, Heighton came to Philadelphia as a youth, and by about the close of the war of 1812, earned his living at a shoemaker's bench.[22] Nothing is known of his early manhood or what became of him after he left the Quaker City in the early 1830s. But during his relatively brief stay in the city, he distinguished himself as its most influential working-class activist and intellectual. He digested the classical thinkers and their critics, including John Gray and Robert Owen, and emerged as the American analogue of contemporary radical intellectuals in England.[23] Like his English comrades writing in the 1820s, he shifted the emphasis of radical discourse from the purely political to a balance of the political and the economic, and popularized ideas that were accessible only to the most literate mechanics. In contrast to Owen, however, he rejected utopianism and the retreat into the wilderness, and yet still managed to retain the admiration of the Owenites. No less a figure than Owen himself judged that one of Heighton's addresses (which he read during a visit to the United States in 1827) imparted more insight than "all the writings on political economy I have met with."[24] This speech and two more Heighton delivered in 1827 and 1828—one of them, it should be noted, in the Second Universalist Church—are among the most eloquent and lucid examples of early working-class radicalism.[25]

Simply put, the labor theory of value insisted that labor was the source of all wealth. Manual workers—and they alone—created wealth by setting their hands to the land or raw materials. Heighton labeled those who performed such tasks "producers," but also went a step beyond current radical thinkers in recognizing two subgroups within this category: *productive labor*, which consisted of those who fashioned commodities and raised crops, or artisans and yeoman; and *official labor*, which included those who transported the fruits of productive labor, or unskilled and casual laborers.[26] The remaining socioeconomic groupings and classes—bankers, merchants, landlords, military officers, professionals, clergymen—fell into the category of "absorbents" or "capitalists," or more commonly, "accumulators." They exchanged and lived off wealth, but did not produce it, and here was the central paradox. Those who made the goods and commodities and who were entitled by right to the "full product of their labor" existed on the edge of subsistence, while those who produced nothing lived in affluence.[27]

Heighton traced the source of this paradox to economic and political arrangements. The political root of exploitation was monopolistic or aristocratic legislation, chiefly charters of incorporation, which empowered a privileged few to engross markets, and banking charters, which gave legal life to the most hateful of all enterprise. Class legislation of this kind, however, simply aided the machinations of accumulators. The degradation of labor was inherent in the economic order because capitalism, or so Heighton believed, reversed the "natural order of things":

> the *production of wealth* . . . which must take place before it can be either exchanged or distributed, and which is of necessity *first* in the order of nature, instead of being made an employment of the *first importance*, held in the highest estimation, and the surest means of a gradual and certain accumulation, is on the contrary rendered one of the meanest, most precarious, and most unprofitable modes of

obtaining a subsistence; while the *mere exchange and distribution of it,* is made, to the greater part of mankind, the only possible means of accumulation, or even of ordinary enjoyment.[28]

Since exchange yielded a greater and surer return than production, commerce and merchandizing called forth more and more rivalries in an endless "struggle to undersell . . . and this struggle is called *competition.*"[29] This pervasive competitiveness was the bane of the workingman.

In fleshing out the social costs of competition, Heighton consulted the latest word on the subject, John Gray's "Lecture on Human Happiness" published in 1825. Gray maintained (and Heighton echoed) that there was no natural limit to production except *"the exhaustion of our productive powers* and *the satisfaction of our wants.*"[30] But under the imperatives of captialism, output was ruled by demand, and demand by competition. Thus the "quantity of wealth" accruing to journeymen in the jungle of the market plummeted because the competition both among them and among employers, depressed wages, usually to subsistence levels. All employers, however, were not equally at fault. Manufacturers who no longer worked with their hands relinquished any claim to producer status, but master craftsmen were excusable and qualified as producers for two reasons: they still performed manual labor and were forced to reckon with "accumulators more powerful than themselves," who lent capital and extended credit at usurious rates.[31] This distinction between dishonorable employers, or accumulators, and honorable masters, or producers, though implicit in Heighton's work, was quite explicit in the polemic of a fellow cordwainer. This journeyman perceived a "vast difference between an employer and a master":

The duties of one are to devise, lay out, and direct the labor of those in his employ, and if they do not comply with his directions, he has a remedy always at hand—he can discharge them; whilst the other can *command* an implicit obedience to all his decrees, whether right or wrong, and can enforce them by various punishments. In the one case there are two parties to any rule to be established, and the strict rules of equity would seem to require that both parties be consulted before a rule is permanently established.[32]

True enough, there was the master who respected the traditional prerogatives of journeymen and honored the maxim that they were "worthy of their hire." But he employed a diminishing proportion of them and was himself joining their ranks in growing numbers.

Time and again radicals returned to these motifs of dependence and the diffusion of marketplace values. They decried the "system of individual interest and competition," which not only demoted independent artisans to wage earners, but also eroded the autonomy of individuals outside the workplace, and constrained a more general form of dependence. Sturdy and autonomous citizens who once possessed a rudimentary understanding of simple mechanics, medicine, and other skills gradually grew more reliant upon specialists and professionals who monopolized knowledge and, worse yet, peddled their training for a fee. Survival skills, like manual labor itself, became commodities; doctors, lawyers, and others practiced their professions "not for the purpose of alleviating human suffering, but for lining [their] own pockets."[33] And this mounting dependence on professionals, argued radicals, dampened the inquisitive spirit in all individuals.

This critique of rising industrial capitalism should not be confused with an argument for socialism. The radical agenda listed state sponsorship of education and public ownership and distribution of fuel and certain foodstuffs, without proposing state control of the means of production. Radicals had no qualms about private property, but they did object to excessive accumulation on the part of individuals and corporate entities and to the concentration of power at the top of society. Doctrinaire egalitarians imbued with a cooperationist ethic, Heighton's minions despised economic individualism and proposed to redress the growing maldistribution of wealth and power through collective worker action at the polls and at workplaces. They thus looked forward to impressing workers of other subcultures with the value of cooperative production; the burning question was how to marshall support for so lofty a goal.

The question of support necessarily raised the issue of worker deference and impotence. Ignorance and intraclass divisiveness are obvious answers, but radicals were not content with such explanations. They probed the reasons behind both and, in so doing, evinced a keen understanding of their differences with other workers (and in the process took cognizance of approximately the same cultural groups examined in this study, even though they did not use the labels of traditionalist and revivalist).

In 1828, for example, Heighton editorialized on the causes of labor's recent organizing. Predictably, he cited the need to combat "monopolistic legislation," which concentrated the wealth "in a few rich hands," and to lobby for free public education, which would help bring workers out of darkness. He also showed awareness of traditionalist culture. Having listed the evils of monopoly and a false promise of education, he went on to argue that workers who frittered away their time in bars and gaming rooms instead of searching out the causes of inequality and taking remedial action unwittingly abetted the ignorance that enthralled them. Sheer numbers made such workers potentially important allies, but radicals could not hope to reach and educate them without lending a sympathetic hand and offering alternatives to what Heighton called the extensive "facilities for vending 'ardent spirits'" and for "Lottery Gambling."[34] Radicals thus intended the labor movement to be an educative enterprise for the moral and intellectual uplift of the ignorant, without subjecting them to the harsh moralizing and humiliation of revivalism.

Radicals were even more concerned with revivalists and especially with the Presbyterian ministry. The more daring of them challenged evangelical spokesmen in public, as did Thomas and Fuller during the cholera epidemic. Others eschewed such confrontation and directed a torrent of abuse against their opponents in editorials and letters to editors of their press. They were predisposed to stress the darker side of the Protestant establishment, but the excesses of evangelists reinforced this instinct.[35] Radical spokesmen never let their followers forget that Ezra Styles Ely, one of the city's leading clergymen, unabashedly called for a "christian party in politics" in order to promote Protestant interests.[36] Ely's coreligionists, they charged with some accuracy, presided over the "benevolent empire"—that solvent and ubiquitous matrix of reformist groups blanketing Philadelphia with evangelical propaganda and flexing its political muscle at all levels of government. Bible and tract societies, temperance organizations, and other Presbyterian auxiliaries—derisively known to radicals as "tributaries of the great machine"—

were disconcerting enough.[37] What made them truly alarming was their subsidy by the industrial elite, the avowed foes of radicalism. The combination of "proud ecclesiastics and rich civilians" convinced radicals that revivalism was not the innocent emotionalism of an evangelical ministry, but a front for clerical and lay boosters of evangelical capitalism.[38]

Radicals did their best to expose the nefarious designs of the Presbyterian hierarchy. They mocked the inhumane methods of ministers who used every pernicious gimmick, including fear, simply to fill their pews. Their version of the Declaration of Independence likened clerical tyranny to that of George III, and accused evangelists of bringing together "large numbers of . . . citizens at places uncomfortable, unusual, and distant from their houses for the purpose of . . . *scaring* them into a belief of their holy fables."[39] In a more serious vein, John Gihon, a printer by trade and Universalist "minister" by avocation, scorned those who "frighten[ed]" Philadelphians into church.[40] He and other radicals made a point of condemning evangelical efforts to proscribe working-class pastimes under the guise of humanitarism. Their favorite target in this regard was the American Temperance Society (A.T.S.), an ostensibly humane group whose activities were no more enlightened than those of its parent, the Presbyterian church. The radicals detected Presbyterian influence in the A.T.S.'s "fanatical" campaign for total abstinence and its studied refusal to minister to the real needs of the poor drunkard, his "miserable wife," and "beggardly children." They described the A.T.S. as another appendage of the benevolent empire, "that hydra-headed monster" that invested more energy in filling its treasury than in alleviating the plight of the poor.[41] Sabbatarianism, the handmaiden of the temperance movement, also aroused radical ire. An angry contributor to the *Mechanics' Free Press,* apparently sympathetic to wholesome working-class recreation, railed against churches for deterring travel by enforcing a blue law that allowed them to stretch chains across public streets on the Sabbath. He extended this attack to include clergymen who scowled at "the proprietors of steam boats, stages, etc., who afforded facilities for recreation of the many who are occupied the entire week."[42]

Radicals saw Presbyterian chains elsewhere as well. They imagined the values promoted by the Presbyterian clergy and its wealthy lay advocates as the fetters of working-class discord and deference. To their way of thinking no other group bore more responsibility for dividing workers into hostile camps of feuding sectarians. John Gihon contrasted the gentle persuasion of Universalist usage with the ravings of Presbyterians, who enlisted converts with "terrific appeals to their baser passions . . . and slander of other denominations."[43] Other Universalists, pursuing this comparative theme, stressed the toleration and liberalism of their faith, and rose to the defense of the victims of Presbyterian invective—both Protestant and non-Protestant. Universalist–turned– Free Thinker Russell Canfield even sided with Catholics, who routinely bore the brunt of evangelical bigotry and conspiracy charges. "With Catholics, as mere religionists," he once wrote, "we have no sympathy; but as men, as republicans, and as members of a persecuted sect we have much—and as such, we extend to them the tokens of fellow feeling, and so far as power extends, of protection."[44]

Judging from the intensity of their polemics, radicals were especially troubled by the apparent deferential teachings of Presbyterianism. Time and again they accused Presbyterian and sometimes evangelical theology in general of stripping individuals of their capacity for critical thought, and of fostering resignation to injustice. "When you have complained of oppression," barked an irritated radical ventilating his feelings about ministers, "they have told you that such was the dispensation of Providence, and you must be obedient."[45] Heighton sounded the same argument with even more indignation, venomously concluding an editorial with the exclamations," *Resignation! Economy,* and *Industry!!! Resignation!—* What Stuff!"[46]

Whether they leveled their guns on accumulators or ministers, radicals subsumed their phillipics under the broader context of republicanism. As other historians have observed, radical workers were not the only upholders of republicanism or the only Jacksonians claimants to the Revolutionary faith. Republicanism was a popular creed espoused by Americans of all classes and continually celebrated in the oratory and iconography of the many national holidays and patriotic observances that packed the calendar of the early republic.[47] The consensus understanding of it implied a belief in (white, male) equality of opportunity and freedom from arbitrary rule, or much rule at all, and a justification of action in pursuit of these ideals. But each working-class subculture emphasized different facets of the republican ideal. To revivalists, republicanism affirmed a fluid and culturally homogeneous social order and the obligation to preserve it from foreign and domestic enemies. As it turned out, they usually saw such threats as external or foreign, and endorsed such corrective measures as tariffs and moral legislation of one sort or another. To traditionalists, it meant the duty of voluntary service in militia units and fire companies and the right to resist the encroachments of the state.

Republican feeling ran deeper in radical circles. In addition to celebrating national holidays with paeans to republicanism, radicals showed their republican-revolutionary spirit by dating their correspondence in terms of the years following 1776 and signing their publications with the pseudonyms of Revolutionary heroes.[48] "Sherman" and "Jefferson," as opposed to "Franklin" who was worshipped by revivalists, were favorites along with such classical appellations as "Publicus" and "Rusticus"[49] They considered themselves not only the direct ideological heirs of the patriots of '76, but also locked in struggle to complete the work of the Revolution. Where their forefathers threw off the yoke of English rule, they would strike at the ramparts of competetive capitalism, in behalf of economic independence and social equality.

These dissidents thus infused republicanism with the same meaning as economic radicalism. They looked upon producers as the "bone and sinew" of society and linked the fate of one to the other: no independent producers, no republican order. Such radicals convinced themselves that to do battle for the full proceeds of labor's toil was to strive for the preservation of republican society itself. Their view of republicanism in effect confirmed the right to equality, not simply equal opportunity, and laid the blame for social injustice at the same doorsteps as the labor theory of value.[50] Their adversary was not the immigrant or foreign-made product but the corrupt politician, the accumulator, and the revivalist clergyman colluding to reduce free and independent workingmen to spiritual and material dependents. No republican worthy of the name could suffer such sinister forces lightly.

Radicals, in sum, constituted a subculture apart from traditionalists and revivalists. They were seasoned artisans of urban birth or upbringing who identified themselves as republican workingmen. Literate and conversant with a wide range of literature, they were singularly sophisticated and cosmopolitan. Above all else they were radicals and rationalists with a political perspective that imparted an acute awareness of inequality, a unique interpretation of its cause, and a comprehensive program for its cure. They located the origins of inequality and deference in the behavior of accumulators and their religious colleagues, just as they found the cause of cholera in the workings of biological processes. Both were different sides of the same rationalist coin; neither divine intervention nor depraved souls, as revivalists would have it, had much to do with social or natural phenomena. In proposing a tonic for inequality, radicals spurned the violence of traditionalists for effective organization. Their remedial program provided social alternatives, both to the pub of the traditionalist and to the church of the revivalist, that they hoped would spread the influence of their politics, if not their controversial religion, to expand the base of radicalism. They would reach some members of both groups in the 1830s under the aegis of the more expansive representation of their culture—the General Trades' Union of the City and County of Philadelphia.

"We Are All Day Laborers": The General Trades' Union of the City and County of Philadelphia, 1833–1837

5

William Heighton's dream of mounting a radical counterpoise to the depredations of capital suddenly seemed possible in the spring 1827. His rousing speeches goaded workingmen into coming together in the Mechanics' Union of Trade Associations, the nation's first bona fide labor movement, and then organizing their own press and reading rooms. The following year they extended the front of struggle to politics and formed the Working Men's party, the M.U.T.A.'s political arm. But the optimism that inspired labor's awakening quickly turned to despair. Radicals neglected the Mechanics' Union upon plunging into politics, and the party itself ran poorly in 1830 and even worse in 1831, its last year on the ballot.[1]

Even at the height of its power in 1827–1828, the Mechanics' Union scarcely represented Philadelphia's working class. A union of artisans, it overlooked unskilled workers, factory hands, and specialized craftsmen, owing to the inertia of these workers and to the policies of some member unions. Such unions honored the custom of limiting membership to trained journeymen. The members of the Association of Journeymen Hatters, for example, barred non-apprenticed workers and tradesmen working "on any machinery that has a tendency to reduce the manual labour required at the business."[2] Machinery was inconsequential to the followers of the Journeymen Tailors' Association, but the quality of work and workmanship was very much on their minds. The unquestioned aristocrats of their trade, they considered "costly broad cloth" and other fine garments made to order worthy of their skillful hands, but not "a light summer coatee" or slop work, which they demeaned as the "work of women, and . . . not . . . so dignified a subject of employment as the former, which men alone have the honor to make."[3] Men or women making up cheap clothing were unwelcome in this union.

Radicals of a more democratic bent discouraged such restrictions. They determined to expand the scope of unionism, and urged the organization of semiskilled workers in the crafts and of wage earners in vocations without traditions of collection action. They were especially attentive to the plight of the millhands. Heighton published the letters of protesting operatives in the *Mechanics' Free Press*, and editorialized on their behalf.[4] But this was a brief interlude in the short life of the Mechanics' Union. The drive to democratize unionism was aborted when the leaders turned their attention to politics and the Mechanics' Union remained the preserve of radicals and a handful of followers; traditionalists and revivalists stood outside the fold. Wary of the radicals and suspicious of one another, they continued to be more responsive to fire alarms and church bells.

The apathetic mood of working-class Philadelphia and the desultory state of unionism shifted dramatically in the years immediately following the end of the Working Men's party. Rumblings of change appeared in October of 1833, when a group of shoemakers, tailors, and bookbinders met to assess the past and weigh the prospects of revitalizing the labor movement. Heighton was not in attendance. He left Philadelphia forever at the beginning of the thirties, passing the baton of leadership to his former colleagues in the Mechanics' Union, who turned out in force. These veteran unionists spoke against mixing politics with unionism for fear of rehearsing the mistakes of the past and their view held sway.[5] Delegates agreed to effect a nonpartisan labor movement and summoned area workers to assist in drafting a constitution and bylaws. In the spring of 1834 they completed their work and unveiled the General Trades' Union of the City and County of Philadelphia, which soon became the most impressive city central union in Jacksonian America. Within two years the G.T.U. grew from an embryo of seventeen affiliates (the Mechanics' Union had only eighteen member unions) and about 2,000 members, to a giant of more than fifty unions representing over 10,000 wage earners.[6]

The G.T.U. seems to have been more highly structured than the Mechanics' Union. There were five executive officers elected semi-annually, two deliberative bodies, the General Assembly and Finance Committee, and a wealth of elective and appointive committees. Each affiliate had proportionate representation in the Assembly, the major decision-making body, which met weekly, and a single deputy on the Finance Committee. Unions were admitted and decisions reached by a majority vote of the Assembly, and funds were raised by assessing each member 6¼¢ a month. Financial matters received close attention. The Treasury Committee could not make disbursements "unless by authority from the Union, under an order from the President, attested by the Secretary," and the Finance Committee scrutinized the books of each affiliate "at least once in three months."[7]

Conservatives often attacked the G.T.U. for being "undemocratic." Union spokesmen answered such charges in letters to the local press that emphasized the semiannual election of officers and union delegates, and the institutional checks on the abuse of power. "The funds of the Union," wrote one leader in response to a detractor, "are . . . secure against the powerful representation of the larger societies, (for) each . . . [union] selects one individual to transact the money matters of the institution, denominated the Finance Committee, and this alone is under their control, so that the society of fifty members have [sic] the same responsibility and interest in the funds that the society of nine hundred and fifty have [sic]."[8] Another officer pointed to the bicameral governance structure as further evidence of democratic rule and boasted that this arrangement approximated the "system of our *National Government.*"[9]

Like any organization, however, the character of the G.T.U. is reflected more accurately in its behavior than in such roseate rhetoric. There was substantial turnover in leadership. Twenty-three men

filled its executive offices from 1834 to 1838 and thirteen served only
one term. But the Union's scanty records disclose that some
individuals exerted outstanding influence. John Ferral, William
English, William Thompson, and Edward Penniman were especially
active and energetic within the Assembly and on committees, and
some trades were over-represented in the highest offices. Seven, or
nearly a third of the officers, for example, were men's and ladies'
cordwainers.[10] Nor did the checks and balances of governance
prevent the Union from acting with vigor and dispatch. Authority
was frequently delegated to committees whose jurisdiction ranged
from mediating disputes, both between affiliates and between unions
and employers, to organizing workers and investigating the con-
stitutions of applicants for membership.[11]

The G.T.U. diverged from the Mechanics' Union in ways other
than scale, structure, and political orientation. In attracting more
members, the Trades' Union represented a wider constituency of
occupational and cultural groups. In part this was the result of the
affiliates' relaxation of membership standards and efforts to organize
semiskilled workers. The house carpenters, for example, had a
reputation for scorning "half-trained" workmen, but broke with
tradition in bracing for a confrontation with contractors over the
length of the workday in the summer of 1835. Preparing for the strike,
they divided the city and county into three zones, and dipatched
teams of organizers to shops and construction sites in each. The
committeemen canvassed fellow tradesmen to "persuade them if
possible to unite . . . in obtaining the object."[12] Cordwainers,
cigar makers, and others in the sweated trades worked assiduously
to bring the unorganized into their fold.[13] The men's and ladies'
cordwainers (men working on women's footwear) concentrated
their organizing drives in the suburban districts which housed
large groups of Irish and native-born traditionalists. The men's
branch apparently excelled in integrating the foreign-born into their
union, for these practitioners of the "gentle craft" elected Irish
immigrant John Ryan president.[14] The spirit of mobilization also
gripped nonradical workers in occupations without histories of
unionism or informal collective protest. Traditionalist frame tenders
and revivalist millhands of both sexes organized for the first time and
joined with radicals in the G.T.U.[15]

The ecumenicalism of the Trade Union derived from the convergence of several factors. Drastic economic change made the late twenties and thirties a difficult period for all wage earners. Rising prices and declining earnings compounded the problem of making ends meet, and the early stages of production for mass markets triggered a general deterioration of working conditions and a tightening of work discipline. Such developments encouraged feelings of mutualism and grievances in common. The division of labor and cheapening of skills, for example, prompted skilled tradesmen to reassess their policy of limiting union membership to their own kind. The influx of specialized workers gave them the choice of either maintaining exclusivity and inviting trade-union obsolescence or adjusting to new realities; evidently, most adjusted. Workers also lost a measure of autonomy, as employers extracted extra effort by extending hours or by cutting piece rates, and as production moved from homes and small shops to the advanced settings. Traditionalist workers who had battled one another and racial foes in earlier years suddenly turned against employers in resistance to excessive toil.

The traits of modernizing production even aroused revivalists by the mid-thirties. Some clerical proponents of the Protestant work ethic now detected ravelings of the moral fabric in unbriddled acquisitiveness and single-minded attention to work. They employed the occasion of a circular letter on Sabbatarianism to reprimand overwork as a sign of "avarice" and a cause of immorality and familial decay. Everyone required an "occasional respite from labor" in order to maintain health, observe the duties of parenthood, and ensure individual and national prosperity. "Our own property, ... our domestic comfort, and our children's happiness and security," they reasoned, "are dependent upon the blessings which distinguish us as a people."[16]

Their working-class constituents, usually quite obedient, appropriated this reasoning for their own ends at a temperance rally on the Fourth of July. The "Glorious Fourth" marked a day of commemoration, and the celebrants in 1835 included the Mechanics' and Workingmen's Temperance Society, whose followers were among the most forceful proponents of the new industrial morality. Albert Barnes and other notable evangelical clerics and laymen delivered speeches touting the virtues of hard work and led the gathering in songs written for the occasion. But the class unity was shaken when workers in the audience submitted songs of their own, one of which expressed solidarity with fellow wage earners striking for a ten-hour day. Entitled "The Temperance Strike," it reads:

> His chains the tyrant rum, too long
>   Has tried to cast around us,—
> Shall not Mechanics prove too strong,
>   When any would confound us?—
> We shall! we shall! we feel our strength
>   And who no sword will draw,
> When we for freedom strike at length?
>   Hurrah! hurrah! hurrah!
>
> Our Fathers—who may see their like!
>   When trodden down as cattle,
> For liberty knew how to strike,
>   And win the righteous battle!
>
> And shall their sons be slaves to drink?
>   O never! never! Nor
> Will Working Men like cowards shrink,
>   No boys!—hurrah! hurrah!
>
> The pledge to Temperance we renew
>   For she is Freedom's daughter—
> In generous draughts of mountain dew,
>   In cold and limpid water!
> Strike hands with us!—for wine like this
>   The toper never saw;
> E'en Woman's lip such cup may kiss
>   Unstained, hurrah! hurrah!
>
> Some strike for wages, some for hours,
>   Shall we refuse?—O never!
> For time and cash we pledge our powers,
>   And strike for both for ever!
> Then strike who will for "6 to 6,"
>   We flinch not in the war;
> For Temperance and for Seventy-Six
>   We strike—hurrah! hurrah![17]

The event referred to in these lyrics, the strike for a ten-hour day, offers the best evidence of the depth of worker unrest. It began

inauspiciously in late May of 1835, when the coal heavers on the
Schuylkill docks left their jobs in protest against long hours.
Parading through the city on June 3, they caught the eye of
cordwainers peering through workshop windows. The cordwainers
threw down their awls and rushed to join the procession, shouting
"We are all day laborers!"[18] The mushrooming line of march
attracted carpenters and other tradesmen in quick succession and
precipitated spontaneous rallies of artisans throughout the city.
Smiths, leather dressers, plumbers, painters, and cigar makers among
others voted to standout by the end of the week. The republic's first
general strike was on; and general it was. The fervor reached into
textile mills around the county and into the homes of outworkers,
who normally had no interest in the hours question. But rate cuts
forced the cottagers to work longer and faster The only form their
struggle for shorter hours could take was a wage increase, and they
struck for rate advances. A festive air prevailed. There were great
parades and rallies uniting workers with master craftsmen and other
middle class sympathizers all bearing banners with variations of the
motto "6 to 6."[19] Friendly shopkeepers displayed this battle cry in
windows and youngsters chalked it on fences.[20] Wage earners were
seen everywhere except at their workplaces, which moved the *United
States Gazette* to note the obvious: "Our buildings are at a stand, and
business generally is . . . impeded."[21]

No one knows how many workers walked off their jobs or won
their point through negotiation. On June 10, after some mechanics
celebrated victory and others prepared to standout one newspaper
counted twenty trades still on strike.[22] At least double that number—
possibly as many as 20,000 workers—participated in walkouts, and
all were successful, though the millhands compromised on an eleven-
hour day and some trades waited until the fall and following spring
before announcing a ten-hour day.[23] The laborers who had sparked
the strike were among the most triumphant of all. Those toiling on
public projects in Southwark extracted a wage increase as well as an
ordinance making ten hours a legal day's work.[24]

Irish hand loom weaver John Ferral correctly pronounced the
general strike an unexpected boon to the General Trades' Union.[25]
Membership, he happily observed, soared in the wake of the standout,
as ad hoc strike committees created in the fervor of the moment

turned into unions, and established societies inducted scores of journeymen. The inflow of new recruits, most of whom were strangers to trade unionism, transformed the G.T.U. from a small clique of radicals into a diversified union representing workers of various cultures.

Though declining working conditions pitted traditionalist and revivalist workers against employers, and propelled them into the Trades' Union, neither these conditions nor the euphoria of the general strike alone shaped the G.T.U. or sustained class unity. Such solidarity, in the 1830s, as in any period, could not be sustained without the cultivation of talented leadership.

Trades' Union radicals were uniquely equipped for the task of fostering intraclass harmony. They appreciated the competing political and religious loyalties of their followers, and judiciously eschewed fractious issues for the sake of unity. Most of them, for example, supported the Democratic party, following the collapse of the Working Men's party. They vied for public office under the Democratic banner and served as party officials, but studiously refrained from pressing partisan causes at Union gatherings and steadfastly resisted the temptation to convert the Union into a party adjunct. When a well-meaning but misguided critic recommended allying with the Democrats, a Trades' Unionist rejected the idea with the explanation that the G.T.U. welcomed "men of every party. A thousand different ideas would clash together and annihilate the institution in the moment the attempt [to merge] was made."[26] Union leaders also toned down their hostility toward organized religion in recognition of the volatility of the issue and in observance of Heighton's injunction: *"Let the subject of religion alone*—or the death knell of our Associations will soon be sounded."[27] With this in mind radical saddler and G.T.U. official John Crossin explained that the "followers of Christ acknowledge a time for all things—we do the same."[28] Affiliates of the Trades' Union thus barred the discussion of religion and the Union itself, "asked no qualification of birth or parentage—nor sign nor token to gain admission."[29]

Radicals hewed to this policy outside the G.T.U. They were especially watchful of employers, politicians, and clergymen given to fomenting intraclass discord by exacerbating religious and ethnic tensions. John Ferral stood out as a voice of moderation and conciliation. In March of 1834 he and William Gilmore, a cordwainer and close friend, came to Manayunk, where an operatives' strike was in progress. The stoppage had been called to contest a wage reduction that slashed earnings by a substantial 30 percent. This pay cut united the entire workforce at Jospeh Ripka's Schuylkill factory and the strikers held firm throughout March and April, even though Ripka hired a small force of strikebreakers and protected them with armed guards. In mid-May Ripka turned in desperation to Manayunk's Protestant clergy, who dutifully urged the operatives back to work. Ferral and Gilmore responded with a mass meeting and a list of resolutions, one of which tactfully chided the ministers for the "recent attempt made by certain persons in this place, to force some to go back to work at the reduced prices, and more so because they are religious pastors, from whom better might be expected."[30] The millhands not only endorsed the resolutions, but stayed out for two more weeks, then returned to work with a wage increase.

The following fall brought Ferral another opportunity to act the part of conciliator. Whiggish politicians, who were rapidly earning a well-deserved reputation for exploiting sectarian differences, performed up to standard in the local elections. Hard-pressed to break the Democratic strangle hold on the suburban districts, they nominated an Irish Protestant for the state Senate and campaigned for Protestant votes with nativist slogans and anti-Catholic epithets. Their strategy reminded Ferral of the Old World's hateful politics and moved him to convene a meeting of Irish Americans, without regard to religion. He beseeched his listeners to recall their past experiences of Ireland, where "aristocracy" exploited religious hatred in order to "keep the honest and industrious population divided, rendering them . . . an easy prey to their enemies."[31] Such appeals on the part of radicals countered the polarizing force of the politicians, and their leadership helps explain why areas like Southwark, Moyamensing, Kensington, and Manayunk, which mixed together Protestant and Catholic workers, resisted the politics of ethnicity and returned solid Democratic majorities during the thirties.[32]

Radicals worked to direct the class unity that they had done so much to encourage into trade-union channels. They traveled across the county spreading the gospel of organization. Edward Penniman (of the Coachmakers', Painters', and Trimmers' Union), John Crossin (of the Saddlers' and Harnessmakers'), Thomas Hogan (of the Printers'), and William English (of the Ladies' Cordwainers), to name the most active, helped unionize fellow tradesmen and staffed the executive offices of the unions in their respective crafts. They also ventured outside their own callings in a concerted effort to organize noncraft and industrial workers. Ferral and Gilmore assisted and, perhaps, even precipitated, the unionization of Manayunk textile hands. And English and Hogan took some credit for the emergence of a combination of paperworkers at Mill Creek in the mid-thirties. A terse account of their exploits thus reads, "met an assemblage of individuals engaged in the manufacture of paper, who after hearing addresses . . . formed themselves into a Trade Society."[33]

Not even the imposing barrier of sex dampened the enthusiasm of radical organizers, even though they did not regard women as equals. Radicals, in fact, took a dim view of women as employees. Like most male workers, they decried the "multiplying descriptions of labor for females" as a "pecuniary injury" to men, because of job competition, and a "moral injury" to women, because gainful employment transferred them from the protective isolation of the home to the inelegancies of the workshop, where they rubbed shoulders with crude and vulgar men and risked acquiring "ruder habits" and "losing all that sacred influence which it is the peculiar prerogative of woman to exercise over man."[34] This point of view conformed to the "cult of the true womanhood" then being popularized by clergymen and writers, but was only one source of radical antipathy to women's employment.[35] The other was rooted in radical fascination with the physiological literature that depicted women as the weaker sex, and more inclined to nervous disorders. Such "wisdom" convinced radicals that women needed sheltering from the "overstimulation" of gainful employment, and were best off in the home rearing rationalist children.[36]

Despite such patronizing attitudes, radicals appreciated the hardships of women who did work and did not hesitate to applaud their unionizing or assist their struggles against rapacious employers.[37] (Blacks, of course, were another matter entirely. There is no evidence of radicals endorsing the rights of Blacks, either as workers or as citizens.) Thus the printer Thomas Hogan and the hand loom weaver John Ferral spoke on behalf of women textile operatives and paperworkers and proved instrumental in organizing both groups.[38] Radical cordwainers had a selfish reason to oppose female employment: their employers hired them by the score when they divided up the work. But when the male members of the Union Beneficial Society of Cordwainers, Ladies' Branch, learned of a strike conducted by a struggling union of female corders and binders, they closed ranks behind the beleagured women. The union's leaders pilloried "heartless" employers for conspiring to "crush a suffering class of females" and, resolving to take the binders "under our wing to sink or swim with us," organized a solidarity committee to coordinate a joint strike and solicit donations.[39] The same spirit animated a meeting of the cigar makers that produced a resolution sympathizing with the women of the trade whose "earnings fell below a just compensation for their labor," and inviting them "in a body to strike with us."[40]

As these incidents imply, radicals were effective organizers because of their remarkable ability to relate to the inarticulate. In an age when the spoken word carried a powerful inspirational thrust, their forceful oratory mobilized workers of varying occupations and cultural origins. If we are to believe eyewitnesses, nearly all Trades' Union leaders shared this oratorical skill; among them, however, William English surpassed all rivals. His charisma and command of language dazzled the most skeptical and astonished Trades' Union critics. A favorite speaker at Union rallies, he once addressed a meeting in support of Boston strikers. Two reporters from the city's conservative *United States Gazette* were present. Though inclined to reflect the *Gazette*'s antilabor bias, they grudgingly conceded to have "rarely listened to more effective eloquence." English in particular evoked their amazement and admiration. He eschewed "grandiloquence," "ranting," "farfetched figure or long quotation," and other expectations of an unlettered stump speaker in favor of a "direct appeal, in vigorous language, to the experience and attachments of the audience." Upon scanning the crowd, they marked "upon the countenances . . . the changes which each effective sentence operated, and then . . . understood the secret of . . . [the] effects which popular orators of olden times were wont to work on the minds of the people."[41]

The substance of the speech is unknown, but most likely English identified the ten-hour movement with the protection of republican liberties. Radicals routinely invoked the republican idiom on such occasions and during their own "standouts," as their strikes were called. The members of English's own union equated their work stoppage for a rate increase with the struggle of the "toil-worn veterans of '76 *who nobly moistened the soil with their blood* in defense of equal rights and equal privileges."[42] A radical shoemaker contested the arbitrary imposition of work rules in a similar fashion. The right to "require strict observance of such . . . regulations," he insisted, was not absolute because journeymen were republican citizens whose rights carried over to the workplace and, therefore, should be "consulted before a rule is permanently established." Nor did the employer have the "right to charge the Journeymen in his . . . trade or art, with unsurping a control over his business when they merely refused to be governed by rules or laws which they may deem to be despotic. . . . And when . . . Journeymen have resisted the enforcement of such rules and have brought the subject fairly before all the members of the same trade and they in turn make common cause in resisting what they conceive to be tyranny and oppression, are they not strictly justifiable in making such resistance?"[43] A Manayunk cotton spinner answered this rhetorical question in the positive and raised precisely the same point in condemning work rules. "In spite of all that is or may be said on the contrary," he affirmed, "they are not the offspring of mutual consent."[44]

This invocation of republicanism served a dual purpose. As E. P. Thompson observes, popular protest rests on some "legitimizing notion" of right. In this respect, radical republicanism was analagous to the "Rights of Freeborn Englishmen," the slogan appropriated by English artisans of the time.[45] It justified dissent around immediate issues, as well as the larger movement for social equality. It also operated as a bridge between radicals, on the one hand, and revivalists and traditionalists, on the other. All workers spoke the language of Republicanism, even if they attached slightly different meaning to it, and by summoning republican metaphors, radicals provided a substantive and symbolic rallying point for their class.

It would be foolish to contend, however, that the chemistry of worker degradation and skillful leadership dissolved all points of conflict among the G.T.U. membership. Internal squabbles arose from time to time over several issues, the most predictable of which was union jurisdiction. Trades undergoing the division of labor were especially inclined to jurisdictional disputes. The ladies' cordwainers discretely avoided one in cooperating with the women binders and corders, but the blacksmiths objected when a union of horse shoers— comparable to the binders—applied for membership in the Trades' Union. The Union leadership appointed a mediation committee, which only confused matters further by submitting minority and majority reports. The delegate Assembly rejected both documents and ordered the committee to reconvene. It reached consensus the second time, but its report produced such acrimony that the Assembly adjourned "without coming to a decision." And the disappointed horse shoers withdrew their application.[46]

Trades' Union leaders recognized the recurring problem of competing jurisdictional claims. A Union-appointed committee that met in 1839 to consider structural reform drafted a report that lamented the "indiscriminate association of trades without any regard to affinity." The report hinted that the building tradesmen, chronically involved in jurisdictional infighting, were particularly displeased with this arrangement, and it recommended reorganizing the Union along the lines of the later American Federation of Labor, that is, with councils or associations of kindred trades with "supreme" authority in their "own sphere of action."[47] The 1837 panic had already greatly weakened the Union, however, and the proposal was a dead letter.

Controversy also developed over guidelines for dispensing benefits to striking affiliates. Member unions were spared the bureaucratic nightmare of the Knights of Labor, but they still had to contend with strict procedures. Applications for strike payments required the approval of a Union-appointed committee, which investigated the cause of the dispute, the means employed, and the "probable chances" of successful negotiations, and the sanction of a two-thirds vote of the general membership. "Sherman," writing in the popular press, detected an "advantage" in the Union's negative rulings "in more than one instance," but some union deputies disagreed.[48] They settled upon streamlining procedures and presented a resolution ordering a

committee to develop a "more certain and effectual plan in sanc-
tioning strikes and granting assistance to Societies on stand."[49] Its
fate, however, is unknown.

Much of this infighting was inevitable in an organization as large
and diversified and, one might add, as primitive as the Trades' Union.
But disputes over jurisdiction and Union policy were more irksome
and time-consuming than consequential. None were serious enough
to threaten the unity that was the G.T.U.'s hallmark. "Sherman's"
assessment that the Trades' Union was the "only system yet devised
which has been able to harmonize all parties and sects" was not the
idle boast of a partisan.[50]

The cohesiveness that prompted "Sherman's" appraisal was
evident after the dust of the spirited summer of 1835 had settled.
Worker struggles in the following years, though far less dramatic
than the general strike, demonstrated ongoing solidarity. In January
of 1836, for example, the journeyman bookbinders embarked on a
protracted strike when the master binders abrogated a wage agree-
ment. Faced with both a rate reduction amounting to 30 percent and
formidable foes who organized a masters' association and issued a
blacklist, the journeymen won the sympathy of the G.T.U., local
unions, and area bookbinders. All of these groups, including twenty-
one Philadelphia unions, contributed in excess of $3,400 to the
bookbinders' war chest.[51] Even Moyamensing's impoverished hand
loom weavers felt an identity of interest with these prestigious
strikers. Barely able to support their own families, the frame tenders
donated $100 to the cause "in order to show our marked hostility to
this claim of *Mastership* on the part of the Employing Bookbinders."[52] Later that year it was the hand loom weavers' turn to test
the good will of fellow Trades' Unionists. Moyamensing and
Kensington weavers struck to resist rate cuts in the fall and asked the
Union for financial assistance. They were voted a total of $1,500 in
strike benefits, which sufficed for the loom tenders in Kensington,
but left those in Moyamensing short of funds.[53] When they appealed
for additional aid, a group of cordwainers, saddlers, and carpenters,
reflecting the Union's mutualist ethic, organized a three-man
committee to solicit donations.[54]

If traditionalist Irish hand loom weavers seemed to be unlikely
recipients of artisanal sympathy, so were the day laborers. Despite

the unpopularity of their religion, the weavers had at least some claim to membership in the fraternity of artisans; but the unskilled were seen by nonradicals as a group apart, which is why tradesmen who banded together with them during the general strike balked at admitting them to the Trades' Union despite the advocacy of some radicals.[55] But these opponents had a change of heart in the spring of 1836, when they not only welcomed the day laborers, but rushed to their defense.

The admission of the laborers to the Trades' Union came in the course of a stirring struggle between the Schuylkill dockers and the coal merchants. The lines were drawn when the merchants rejected the dockers' request for a rate advance. A strike followed in which the merchants posted advertisements for strikebreakers. Because few scabs were willing to brave the laborers' picket line or intimidations, the merchants looked to the courts and public officials for relief, charging the strikers with breach of the peace. They had the backing of Whig Mayor John Swift, who ordered the arrest of eight laborers and a tavern owner, an appropriate leader of a protest march staged by these traditionalist workmen. Bail was set at $2,500 each, an impossibly high amount, and it broke the walkout. Swift, in setting bail, delivered a blistering attack on the Trades' Union. It was held to blame for recent "mischiefs," and Swift threatened, so reports had it, to strike at its "root" until he "felled the tree that it might lay and rot."[56]

Swift failed in this clumsy attempt at discrediting the Trades' Union. The imprisoning of the day laborers created martyrs, not pariahs, and played into the hands of the radicals, who had sought to get them into the Union for the greater part of a year. His menacing conduct was interpreted as an assault on all workers, and generated such support for the embattled laborers that the Trades' Unionists arranged for their legal defense as well as voting to admit them. Their trials had a happy ending as well, for the court twice acquitted them — once for breach of the peace and once for conspiracy.[57]

By embracing the laborers, Philadelphia artisans became the first skilled workmen to join with the unskilled in the same union. Their feat would not be repeated until the 1860s, when central labor unions united combinations of casual laborers with those of craftsmen. Radicals took some pride in this achievement and in the G.T.U.'s stunning record. Trades' Union muscle helped establish a ten-hour day, organized labor's burning issue, and every walkout subsidized by Union funds in the seven months following the general strike ended in victory.[58]

Yet no radical envisioned class cohesion or even trade unionism as ends in themselves. Repelled by the horrors of poverty and the intellectual deadening produced by overwork, they endorsed any form of collective action that might alleviate these conditions. As radicals with dreams of reorganizing production along cooperative principles, however, they expected meager returns from trade unionism if workers continued to squander hard won leisure hours by fraternizing on street corners, in pubs, or at fire houses, or in churches and Sunday schools. According to the radicals, such activities retarded moral and intellectual advancement and cancelled the gains extracted at the workplace. They pressed for constructive uses of leisure, which involved cultivating tastes for reading and discourse and transforming class feeling, expressed through trade unionism, into radical consciousness.

The didacticism that punctuated the private life of radicals imbued their public life as well. Convinced of the need to lure revivalists and traditionalists from their chosen pastimes, they sponsored a range of functions and organizations designed to replace or at least compete with pub and pulpit. Rallies, meetings, and picnics with agitational speeches were complemented by debating clubs, lyceums, and reading rooms where workers could hear lectures and debates or consult radical literature, including the *Radical Reformer* and the *National Laborer,* organs of the G.T.U., in relaxed surroundings.

The Society for the Diffusion of Useful Knowledge (S.D.U.K.), the major educative auxiliary of the Trades' Union, demonstrates the emphasis on self-improvement, radical style. Union leaders gave lectures twice monthly on topics of interest such as radical political economy, temperance, and the relationship between them.[59] Records of these meetings do not survive, but the proceedings probably conformed to what we know of the "Moral and Physical Improvement Club," a local expression of the S.D.U.K. Speakers conveyed the essence of the labor theory of value and principles of primitive socialism through vivid example rather than abstraction. One lesson, we are told, went as follows:

If A goes to Germantown, for instance, and agrees with B to make him a gig, price asked, $200, which A agrees to give; he receives the gig, pays money for it, all right and fair; but he afterwards sells this gig for $220—their argument . . . was, that A is a scoundrel, rogue, robber . . . if he does not give B $10, half the profits made on it, as it was the production of his labor.[60]

Workers who did not attend such sessions but shared workplaces with radicals heard much the same thing. Radicals employed in small shops would read newspapers and hold informal seminars during the frequent dull spells in the course of the day.[61]

The impact of radical education is difficult to gauge. There is compelling evidence that some members, whose number defies quantification, refrained from this facet of G.T.U. activities. Such workers were driven to trade unionism by the polemics of the leaders and by the deterioration of work. They flocked to established combinations or formed their own loose organizations on the spur of the moment, but left the union fold when immediate grievances were satisfied or unionism showed signs of weakness. Their behavior accounts for the fitful rhythm of union membership, which swelled in the inspiring nine months following the general strike and fell off thereafter when employers in some trades came together in masters' associations and defeated key strikes.[62] These defeats so dampened the enthusiasm of some wage earners that membership thinned and the number of affiliates dropped from fifty-one in the spring of 1836 to about thirty a year later.[63] It is impossible to know the cultural identities of these defectors, but one may assume that a disproportionate number were revivalists: their initial commitment to unionism was tenuous, and they were exposed to the potent countervailing force of their own political and cultural leaders. Evangelical ministers and Whiggish editorialists, stepping up their war against the Trades' Union in the spring of 1836, stigmatized the Union as "radical," "Jacobin," and the standard epithet of all conservatives, "foreign import," and posed as defenders of the sacred rights of property against the levelist thrust of labor.[64] These fulminations were subject to lengthy rebuttals, but there seems little doubt that they tainted the G.T.U. for some evangelical workers. One of them, writing under the fitting pseudonym of *"True American,"* endorsed the jaundiced views of Union opponents and, sounding the alarm against the specter of godlessness and agrarianism, called upon fellow workers to *"Strike for your altars and your fires, God, and your native land."*[65]

Yet there is good reason to conclude that the G.T.U.'s agitational and educative activities were of considerable importance. Union rallies consistently dwarfed those of political parties, even in this age of mass politics, and exposed workers to critical modes of thought. Lectures and debates also played to healthy audiences. And while no revivalist or traditionalist testified that the persuasive oratory at such conclaves swayed him to radicalism, Union leaders reported a change in the leisure tastes of their followers. Workers who had once socialized in pubs and other settings, said a Trades' Union official, now gathered together "for the purpose of deliberating upon measures for their mutual advancement."[66]

The best evidence of the growing popularity of radicalism is recorded in the behavior of Union members. Affiliates with factions of radicals and new converts such as the men's and ladies' cordwainers, saddlers, tailors, and hand loom weavers, put radicalism into practice beginning in the summer of 1836 by experimenting with various kinds of cooperative production.[67] As might be expected, however, their cooperatives ran into financial difficulty and they then turned to the G.T.U. for assistance. Their editorials and letters in the Union press and speeches to the delegate assembly proposed Union loans for cooperative ventures. Union delegates warmed to the idea, passing a radical-sponsored resolution that charged a committee of nine with drafting rules governing a "Savings and Cooperative Loan Fund" and consenting to a committee stacked with partisans of the plan. They voiced additional approval at the end of the summer upon endorsing the committee report.[68] But there was another hurdle: in order to be implemented, the plan required the amendment of the by-laws by a two-thirds vote of the affiliates, and some unions were divided on the question.

The opponents came from two quarters. First, there were some traditionalists and revivalists who rejected cooperation as "impracticable" and who preferred to fight for their rights through unions and strikes.[69] Second, there were some workers, largely revivalists, who opposed cooperation on ideological grounds. They showed their displeasure with the drift toward radicalism by deserting unions that had transformed themselves into cooperatives. Revivalist tailors, for example, left the Association of Journeymen Tailors for this reason.[70]

Nonetheless a large segment, and perhaps a majority, of the G.T.U.'s societies favored cooperation. Twenty-three of twenty-nine member unions, some of which had already organized cooperatives, attended (in the winter and spring of 1837) meetings on non-competitive production and the procedures involved in initiating and sustaining cooperatives.[71] Enthusiasm ran high, diminishing only with the 1837 panic that idled thousands and destroyed or debilitated unions and cooperatives alike. A shrinking band of loyalists continued to meet without voting on whether to make Union funds available. But the depression rendered the issue irrelevant.

The economic downturn of 1837 could not have been more inopportune. It delivered the decisive blow to the weakened Union and the symptoms of irreversible decline were soon apparent. Workers now watched helplessly or put up token resistance as employers ignored wage agreements. The house painters turned out in May, but, noting the "manner in which business of every kind is depreciating," then conceded defeat.[72] The printers summoned tradesmen "wishing to join the Association" and protect the "present" bill of prices, but failed to raise any volunteers.[73] Even the mighty cordwainers, whose unions had been the showcase of strength and unity, were now powerless. Both groups sharply attacked employers for violating price lists, but mustered only empty threats to defend wage scales and equally empty promises to find work for the unemployed of their trade.[74] The ladies' branch, innovative to the end, charted a new course in changing their union into a benevolent society. Other trades followed suit.[75]

With or without benevolent societies, wage earners took whatever work they could find. As unions atrophied, so did the G.T.U., and "A Workingman" penned a fitting though slightly premature epitaph for the Union in December of 1838. "Circumstances . . . beyond the control of any," wrote the saddened warrior, "have in a degree retarded, if not entirely broken up that system; so much that . . . the *head* is left to support itself without the members performing their proper functions. In other words, the *body* is dead."[76] Four months later a cadre of weary radicals announced the official death of the Trades' Union.

In one blow then, the panic of 1837 crushed working-class Philadelphia's initial experiment with trade unionism and radicalism. Their combinations, cooperatives, and umbrella organization, the G.T.U., in a shambles, workers were stripped of their agencies of struggle, unification, and critical thought. But while the organizational network of radicalism crumbled, radical nostrums would persist in transmuted form and exert a profound impact on worker culture. Just as evangelical divines imbued some wage earners with the principles of industrial morality, radical leaders, aided by class conflict itself, passed on radicalism to revivalists and traditionalists.

Labor's immediate task, however, was not to lament the end of the Trades' Union. Rather, it was to survive in the midst of the most prolonged economic downturn in memory. Few emerged from this dismal period unscarred.

Part Three:
Hard Times
1837-1844

"The Uses of Adversity"

6

Jacksonian Philadelphia had grown accustomed to fluctuations in trade. Periodic downturns, such as that which occurred in the spring of 1837 following the bank failures and suspensions of specie payments, were endemic to an age of reckless acquisitiveness, and many Philadelphians expected to be back at counting houses and workshops by summer. The *Board of Trade and Commercial List*, a leading businessmen's sheet which closely monitored the fitful economy, predicted a bright future, which seemed confirmed by the upturn the summer months ushered in.[1] But the banks commenced another round of defaults and suspensions by the end of the year and once again plunged the economy into the doldrums—this time for six long years.

No one knows precisely how many wage earners lost their jobs, but sources convey a picture of widespread and prolonged distress. Conservative diarist Sidney George Fisher found little cause for hope as late as the summer of 1842. "The streets seem deserted," he wrote, "the largest houses are shut up and to rent, there is no business . . . no money, no confidence." The busiest man in town was the sheriff, who "every day" auctioned off property "at a 4th of the estimated value a few years ago."[2] The *Public Ledger's* economic survey in 1842 was equally bleak. It could "not mention a mechanic trade or branch of commerce which was not crowded in 1835 and 1837 and which is not completely desolate now."[3]

While Fisher's wealthy friends watched their investments depreciate, wage earners strived to feed their families. They adopted several time-worn strategies. The usual safety-valve of tramping, which sent a steady stream of workers ebbing and flowing between urban centers, assumed new popularity in the crisis. Perhaps as many as a third to a fourth of the working class left the city to forage for work elsewhere.[4] Those who weathered hard times in Philadelphia worked part-time at their trades, occasionally doing repairs, or shifted into casual labor of one sort or another. They also cut back on consumption, and many shared costs through cooperative living. Some, for example, "broke up house keeping" and boarded with friends and family, which allowed the pooling of resources but at the expense of crowding four and five families in single-unit dwellings.[5]

Such survival tactics were essentially defensive and probably cut across worker subcultures. No group necessarily left Philadelphia, searched for work in the Quaker City, or combined meager resources with greater frequency than another. But the uniformity of short-term tactics broke down when workers looked to long-term solutions to the lean years. There were, in fact, three responses to the depression—one by the radicals, another by the revivalists, and a third by the traditionalists—that derived from the ideological content implicit in each culture.

Radicals

Radical perspectives on the 1837 crisis flowed from the assumptions of rationalism and the producer ideology. The rationalist side of radicalism, which linked socio-economic affairs to human action and natural phenomena to natural laws, pointed to the behavior of groups and classes. Aggregates of human beings, not an avenging deity or immoral individuals, brought on hard times (just as natural laws and not an angry God explained the causes behind the cholera epidemic of 1832). This analysis prevented individuals from blaming themselves for their plight at the end of the thirties, but offered no guidelines as to who was responsible for the panic and ensuing depression. Here radicals turned to the producer ideology. Just which group caused the privation was no mystery to them. The labor theory of value, the first axiom of radical ideology, provided the answer or at least offered a clue. This theory imparted a pre-Marxian notion of class and inequality. Instead of bifurcating society into classes of workers and employers, and locating exploitation exclusively in production, it loosely distinguished producers from accumulators, and emphasized the exploitation in exchange. This formulation all but absolved employers of responsibility, and focused attention on accumulators or bankers and merchants. Such financiers, reasoned John Ferral, alternatively provoked booms and busts, periods of "wreckless expansion" and "cruel contraction," by manipulating the money supply.[6] They were directly at fault for the latest downturn.

Radicals also believed that economic issues were inherently political. They established an intimate relationship between the economic and political spheres in which decisions fashioned by legislators determined material arrangements. Legislation, in turn, usually worked to the disadvantage of producers because financiers controlled the machinery of state and thereby could legitimize all manner of injustice, the most egregious of which were banking charters and general incorporation laws.

The lesson of this was clear. The struggle for social justice would fall short if confined to trade unionism and cooperation. Neither activity, it was thought, addressed the twin needs of countering laws of privilege and enacting legislation that reflected the true interests of producers. This perspective made some form of political activity inevitable; and the depression raised the political dimension of radicalism to the forefront.

Mass action was the immediate tactic radicals adopted following the suspension of specie payments in the spring of 1837. They called a series of massive rallies and demonstrations designed to denounce "shin plaster" Philadelphia and map remedial action. Committees appointed at these gatherings drafted resolutions demanding state suppression of small notes and a moratorium on bank charters, served local bankers with petitions bearing thousands of signatures and insisting on a return to specie, and, demanding action on the national level, endorsed President Van Buren's sub-treasury plan.[7]

Nonpartisanship was the common denominator of these demonstrations, quite apart from the antibank feeling. Speakers routinely expressed "no confidence" in either party as "presently constituted," even while they praised Van Buren.[8] They drew attention to issues and accented the Union's political neutrality. A hostile critic who tried tarring the G.T.U. with the brush of partisanship was told that it "spoke independently of all parties and owed allegiance to none."[9] "A judicious selection of law makers," said John Ferral, guided its politics.[10]

Ferral aptly captured the formal policy of the G.T.U. Outside the halls of the Union, however, he and other radicals were partisan Democrats thickly involved in the party. At least thirteen of the G.T.U.'s executive officers and numerous leaders of its affiliates served the Democracy in one capacity or another during the thirties. (One was a Whig and the remaining ten ignored political activism altogether or were so marginally involved in party life that their names do not appear on conventional party rosters.)[11]

Radical affinity for the Democracy is easily explained. It derived in part from the rough correspondence between party policy and radical views on culture, on the one hand, and political economy, on the other. Most Democrats endorsed cultural pluralism and were seen as the sentinels of religious freedom and toleration. As the champions of "freedom of conscience," they resolutely opposed prohibition, Sabbatarianism, and other reformist impulses that grew out of evangelicalism and found political expression in Whiggery. They thought of their party as a refuge for antievangelicals and antiPresbyterian Protestants of all sects, which endeared them to the Free Thinkers and Universalists (as well as to some Methodists, who saw the Whigs as the representatives of the haughty Presbyterians).[12]

Democratic policy on economic and social issues was another matter. Party loyalists who agreed on freedom of conscience were of mixed minds on noncultural issues. Two factions, radicals and regulars, emerged in the course of the thirties, and carried on an intraparty feud that occasionally flared into open combat and split the Democracy in two. Party regulars were a diffuse group popular in the city of Philadelphia and in rural counties outside of the southeast. They opposed or paid lip service to debtor relief, mechanics' lien laws, and other reforms raised by workingmen, and took moderate to conservative positions on the major economic issues. While some even favored Biddle's Bank of the United States, the typical party regular promoted state banks and easy credit in order to spur growth.[13] Their views put off the self-styled radicals, whose electoral base lay in the southeastern region and in suburban Philadelphia, with its teeming population of Trades' Unionists. Radicals were the progenitors of the meliorative measures for the popular classes and enthusiastic champions of free public education, but it was their stand on the controversial economic affairs of the day that really distinguished them from regulars. They took to the hustings in the name of the producing classes—yeoman farmers, master mechanics, and journeymen—and, in the language of radical republicanism, decried the hydra-headed monster of banking, corporate charters, and easy credit.[14]

Radicals in office were not always loyal to their creed; they often compromised their principles in the give and take of legislative bargaining. Radical legislator Samuel Stevenson, to cite one of many examples, traded off the struggle to abolish banks for an effort to regulate banking abuses, as did radical representatives to the state constitutional convention in 1838.[15] Such compromises disappointed constituents outside the State House, but the coinciding interests and rhetoric of both groups produced a loose alliance.

What cemented the bond between the Democracy and radical workingmen was the posture of the party at the local level. In suburban Philadelphia, birthplace of the workingmen's movement, master mechanics Lemuel Paynter and Thomas Grover, lawyer William F. Small, and other radical Democrats of middle-class status eagerly courted working-class voters. They gave their blessing to the ten-hour day, public ownership of granaries and coal yards, and other popular measures, and carved out a niche for radicals in their party.[16] Working-class leaders, in turn, took advantage of the party's openness. Joshua Fletcher, William Thompson, Israel Young, and John Ferral, for instance, headed ward committees and canvassed voters in elections; Young and Ferral ran successfully for borough offices in Moyamensing and Southwark; William English, Edward Penniman, and leaders of local unions entered the state legislature in the late 1830s.[17]

This axis of middling and working-class radicals evolved into a potent political force in some suburban districts. Southwark radicals, their growth enmeshed with that of the Trades' Union, pressured the district Commissioners into passing a ten-hour law in the summer of

1835. They gradually amassed enough support within the party to challenge the rule of the boss Joel Sutherland, a regular Democrat and Congressman who had run the party uncontested since the late 1820s. Radicals jousted with Sutherland's men over ideology and broke with them in the 1835 gubernatorial race, when each wing endorsed rival candidates. They bolted again in the spring, following Sutherlands' ringing endorsement of state Senator Jesse Burden, who voted to recharter Biddle's Bank of the United States. Radicals ran a slate of "Antibank" office seekers and deftly exploited popular antipathy toward financiers, sweeping every ward and placing such trusted allies as Thomas Grover on the borough Commission. This stunning victory was the prelude to a weightier battle against the real radical targets—Sutherland and Burden, whose renomination for Congress and the state Assembly, respectively, were pending at the upcoming county convention. Radicals husbanded their forces through the summer with mass meetings and engineered a supportive delegation which dumped Burden and replaced Sutherland with Lemuel Paynter. The incorrigible Sutherland refused to concede defeat and sought his office as a Whig, but Paynter capped the radical insurgence with a sound victory.[18]

Radical Trades' Unionists thus operated on two fronts in the thirties—one foot in the labor movement, the other in the Democracy's radical wing. Maintaining a delicate balance between the two, they managed to keep their political and union commitments separate. In this sense the labor movement governed the political practice of the radicals. As long as the Trades' Union continued to be a vital force with a heterogeneous constituency, the leadership was deterred from mixing partisanship with unionism or giving disproportionate attention to the political realm.

The G.T.U.'s collapse and its leadership's romance with the Democratic party combined to tilt the balance. Divested of their trade-union functions by the panic and depression, the leaders could turn only to politics and, in the late 1830s, they pitched into party work. Ferral, for one, struck up a correspondence with the future Democratic leader, James Buchanan, and in a revealing letter written in the cold winter of 1838, confessed that he measured the political health of wage earners in terms of their party loyalties. He told Buchanan of a meeting chaired by party regulars who rejected

President Van Buren's sub-treasury plan over the shouting objections of workingmen in the audience. But when another "shin plaster" (probank and soft money) Democrat rose to censure the President himself, the workers reacted with such anger that regulars adjourned the meeting. Such "spontaneous effusion" on behalf of radical Democracy convinced Ferral that "all is well with the bone and sinew" and marked a shift in the political tide that party "schemers will not be able to turn aside [,] . . . and for every shin plaster Democrat we lose, we shall gain ten honest workingmen who now keep aloof by reason of their knowing the baseness of those whilst pretending democracy only used the power obtained by duplicity to fasten upon the people a deeply demoralizing rag aristocracy."[19] Such reasoning was also manifested in the Trades' Union rallies during the closing years of the decade. Union leaders gave up all pretense to political neutrality and invited radical Democrats to share their speaking platforms at antibank gatherings.[20] Radical unionism and the Democracy were joined together more closely than ever.

A further step in the politicization of labor took place at the 1839 Workingmen's Convention. Composed of dispirited Trades' Unionists who gathered to appraise the condition of the labor movement, the Assembly consisted of thirty delegates representing skilled and unskilled workers.[21] Seven of the most active participants were former Trades' Union officials and loyal Democrats, and their intention of fusing the shattered G.T.U. with the Democracy was apparent from the beginning.[22] They invited "Persons not delegates from Societies or Associations, but who are favorably disposed to the advancement and interest" of working people.[23] This thinly veiled appeal to middle-class radicals violated a basic Union tenet that restricted formal Trades' Union assemblies to bona fide wage earners, and a majority of the delegates rejected it, voting to limit admission to workers. Thomas Fitnam, a former Trades' Union member turned master craftsman and Democratic politician, protested to Convention president Henry Scott. He questioned the "logic advanced by your erudite spouters, [that] no workingman can, the moment he betters his condition by applying to himself the fruits of his own toil, be any longer a friend to those he happened to leave behind."[24] The missive failed to alter Fitnam's status as *personna non grata,* but he nevertheless offered advice. He recommended

converting the depleted G.T.U. into a "Trades' *Political* Union"—
advice which accorded with the Democratic standard bearers but
which the majority scrapped upon banning the likes of Fitnam.

Though thwarted, the Democratic workingmen still left a mark on
the proceedings. The final report summed up the essence of working-
class radicalism. It called for a "*more equitable distribution of
wealth*" and for the intellectual advancement of workingmen and
their children through autonomous education institutions and a
Democratic "Republican" system of public instruction that supplied
"food and clothing" to the needy. There was no disagreement with
those noble planks or with the assessment that the G.T.U. was
beyond resuscitation—that sad conclusion was hardly new. The
innovation cropped up in the political proposals and here the
influence of the radicals was unmistakable. They bowed to the
majority will and arraigned both parties, but underscored the
primacy of politics by counseling workers to "participate in the active
business of party if you expect any benefit therefrom" and by urging
the "pursuit of the honours of government."[25]

These political prescriptions were as portentious as they were
autobiographical. During the depression Philadelphia's radical
workingmen doggedly pursued public office, both elective and
appointive, on the Democratic ticket; and, in these years, growing
numbers of them attended party conventions where their names were
placed in nomination for local and state-wide positions. Suggesting
their obsession with party affairs in 1838, Edward Penniman
withdrew from the race for Assemblyman at the insistence of the
regulars, explaining that the "*good of the party*" was his "*primary
concern.*"[26] John Ferral regularly sought the nomination for
Assemblyman and Senator and even publicized his candidacy with
advertisements in the local press. Samuel Thompson did better,
capturing the nomination for Assemblyman on a number of occasions. But he had the misfortune of running in a Whig district and
never won an election. Even more successful was Penniman, who,
undaunted by the rebuff in 1838, was nominated in 1839, and would
serve four terms in the Assembly. Much like William English and
other victorious candidates, Penniman made a career out of politics
and never returned to his former trade of coach making after being
elected. Shoemaker William Gilmore followed a slightly different
route out of the working class. A party functionary in Southwark

from the mid-thirties, Gilmore was rewarded for his efforts with the patronage position of Clerk of the County Commission, a job that also lifted him out of the artisan ranks.[27]

It is ironic that while the Democracy drained off the cream of radical working-class leadership, it resisted their ideas. Radicals always constituted a small minority of the party and made little impact on policy. Nor did they arouse much enthusiasm among rank and filers for radical solutions to the depression. Antibank meetings attracted thousands of disgruntled workingmen in the late 1830s, but scarcely deserved newspaper attention by the early 1840s.

Not all radicals found the Democracy as compatable or accessible as Penniman and Gilmore. A large group, frustrated with indifference to their program and with party rules that protected functionaries from insurgents, agitated for internal reform. In 1842 they organized an Equal Rights rump and campaigned for greater party democracy and against party inertia in the face of continued unemployment. But they were no more successful in sustaining mass protest than those who had captained the antibank movement. Equal Rights demonstrations were hardly worthy of the name and voters ignored Equal Rights candidates at the polls in the winter of 1842.[28] Radicalism lost whatever grip it had on the imagination of working-class Philadelphia, at least for the moment; the day belonged to the revivalists.

Revivalists
Alexander Fulton was among those wage earners who brushed aside radicalism in the midst of the Great Depression. Born in (northern?) Ireland around 1805, Fulton arrived in Philadelphia in the mid-thirties and took his place among his countrymen tending weaving frames in the traditionalist district of Moyamensing. There he shared a house with other families also headed by Irish hand loom weavers. Fulton's average earnings of from $4.00 to $5.00 a week in good times fell short of supporting his family; and it compelled his wife and daughter to wind yarn, and his two sons to work at an early age.[29] But even with the entire family as wage earners, the Fultons lived in the chronic poverty of hand loom weavers. The depression made a desperate situation even worse, but it drove Fulton into the church rather than into radical action.

Fulton's arrival coincided with the return of Reverend William Ramsey, the young Presbyterian minister who had spent the early thirties in India, after a year or two at Southwark's First Presbyterian Church. Anxious to pick up where he had left off, Ramsey took on the difficult task of revitalizing the Twelfth Church, a once-prosperous congregation whose members had lost enthusiasm and drifted apart in the early years of the depression. Ramsey warmed to the challenge with the single-minded zeal that had distinguished his earlier endeavors in Southwark and India, and shook the neighborhood with a spate of revivals in the late thirties. His message reached the beleaguered Fulton, who experienced a quickening of faith, confessed his sins, and was enrolled on the books of the revivified Cedar Street Church, as the old Twelfth was renamed under Ramsey's tutelage.[30]

Ramsey's India travels obviously did nothing to dampen his evangelical flame. "We are a temperance church," he wrote. "And although no one is required formally to sign a temperance pledge . . . the distinct understanding is, that every person who unites with the church . . . shall abstain from intoxicating drinks as a beverage," as well as from dancing, using profanity, and other revivalist taboos.[31] He continued to force these injunctions with the aid of communicants who reported cases of backsliding and sat in judgment of the accused. Transgressors were usually suspended and those wishing to rejoin the church had to confess before the session and show evidence of regeneration.[32]

As in the past, converts usually found adherence to this moral code difficult. It was singularly so for workers like Fulton, because of the rigid standards of behavior, the surveillance of minister and congregation, and the cultural milieu and work setting of hand loom weaving. Fulton's was a quantum leap from the culture of traditionalism, with its lax work ethic and closely knit, reinforcing fraternal groups, to the world of revivalism. The difficulty of negotiating this wrenching change—of severing friendships developed in bars and on street corners—must not be underestimated. Community networks discouraged Fulton's new life, as did his work experience. The poverty and irregular work routine of outwork impeded the self-discipline and steadiness of purpose that meshed with and fostered the morality of revivalism. Frequent unemployment, as observers of working-class communities have pointed out, had a way of encouraging reliance on drink.[33]

These circumstances and the untimely death of his young wife, weakened the resolve of the struggling hand loom weaver. Fulton lapsed shortly after conversion and was suspended; but he showed remarkable tenacity. Readmitted to the church after vowing to mend his ways, he succumbed to drink on three separate occasions between 1845 and 1855, but each time mustered the determination to swear off and was again inducted.[34]

Fulton represented a new evangelical constituency. He was one of thousands of wage earners who converged on Protestant pews during the depression; their turning to revivalism made the evangelical tide of the period qualitatively different from the Finneyite wave of the late twenties. The working classes of poorer suburban districts displaced the middle and upper classes of the old port as the chief evangelical legion; relatively anonymous ministers such as Ramsey, Robert Adair, William Elliott, and Pennell Coombe succeeded the established Presbyterians who had stood out in the earlier revivals; and the popular sects, peripherally involved in the previous surge of evangelicalism, now assumed the lead.[35] Reverend Pennell Coombe of Southwark's Ebenezer Methodist Church conducted such electrifying prayer meetings that a veteran class leader wrote in amazement to a relative, "I have never heard such a revival."[36] Coombe converted over a thousand souls in just two years, and swelled the membership beyond the capacity of the fifty year old church.

The reborn Methodists without pews organized their own congregation at Wharton Street and staffed a mission at Bedford Street. William Elliott took charge of the Wharton Street pulpit and matched Coombe's achievement, "quickening" five hundred Southwarkians in 1842 alone.[37] Their endeavors and those of fellow ministers throughout the county fired unprecedented growth in Methodist membership. Nearly 540 Philadelphians a year entered the Methodist church between 1837 and 1843, or double the yearly increment of the previous two decades.[38] The increase of New School Presbyterians was even more striking. Their congregations admitted nearly 900 converts each year in the depression, compared with a paltry 240 per year between 1815 and 1836.[39] Untold numbers of both sects were redeemed, it should be added, but did not enroll in churches. (And when prosperity returned in 1844 revivals flared for a brief time, but failed to have much impact and the annual increases of both sects fell to predepression rates.)

The Great Depression was the source of this renewed religious awakening. No single force, apart from the advent of industrial capitalism, did so much to break down the resistance to the new Protestantism and diffuse it among the clergy and laity. As we have seen, prior to the downturn, ministers were of different minds on the efficacy of revivals and the value of industrial morality. Methodist proponents of Finneyite measures, for example, were a minority of their church and at loggerheads with those who appealed to the emotions without resorting to formal revivals and who saw nothing wrong with drinking in moderation or even selling liquor. But the perspective of "new wave" Methodists was confirmed by the economic collapse. Such ministers (as well as those of other denominations) interpreted hard times as divine retribution for man's depravity and they proved to be remarkably persuasive.[40] More and more fellow divines joined together with them in a frenetic movement of atonement that took the form of a rash of revivals and temperance meetings, many of which united Methodist with Presbyterian in a burst of ecumenicalism. Their forces strengthened, the Methodist reformers won a key battle against their "old guard" at the annual meeting of the Philadelphia Conference in 1841. Under their influence, the Conference suspended a rule permitting the consumption of spirits for medicinal purposes and passed a resolution recommending "total abstinence from all intoxicating liquors."[41] Seven years later they would finally restore John Wesley's stronger language.

These clergymen, in turn, effectively exploited the psychic torment imposed on working people by the depression. Few contemporaries had a keener appreciation for the vulnerability of wage earners in periods of stress. Witness, for example, an intriguing primer on evangelical methods written by Reverend James Porter, a Methodist who journeyed through the East during the decade. Porter posited a causal link between personal and collective distress of workers and their propensity to religion. He saw hard times as especially opportune in this respect because extended unemployment evoked solemnity and introspection, the precursors to conversion. Porter challenged the ministry to make the most of such "providential occasions which seem to compel them to be serious and to regard religion as the paramount interest." "The most buoyant and reckless spirits," he stressed, "have times of depression, and solemn review."[42] The city's leading newspaper, elated by the recent upsurge in church membership, endorsed this point. "The most valuable result of the calamities of the times," the *Public Ledger* editorialized in 1843, "is . . . to be found in its moral influences." "'Sweet are the uses of adversity . . . ,'" it added and continued:

> That the zeal of the ministry and efforts of the pious have effected much cannot be doubted: nor is there doubt that the depression of the times, the anxiety and affliction which have prevailed, and which have induced reflection . . and self-reproach, have tended in a great degree to direct serious attention of the mass to their religious interests.[43]

Workingmen were not simply pushed into the church by the destitution accompanying hard times; they were also pulled there by the polemics of pastors. In attributing the depression to moral depravity, the clergy apparently put forward a more compelling argument than the radicals. The radical formulation, which traced the depression to the machinations of bankers, left workers relatively powerless to effect much change. Legislators in far-off Harrisburg and Washington made the decisions, but their remedies, radical or not, brought no relief. Clergymen singled out the behavior of individuals and, in so doing, offered an easier solution, or at least one that left room for individual effort. They maintained that he who came to Christ on their terms not only appeased the Lord but also regenerated himself and gained the moral fortitude to weather perilous conditions.

It comes as no surprise that a refurbished temperance movement swept Philadelphia. Like the revivalist upsurge, this crusade differed from its predecessor with regard to leadership, methods of operation, and constituency. The pioneer temperance leaders, as we have seen, were interchangeable with early revivalist ministers. They gave the movement an elitist coloration and, with a few exceptions, kept it distant from the popular classes. Rarely, if ever, having contact with the masses, they restricted their activities to collecting signatures on temperance pledges, distributing literature, and lecturing on the evils of drink and the glories of abstinence. They seemed to be preoccupied with raising funds ear-marked to defray the costs of the endless polemics and tracts that were churned out; and their societies were loosely organized affairs that held infrequent meetings. Some workingmen, it is true, had joined local organizations aligned with churches, but it is difficult to conceive of this earlier temperance crusade as a movement. Instead, it was more comparable to a highly energetic bureaucracy.

The new movement was very different from its predecessor. On the one hand, its leadership was drawn from the ranks of petty professionals, small shopkeepers, independent producers, and skilled workers, and, on the other, from the ministry of these groups. Men like Lewis Levin, an ambitious small-time lawyer outside the city's legal establishment, and ministers like Ramsey and Coombe supplied the leadership. Such guiding lights ignored the established societies allied with the American Temperance Union and put together separate organizations that were temperance-beneficial lodges and were tailored to the needs and interests of common folk. Their press, in fact, criticized the orthodox groups for neglecting the economic interest of their followers and for lacking the provisions "by which all the members may be brought together at short intervals" so as to exert their "united influence."[44] Temperance-beneficial societies remedied both flaws by combining welfare with reformist functions, so critical in the depression, and by holding frequent meetings. Their gatherings might take place on consecutive evenings when interest ran high, as it often did during the late thirties, and they were convened in the streets as well as in churches and meeting halls. Leaders anticipated the Washingtonians by seeking out hardened drinkers and congenital drunkards, those whom older societies had neglected and who would become featured speakers at meetings, testimonies to the possibility of self-reform under the encouragement of peers. Such tactics yielded striking results. Together with the goadings of the depression, they accomplished what elite temperance advocates had failed to do: bring total abstinence to the status of a mass movement.[45]

Temperance-beneficial societies with billowing memberships shot

up between 1837 and 1841. One observer placed the number of
temperance advocates in the county at 17,000 in 1841, a four-fold
increase since the middle of the thirties, and noted that in the first two
months of 1841 alone, 4,300 Philadelphians enlisted in the crusade.[46]
Most of these acolytes were in temperance-beneficial societies and an
analysis of the membership of two lodges—Southwark Branch No. 1
and Western Branch No. 2 of Moyamensing—underscores the class
nature of the new movement. Both societies consisted of a minority of
small shopkeepers and ministers and a majority of wage earners, both
skilled and unskilled. (See Table 10.)

Table 10

Occupations of the Members of Temperance-Beneficial Associations,
Southwark Branch No. 1 and Western Branch No. 2,
1837–1838

	Southwark		Western	
Occupation	*No.*	*%*	*No.*	*%*
Gentleman	0	0	0	0
Merchant	12	10.3	2	6.0
Manufacturer	1	0.8	1	3.0
Professional	5	4.2	1	3.0
Lesser professional	9	7.8	1	3.0
Public official	3	2.5	0	0
Master craftsman*	5	4.2	0	0
Journeyman	60	51.3	20	60.7
Unskilled laborer and street trade	22	18.8	8	24.2
Total†	117		33	

*See Table 5.

†The original Southwark list contained 148 names along with the addresses and
occupations of most of the members; the original Western list contained the names
and addresses of 64 members. One-hundred-seventeen of the former, or 74.3
percent of names listed, were located in the directories or their occupations were
recorded as they appear on the membership roll. Thirty-three, or 51.6 percent of the
latter, were located in the directories.

*Source: Charter and By-Laws of the Temperance Beneficial Association Western
Branch No. 2* (Philadelphia: T. K. and P. G. Collins, 1837); city directories,
1837–1838. The pamphlet lists the members of both organizations.

Careful scrutiny of temperance-beneficial society rosters indicates that the movement (as well as renewed evangelicalism) cut across cultural lines within the working class. The coachmaker Joshua Fletcher, the tanner Benjamin Sewell, the cordwainer Joseph Hollingsworth, and other former leaders of the Trades' Union and of union locals in the mid-thirties were drawn into the temperance movement, the evangelical crusade, or both in the late thirties and early forties. And they joined former traditionalists like Alexander Fulton in one or both of these. This amalgamation suggests why it was that workers of all cultures lost interest in antibank rallies and spurned the Equal Rights party in the closing years of the depression. Radicalism, at the end of the decade, simply lost out to evangelicalism for the minds of wage earners. Fletcher, Sewell, Hollingsworth, and thousands of other workers who swung to radicalism under their influence during the thirties turned inward upon being evangelized; they pursued self-perfection rather than collective protest against the wealthy. In addition, the resurgence of temperance and revivalism severed whatever ties remained between radical workingmen and traditionalists and revivalists. While the radicals lambasted banks and ran for public office, their former followers gradually fell into line behind middle-class laymen and the suburban ministry. These leaders, consumed as they were with cultural issues, took their evangelized minions down the road to harmony with employers and discord with nonevangelicals.

The leading exponent of this course was Lewis Levin, a South Carolina-born lawyer who tramped the southern back country teaching and practicing law before settling in Philadelphia in the late 1830s. Although admitted to the bar, Levin could not penetrate the polite society of Philadelphia's legal profession. Nor was he temperamentally fit for it. Crude, vulgar, and something of a charlatan with flair for demagoguery and a hunger for political office, he mixed more easily with his social inferiors than with gentlemen attorneys. He never established much of a legal practice and, in the early 1840s, devoted himself to the quest for public office and the cause of temperance, both as lecturer and editor of the *Temperance Advocate and Literary Repository.*[47]

To some extent Levin reflected the apprehensions and anxieties of Philadelphia's Protestant middle class at the end of the 1830s. They had been chastened by the depression and the social disorganization that came in its wake, and could not help but look back to the 1830s with some trepidation. Deeply troubled by the 1830s' class warfare and ideological ferment, they sought a moral equivalent for radicalism that both uplifted their own spirits, as well as those of workingmen, and restored social harmony between the classes. Temperance was a key to this strategy, and Levin's followers packaged total abstinence as a restorative force for both the individual and society. Temperance advocates, boasted a lieutenant in the new cold water army, actuated a revolution in public and private morality that enabled individuals to "maintain their *glorious independence,* which has contributed so essentially to their health, happiness, respectability and worldly prosperity."[48] Another sounded the same theme in a poem describing a downcast soul who

> Knelt and thanked God for the Teetotal Mill,
> The poor were made *rich,* and the weak made *strong,*
> The shot was made *short,* and the *purse* was made long.[49]

Those who worshipped at the shrine of the "Teetotal Mill," combated familial decline and personal hardship, for they transformed themselves into responsible parents and reliable workers. Their honest toil was rewarded with wages sufficient to support dependents in comfort even in the worst downturn in memory. They also partook of the tonic of social cohesion. Or as Levin put it, such workers tracked "evil to its legitimate source—the *Rum Shop,*" and no longer "considered themselves cast off from the sympathies of the upper classes, regarded as tools and machines." Thus the communalism of the temperance cause was the "most effectual means of closing [the] fatal chasm in our social system, of knitting up [the] sympathies again; of reviving between the middle and working classes those healthful and fraternal feelings which the spirit of intemperance has done so much to destroy."[50]

The cultural issues that produced this alliance of middle and working-class evangelicals drove a wedge within the working class itself. Nativist tendencies inhered in the temperance and evangelical crusade from the very beginning. They now became more articulate in the hands of temperance zealots, who directed this heightened sense of Protestant identity against traditionalists. Catholics were especially vulnerable targets for these enthusiasts, not only because of their religion but also because they were easily identified with the liquor interests and had a reputation as a cheap labor pool. All of these issues were charged with emotion, but the labor question was positively explosive during a depression—when the unemployed were not above unleashing their frustrations on scapegoats.

Traditionalists

Traditionalist workers who resisted the radicalism of the thirties and the evangelicalism of the depression were pulled in two directions. The hand-to-mouth existence of hard times, exacerbated by the treatment meted out by loom bosses, drove Irish Protestant and Irish Catholic wage earners together against their own middle class and against Black workers, while the cultural chauvinism of evangelicals drew Catholic workers together with their own middle-class leaders, who built political careers out of defending their cultural integrity from bigoted Protestants. Both courses occurred simultaneously; both were marred by violence; and both strained relations with evangelicals to the breaking point.

No group of white workers bore a heavier burden than Irish hand loom weavers and unskilled laborers. The oversupply of weavers kept wages low and employment irregular, so much so that frame tenders lived at subsistence levels and routinely shifted into casual labor when work was lacking. The protracted depression and continued immigration multiplied the number of hand loom weavers searching for unskilled jobs; and the exodus from weaving to the docks and construction sites irritated racial antagonisms and touched off another round of rioting between the hungry Irish and hungry but employed Black dockers. Sporadic scuffles between the groups burst into a melee on August 1, 1842, when Blacks in the southern ghetto massed at their temperance hall for a parade in commemoration of Jamaican Emancipation Day. The iconography of the procession, which included a flag depicting a slave breaking his chains against the rising sun of freedom, caused a stir among Irish onlookers. Tempers were simmering by the time the marchers reached the public market at Plum and Fourth Streets, in the heart of Irish Southwark. Market vendors and aroused spectators, provoked partly by the flag and partly by the spectacle itself, first hurled insults and then paving stones, disrupting the parade and pursuing the Blacks into the ghetto. Blacks defended themselves against prowling mobs, and some retreated to a house on Bradford's Alley, where they held off their assailants with musket fire and inadvertently incurred more severe treatment. Torches replaced missiles and by nightfall Smith's Hall, an abolitionist meeting place, as well as St. Mary's Church, were reduced to ashes.

Renewed fighting broke out the next morning at the Schuylkill docks, the exposed nerve center of unemployed Irishmen. Club-wielding Irishmen assaulted Blacks reporting for work and, as in other such episodes, then turned against the sheriff's posse sent to quell the trouble. They easily routed the authorities and resumed bludgeoning the Blacks, which inspired the mayor to call out seven militia companies. Composed of over a thousand volunteers, it was the largest peace-keeping force ever assembled and a sufficient show of strength to dampen Irish courage, momentarily at least.[51]

Hand loom weavers also fought running battles with their employers over wages during the next few years. Loom bosses in both districts incited their workers by repeatedly shaving the rates. They slashed the scale on the standard five-shuttle gingham from five to three cents a yard by 1841, but the journeymen were in no position to offer much resistance through most of the depression. Their own poverty and massive unemployment deterred effective action. They were also disarmed by the death of their unions and by the disruption of communal solidarity issuing from the social disorganization of hard times and from the continuous arrival of new immigrants. In August of 1842, however, the weavers took a stand against yet another wage reduction and held out for six long months before returning to work with a compromise settlement. The following spring and summer they staged brief strikes that boosted the rates to predepression levels. But the loom bosses, who had been at one anothers' throats, finally pulled together and resisted weaver demands for another increase in January of 1844. They stood firm for five months and, on top of this, dealt the weavers a devastating wage cut. In May the defeated frame tenders returned to their looms, weaving cloth for 3¼¢ a yard.[52]

Working conditions and the character of the labor force combined to make these strikes as violent as they were lengthy. Scabbing was common because of the oversupply of workers and because weavers like Alexander Fulton were more concerned with the salvation of their own souls than with deprivation. Such workers, as well as recent arrivals who, Michael Feldberg observes, were not yet integrated into the tight-knit weavers' communities, became the most likely strike-breakers.[53] Policing them and enforcing solidarity proved to be arduous. The decentralization of the industry and nature of the work setting obliged vigilance committees, in order to ferret out scabs, to comb the districts and even enter homes. Such painstaking efforts and the frustrations built up in the course of the long standouts put vigilantes in an ugly mood, and they went about their work accordingly. Timid weavers found at work were beaten mercilessly, chains were ripped from frames and destroyed in the streets, wives and children were sometimes intimidated and threatened; resisting employers had property destroyed and their homes sprayed with musket fire.[54]

The rash of violence set the embattled weavers against local authorities. One of many clashes with the police took place in Kensington in January of 1843 when two Alderman in hot pursuit of a vigilance committee were themselves apprehended by the weavers. One fought his way to freedom, the other suffered a severe beating, but managed to seize Thomas Lynch, a strike leader and popular figure in the cottager community. News of Lynch's arrest spread rapidly through Kensington's pubs and fire houses, and it led to a spontaneous rally of weavers and sympathizers at the Nanny Goat Market. Lynch's partisans vowed reprisals against the police, but the meeting was disrupted by Sheriff John Porter, who braved the angry Kensingtonians and, mounting a soap box, ordered the crowd to disperse, but drew the predictable insults and cat-calls. Left without options, he went to raise a posse. Meanwhile the weavers and their partisans armed themselves and greeted Porter's force with a hail of fire, which put most to flight. A handful, the sheriff among them, were stranded and bore the onslaught of the furious weavers. Porter's deputy ordered several militia units into the area and pacified it, while local constables rounded up eight ring leaders.[55]

Ironically, Hugh Clark, the chief arresting officer, was in the middle of the class and ethnic struggles that disturbed the Kensington peace. A loom boss and shrewd land speculator, Clark was busy accumulating a modest fortune (value at $30,000 in land alone by 1850) and becoming one of the wealthiest residents of that poor district. He had counterparts in the south, the most important of whom were Joseph Diamond, liquor dealer and land speculator, and Judge Joseph Doran. Clark, Diamond, and Doran, and other Catholic parvenues represented a breed of ethnic politician and community leader that, together with the Catholic clergy, was displacing class-conscious stalwarts like John Ferral in Kensington and Moyamensing during the depression years.[56] They parlayed the growing ethnic strife into political prominence, exacerbating it in the process, and, at the same time, ignored the economic grievances of their traditionalist constituents. Or, in the case of Clark and Bernard Sherry, they drove their own employees to the wall on wage matters, but staunchly defended Irish Catholic cultural interests. Sherry, for example, tenaciously resisted the wage demands of his journeymen weavers, yet primed them for a battle with nativist mobs by distributing arms.[57]

The Moyamensing Commission, a stronghold of Irish power in the forties, played a similar role. In June 1842, the John Hancock Temperance-Beneficial Society petitioned local officials for the use of the district hall. Such requests by community groups were routinely granted, but the Commissioners, protecting Catholics from nativistic temperance enthusiasts, turned down the petitioners.[58] A few months later the Commission had occasion to enhance this image. Residents living near a Black temperance hall feared that the building would be fired by the mob and thereby endanger their property. They demanded that the Commissioners destroy the hall and the officers complied, sending the case to a friendly judge. The judge then appointed a rigged panel which ordered the building demolished.[59]

The conduct of these Irish politicians produced indignation in temperance circles and in the press, and arrayed popular feeling against Irish Philadelphia. The members of the John Hancock Temperance-Beneficial Society, lodging a complaint that would become the nativist battle cry, bristled at being excluded from their own halls of government and charged the Moyamensing Commission with placing "civil and religious rights in jeopardy."[60] Bushrod W. Knight, a Hancock leader and Commission member, was so em-

barrassed by the patent illegality of razing the temperance hall that he
felt the need to disassociate himself from his fellow Commissioners.
In an advertisement in the *Public Ledger* he claimed to have been
absent during the vote and roundly condemned the decision.[61] The
Ledger itself joined the opposition, observing that the *brick* building
hardly constituted a fire hazard and even if it did, its destruction was
illegal since there had not been a jury trial.[62] But it was Clark who,
wittingly or not, brought down Protestant Philadelphia against the
Irish.

Philadelphia's participation in the state common school system
began in 1834. Discord over its administration was inevitable, given
Protestant domination of classrooms in a city with a growing
Catholic minority. The school day opened with teachers reading
passages from the King James Bible and using it as a text to drill
children in morality.[63] Catholics, however, recognized the Douay
Bible as their scripture, and canon law prohibited their taking com-
munion or engaging in worship, bible reading included, with other
sects. School practice obviously violated rules of Catholic conduct
and of local prelates, who brought this to the attention of the
Controllers of the Public Schools shortly after the inauguration of
free public instruction in 1834. They apparently won their point, for
the Board forbade "any form of religious or sectarian instruction."[64]
The ruling, however, did not pertain to bible reading, which was a
convenient escape for teachers, and was impossible to enforce in any
case.

Protestant control of the schools disturbed Bishop Francis Patrick
Kenrick, but there was no easy remedy at hand. The Catholic church
had not yet constructed its own schools; and the Bishop, cautious and
mild-mannered in temperament, held his peace for fear of creating a
backlash. He tried to buy time until the diocese built a haven for
Catholic children in the form of a parochial school network, but as
the city's Roman Catholic spokesman he had to protect his flock
from Protestant insults. Southwark's Public School Directors forced
his hand in the spring of 1842 by summarily firing a Catholic teacher
for refusing to open the school day with readings from the King
James Bible. Kenrick protested the dismissal in the diocesan
newspaper, the *Catholic Herald,* but did not raise so much as a
whimper among the laity. Many Catholics were preoccupied with the

weavers' strike, but most were not yet incorporated into the institutional life of the church, and their indifference forced Kenrick to change his strategy. He took to the pen and in a letter to the county School Board, set forth a litany of grievances but emphasized the bible reading issue. He proposed a compromise that involved excusing Catholic children from the opening exercises and allowing them to conduct separate services with their own bible.

Kenrick's plan put the School Board in a delicate position. Its members could not help but consider Protestant reaction to the prospect of introducing the Douay Bible into *their* schools, but neither could they ignore the legitimate complaints of the Bishop. Caught between these constraints, they hewed the line of least resistance and agreed to excuse from the bible reading "children whose parents are conscientiously opposed thereto" but refused to sanction the use of the Douay edition.[65] This ruling disappointed Kenrick, but at least it spared Catholic children the indignity of sitting through the reading of the King James Bible. He therefore pressed the issue no further.

Evangelical and orthodox Philadelphia, already troubled by Catholic political power, took a less balanced view than Kenrick or the School Board. They interpreted his letter as further confirmation of a Catholic conspiracy to infiltrate the schools and then deliver the republic into the hands of the diabolical pope. Ministers hysterically "exposed" Kenrick's scheme to "kick the bible" from classrooms and in the fall of 1842, over ninety clerical representatives of nearly every Protestant church and sect—Arminian and orthodox, evangelical and otherwise—coalesced in the American Protestant Association, which blanketed the city with foreboding comments on Catholic designs.[66] Its representatives distributed copies of anti-Catholic literature, hawked Protestant propaganda pretending to uncover the resurgent Catholicism predicted by the prophet Daniel, and, on the lecture circuit, exhorted responsible Protestants to rally in defense of God, country, and republican virtue.[67]

Such feverish rhetoric from the clergy spilled into the political arena and revitalized an anti-immigrant movement which had been operating without much success since 1837. American Republican Associations, the political analogue of the American Protestant Association, awakened new interest in the winter and spring of 1843.

They promoted a measure that would deny suffrage to the immigrants for twenty-one years after arrival in the United States and would also bar them from public office. Their program took on new relevance in the heat of the school controversy and American Republican clubs, heretofore paper organizations, spread throughout the county.[68]

Clark fanned these nativist flames. A member of the Kensington School Board, he was inspecting district classrooms in February of 1844 (and perhaps looking to promote his own political fortunes), when a teacher complained of disruptions that occurred as Catholic children departed prior to the bible reading. Clark might have disregarded the observation, but instead, took it upon himself to order an immediate suspension of the bible reading until the School Board worked out another arrangement. Sensible Philadelphians did not take kindly to Clark's measure. Even the *Spirit of the Times*, a radical Democractic organ that never suffered evangelical excess, scored his "intolerant zeal . . . lamentable fanaticism."[69]

More than any previous event, Clark's ill-timed intervention into the school controversy galvanized Protestant groups among the clergy, the temperance movement, and the larger society into a coherent movement. His action became grist for the mill of demagogues, like Levin, who merged their temperance forces with those of the American Republicans, forming a nativistic phalanx that exploited the event in the March elections. American Republican candidates crying "Save the Bible!" and demanding Clark's dismissal made strong showings in select wards.[70] Emboldened by their success and spurred into provocative acts by their histrionic leaders, American Republicans resolved to test the mettle of their adversaries on Clark's home ground and scheduled party rallies in Kensington.

With these meetings, class and cultural currents of the depression years converged. On one side was Clark, surrogate for Irish Catholicism and the Irish Catholic community, whose weavers were in the midst of a bitter strike against Clark himself; on the other was Levin, Clark's counterpart among evangelical and nonevangelical Protestants, whose own followers had closed ranks behind striking Irish frame tenders a scant seven years ago. In the end, Kensington class cleavages dissipated, as weavers perceived an even greater threat in nativism and sided with Clark.

Angry Irish weavers twice disrupted small American Republican gatherings in mid-April, but failed to discourage nativist chieftains. On the first Friday in May, S. R. Cramer, a rising nativist star who combined house carpentry with publication of the *Native American*, addressed still another meeting. He, too, was driven from the platform by Catholic hecklers and spent the remainder of the weekend strategizing with party leaders. He returned to Kensington the following Monday, accompanied by Levin, who mounted a soap box across the street from the Nanny Goat Market. A cloudburst sent Levin's listeners scurrying for cover in the market where Levin himself put together a makeshift stump and launched into a tirade against "Popery." His provocations were answered with a barrage of rotten vegetables and rocks. Matters took a more serious turn when nativist crowds, allegedly excited by musket fire, stormed the Hibernia Hose house and nearby weavers' cottages suspected of harboring armed assailants. Both sides opened fire, and when the shooting stopped, eleven nativists lay on the ground, wounded or beaten, and George Shiffler, a morocco dresser's apprentice, was dead.

The initial volley and Shiffler's death turned Kensington into a magnet for avenging nativist mobs. They converged on the area and spent the next two days laying waste to buildings, looting, and exchanging gunfire and fistacuffs with its besieged immigrants. Upward of 3,000 troops were called in on Wednesday morning, and took up positions near Catholic churches, the anticipated nativist targets, but they could not (or refused to) block bands of young toughs, who burned two churches and occasionally roughed up residents. By Thursday morning the worst was over. Nativists retreated across Kensington's borders, leaving behind the charred ruins of thirty buildings, and at least sixteen dead.[71]

Nativism surged through the summer and American Republican helmsmen adroitly steered it into displays of political might. The traditional Independence Day parade became a nativist spectacle of at least 5,000 marchers wafting banners with party slogans and promises of electoral victory. Widows of riot victims and their orphaned children marched, as well, evoking special compassion from the estimated 100,000 spectators who lined the streets for the occasion.[72]

Prophesies of political ascendance announced by the parade banners came to pass in the fall elections. American Republicans swept the entire county and old port city, sending Levin to Congress, a delegation of Senators and Assemblymen to Harrisburg, and seating numerous Commissioners in the chambers of local government. A year later the Whigs regained control of the city, the Democrats recaptured the county delegation of Senators and Assemblymen, but American Republicans retained a firm grip on local government in Southwark, the Northern Liberties, Spring Garden, and portions of Kensington throughout the 1840s.[73]

The great depression thus marks a watershed in the making of working-class culture. The prolonged unemployment that destroyed the institutional base of radicalism—unions, cooperatives, debating clubs, and reading rooms—also altered the strategies and cultural commitments of those who had used these organizations as instruments of material improvement and intellectual uplift. Some radicals turned to political activism with renewed vigor. They directed popular discontent against the bankers at a series of massive rallies in 1837–1838. But the antibank sentiments of rank and filers waned and radical rallies became pale replicas of their former selves by the winter of 1838–1839. Radical leaders, having been deserted by their followers, passed the remainder of the depression bearing the standard of the Democrats or assembling an Equal Rights party. Revivalists, traditionalists, and even some radicals—veterans of radical campaigns, as well as the newly converted during the thirties—were more attentive to middle-class temperance advocates and evangelical ministers who trumpeted self-discipline, sobriety, and other facets of the new morality both as the remedy for unemployment and as the road to a competency.

These newly enlisted evangelicals and temperance crusaders fulfilled the worst fears of radicals. Ever since William Heighton had codified radicalism in the twenties, they understood revivalist ministers to be their chief competitors for working-class loyalties. They lived in apprehension of the church, but had the advantage in the thirties. Evangelicalism did not reach very deeply into the social structure and, when touching the labor force, it claimed a small minority only—mostly upwardly mobile craftsmen and workers engaged in the most modern pursuits. It made little sense to the vast majority of workingmen until the depression years. Hard times violated this rough equation between career trajectories or work experiences and revivalist inclinations. Evangelicalism crossed work environments and cultural lines alike, and turned revivalism into a mass movement with a strong working-class base.

Yet, as the return of prosperity would show, evangelicalism did not transform all wage earners into deferential employees or rigid nativists jealousy protecting their jobs from the immigrant hordes. Some workers accepted it selectively: they endorsed revivalistic morality but repudiated its conservative political economy.

Part Four:
Years of Discord
1845-1850

Workers at Bay

7

The years after 1845 were a mixed blessing for working-class Philadelphians. Their despair born of unemployment abated with economic recovery and they could once again look forward to steadier work. Artisans who moved into unskilled work in the dislocation of the depression returned to their trades. Some craftsmen benefited from the showdowns of 1835–1836 over the length of the workday and left their jobs before sundown in observance of that memorable slogan, "6 to 6." But this was one of the few residual dividends of the thirties.

Prosperity may have restored jobs but did not lighten the worker's travail. Making ends meet was more demanding than ever according to "A Reflecting Operative." This embittered worker of 1849 calculated that labor had lost one-third to one-half "its former gain" in the last fifteen years, and he erred only on exaggerating the magnitude of the decline. Most journeymen, he accurately observed, failed to recover the wage reductions imposed by employers during the depression, and those in the sweated trades sustained additional

Some material in this chapter has been adapted from "Fire Companies and Gangs in Southwark: The 1840s," in *The Peoples of Philadelphia: A History of Ethnic Groups and Lower-class Life, 1790–1940,* ed. Allen F. Davis and Mark H. Haller (Philadelphia: Temple University Press, 1973), with permission of the publisher.

cuts in the late forties.[1] They paid more for necessities, owing primarily to rising prices on the open market and partly to the store-order system, which further increased costs.[2] The price of pork, corn, and fuel fell gradually during the depression, before beginning an incremental rise after 1845, which returned prices to 1835 levels by the late 1840s.[3] Workers who were unable to push up earnings during the inflation spiral were worse off in 1850 than in 1835. Most, in fact, lived at or below subsistence levels.

Many tradesmen and operatives toiled longer and harder in order to survive. Textile bosses stretched out the workday to twelve and thirteen hours, and shoe and clothing manufacturers accomplished the same result by holding down piece rates. Journeymen shoemakers and tailors worked late into the night during the busy season of the late forties in compensation for continual rate cuts.[4] With the shift of production from homes and shops to manufactories and garrets, a growing number also faced stricter work routines and closer supervision. Printers and building tradesmen were among the privileged craftsmen who maintained the ten-hour day, but even they experienced erosions of their skills and laboring traditions. Boss printers demoted the all-around journeyman into a specialized worker relegated to setting type when they divided up the craft and staffed press rooms with young women and teenage boys commonly known as "half-trained" apprentices. Publishers on the frontiers of innovation installed power-driven presses, which subjected the women and youths to the regimen of machinery and placed additional pressure on the male compositors.[5] Speculators in the building trades began a radical transformation of housing construction at the expense of the skills of journeymen and the independence of masters. Such entrepreneurs performed no manual labor, nor did they hire their own workers in the manner of the traditional builder. Instead, they let contracts to masters and awarded jobs to the lowest bidder within each calling, which converted masters into intensely competitive subcontractors forced to hire the cheapest labor available. This system spelled the demise of independent masters and the displacement of skilled construction workers by "green hands."[6]

Journeymen with ambitions to establish themselves on their own could not have chosen a more inauspicious time. The conventional avenue of mobility from journeyman to master narrowed appreciably during the forties.[7] Opportunity dried up and failures mounted, which sent even more masters and journeymen into the advanced work environments. The few that did rise to master status did not necessarily achieve independence. Most were more likely to be subcontractors and garret bosses beholden to merchants and manufacturers.

The decline in living standards and deterioration of working conditions did not go uncontested. Skilled and unskilled workers reconstituted their unions or mobilized in make-shift strike committees, but these agencies of struggle paled in contrast to earlier models. Artisan combinations regressed to their pre-thirties form and rarely drafted the semiskilled or expressed solidarity with one another, with industrial workers, or with the unskilled. And they were emphatically less combatative than in the 1830s. Newspapers recorded only eighty strikes in the decade following recovery, compared with thirty standouts in 1836 alone, and such work stoppages usually collapsed within a month.[8] This perceptible falling off of worker militancy derived in part from the want of a central labor union capable of coordinating strike activity and of funding union efforts. Fragmented and disorganized, strikers received no quarter from fellow unionists and more often than not went down to defeat.

Waning worker militancy was not simply the result of weak organization. Instead, both were symptomatic of the impact of immigration, revivalism, and nativism on worker cultures. These forces further balkanized wage earners into hostile camps and solidified the affiliations between native-born journeymen and small producers that had been prefigured in the shifting political alliances of the depression and had fueled American Republicanism. Such factors also spawned new cultural types. Evangelicalism, for example, gave rise to a variant of radicalism—or what we shall call radical revivalism—and immigration reshaped the texture of traditionalism and the old radicalism. Thus, the cultural mosaic of the past assumed a new complexity; it consisted of revivalists, two groups of traditionalists, and two of radicals. The radicals are the subject of the following chapter. Here we explore the revivalists and traditionalists.

Revivalists

The depression's evangelical upsurge swelled the revivalist minority
into a sizable subculture. Revivalists constituted an even larger
faction of the American Republican party, traditionalists and
radicals being the others. They shared the nationalistic and anti-
Catholic sentiments of fellow nativists, but had a unique point of view
and a different organizational nexus outside the party itself. Their
institutional base was the evangelical church of the suburbs—those
congregations that vegetated in the revivals and temperance rallies of
the late thirties, under the cultivation of Ramsey, Coombe, and
others. Such ministers brought their own perspective to bear on the
key issues of the day. They were adept at fomenting strong antialien
feeling with dark forecasts of the consequences of unchecked
immigration. They depicted the foreign-born as competitors in the
labor market, and singled out Catholics as a force that would arrest
progress and reduce prosperous America to the backwardness of
Spain, Ireland, and other lands under papal rule.[9] Some even
rebuked bankers, lawyers, and merchants in the language of the
producer ideology. Methodist minister John Hersey, for one, was
fond of dispensing advice on child rearing and domestic economy. He
once counseled parents against preparing children "for the bar, if you
wish them to live in heaven. Neither can we recommend but utterly
condemn merchandising." He continued with a choice quotation
from Oliver Goldsmith: "Honor sinks where commerce long prevails."[10] The most "honorable and independent employment on
earth," he insisted, "is the cultivation of the ground: next to this
stands plain, useful mechanism [artisanship]."[11] In a similar vein
William Ramsey and other suburban ministers with working-class
congregations sermonized against "speculation" and nonproductive
labor.[12] But reprobations of this sort were rare and should not be
confused with the radical version of the producer ideology.

Evangelical leaders looked at such matters through the lens of the
new morality. Moral considerations, not radical economics, under-
pinned their distrust of accumulators and immigrants alike. Hersey
thus demeaned merchandising and the professions not because they
were unproductive or exploitative but because they could "dissipate
and distract the mind" and, if followed, would lead to vice and moral
languor.[13] By the same token, immigrants aroused revivalist enmity

not so much because they threatened the jobs of Americans, but because they were perceived as degenerates.

This moral critique of accumulators and immigrants was only one aspect of revivalism. For ministers were not only interested in the conduct of nonevangelicals; their own behavior and that of their communicants also concerned them. Attacking the foreign-born and warning of the perils of nonmanual vocations, after all, allowed for the ventilation of frustration and anger, but left unresolved the issue of individual salvation. It involved a dilemma that weighed on the conscience of every Arminian divine and one they invited by rejecting the absolutism of orthodoxy. The orthodox synthesis made no pretense of uncertainty over free will or man's ability to shape his own destiny, which could be a source of comfort to the believer: if salvation were predetermined and man innately depraved, there was no point in striving for perfection in order to please God. Arminians, however, had opened up a gray area by maintaining that men and women were free agents with the capacity for salvation, but were ultimately accountable to God himself and finally uncertain of their fate. And the doubt and irresolution inherent in Arminianism deeply troubled evangelical divines. Their diaries and writings betray continual inner turmoil over one's adequacy as a Christian and servant to God.[14]

This stress on individualism, or "free agency," carried over into revivalist notions of economic justice. Ministers averred that worldly success or failure, like salvation itself, was a matter of individual choice and that those who lived in poverty or failed to improve their station had only themselves to blame. They clung tenaciously to this view, their impoverished parishioners notwithstanding. Confronted by scenes of privation and misery among their communicants, they advised perseverance and held out the possibility of a comfortable afterlife as reward for earthly tribulation. One poor outworker complained to her Methodist class leader, "You don't get abused or knocked about as we do; your temptations are not like ours. What would you think if, after working hard for three days, and living on trust for that time with the expectation of receiving a proper compensation for your labor, you were to receive only 31 cents for the whole?" But her leader replied: "Fannie, I know you have had a hard lot of it; but pray, it will not last for always. This is *your trial,* and if you endure to the end you will have the promise of a crown of life."[15] Ramsey had a similar reaction to the hardship of the poor. He once visited a family of indigent cottagers who had "to work often till late at night . . . to 12, 1 o'clock" and still could not afford "clothes fit . . . for church."[16] But such deprivation evoked nothing more than private confessions of pity to his diary and lectures to the poor laced with the familiar aphorism "What shall it profit a man if he gain the world."[17]

Ministers passed on this preoccupation with self, morality, and salvation to their lay followers. These proselytes, the experience of Alexander Fulton discloses, were stricken with the same internal torment that troubled their clergy. They were at constant war with themselves in striving to honor the moral regimen dictated by their faith and they struggled mightily to be good Christians.[18] They saw evangelicalism as the best hope for a better life on earth as well as in heaven, and entranced by its promise, they rarely strayed beyond churchly moorings. In times of doubt and personal crisis, they sought the counsel of their clergyman.[19] If they joined a teetotal club, which was often the case, they were likely to enroll in church-sponsored societies or temperance-beneficial clubs initiated by activist ministers rather than trade-based groups led by artisans with an explicit sense of craft or class identity. Those who joined fraternal groups outside the orbit of the church preferred the Odd Fellows and Sons of Temperance to beneficial societies of artisans.[20]

Above all, then, the revivalist worker thought of himself as a Protestant. He could be and often was a militant defender of his faith and culture, but on the shop floor he was the most tractable of employees, a firm believer in self-denial, diligence, and individualism. Only infrequently did he question the will of his employer and opposed him only with the greatest reluctance. Poverty to him was literally the "wages of sin," the result of a flawed character.

The deference of the revivalist worker is understandable. He was usually a former traditionalist whose preconversion experiences left him without a critical perspective or that spirit of independence capable of mediating clerical conservatism. When driven to despair by the economic downturn, he rushed to embrace revivalistic morality as well as the ideology of accommodation.

Old radicals were also vulnerable to the paralysis of revivalism. As

Benjamin Sewell's religious odyssey reveals, conversion could in fact eradicate political commitments. A journeyman tanner by trade, Sewell was a leader of the militant Journeyman Saddlers' and Harnessmakers' Union in the thirties. He rose to vice president of the Trades' Union and appears to have been a prominent figure in the G.T.U.'s cooperationist faction. But Sewell succumbed to the evangelical tide of the depression, joined the Methodist church, and, in the late forties, exchanged his saddler's apron for a minister's broadcloth. He signed a portrait of himself on the frontpiece of his memoirs, "Yours in Jesus Christ." His duties took him to the Bedford Street Mission, Philadelphia's answer to the Five Points of New York, where he ministered to the needs of the poor without a trace of his radical heritage. Sewell blamed "demon rum" and "hard living" for the poverty of his constituents. And as befits an enthusiastic evangelical, he wrote, "God pity the suffering poor, and help them to resist temptation, overcome the world, and secure for themselves a place in heaven where poverty will never come."[21] To Sewell and his coreligionists, intemperance was the cause of indigence and not a symptom of it.

Yet evangelicalism fell short of completely depriving workers of critical faculties or totally subjecting them to the behest of employers as Anthony Wallace would have us believe.[22] In the 1840s, as in the past, evangelical injunctions to self-improvement and dutiful parenthood induced worker deference, but at the same time they heightened vigilance against exhaustive toil and the abuse of children. Revivalists employed at home as cottagers had a higher threshold for both since they hired family members and regulated the pace of their labor. But conditions in the textile mills were different and were perceived as such. Operatives could not mistake the fact that employers compelled an extended workday and preferred to hire parents willing to send their children into the grimy mills. When their bosses extended the workday from 11 to 13 hours in the business upturn of the late forties, they stepped beyond the bounds of working-class evangelical propriety and set the stage for another ten-hour movement.

The revitalized ten-hour movement reached into textile hamlets across the state. In the east it centered in Manayunk and in the mill districts of adjoining Delaware and Montgomery Counties. Both areas had heterogeneous populations of English and native-born male Methodists, or revivalists, and male Irish and German Catholics, or traditionalists, as well as large concentrations of women of both religions and all nationalities. Traditionalists entered the struggle on the side of the revivalists, but the latter provided the leadership and directed the movement. Manayunk ten-hour stalwarts were class leaders in the Methodist churches and members of the local lodge of the Sons of Temperance.[23] They transferred their prestige and leadership skills from these institutions to the ten-hour movement and it gave off a revivalist glow from its inception. Manayunk evangelicals, for example, had recently circulated petitions requesting a legislative ban on the manufacture and sale of liquor and they adapted this tactic to the ten-hour movement.[24] They petitioned state lawmakers for a legal limitation on the hours of work, and, as events and their own rhetoric would show, they perceived the issue as a moral struggle between right and wrong and not a battle between classes. Fellow operatives in neighboring Delaware County endorsed this view. "In the contest," read an address penned by their ten-hour committee at a mass demonstration, "we enlist ourselves against no interests or class—assail no one with . . . invective abuse. Detraction and calumny form no part of our proceedings in [the] prosecution of the great question we have in mind."[25] They closed their gathering with the following invocation:

> Press on then, and though you may not share
>   The toil or glory of the fight—
> May ask at least in earnest prayer,
>   God's blessing on the right.[26]

The petitioners received a hearing at the legislative sessions of 1848 and 1849. In the spring of 1848 lawmakers deliberated a bill authored by state Representative and radical Democrat William F. Small of Philadelphia County. It prescribed a ten-hour day for textile mills and kindred factories with the notable exception of furnaces and foundries. The debate divulged, however, that legislators did not agree with the operatives' conception of a legal day's work. The workers demanded a general reduction of hours, but the Whigs and conservative Democrats preferred to ban child labor, grant a ten-hour day to children, and give adults the option of contracting to work as long as they wished. The law which emerged embodied these reserved views. It prohibited the employment of children under twelve years of age in cotton, woolen, silk, paper, flax, and bagging mills and proclaimed ten hours to be a legal day's work, but vitiated this clause with a provision empowering parents and guardians of children over the age of fourteen to make their own arrangements through "special contracts."[27] This loophole presumably applied to adults, as well, and consequently, the struggle was transferred back to the operatives and to their middle-class sympathizers who formed the "Friends of Ten Hours."

Manayunk millhands and their "Friends" held jointly-sponsored rallies at which they formulated long and short-term tactics. Expressing disappointment with the law, they announced still another petition insisting upon deletion of the contract provision at the upcoming legislative session. Both groups, in effect, looked forward to a legal resolution. Neither of them, least of all the "Friends," relished the thought of a strike.[28] Class conflict was precisely what they wished to avert, but there was no escaping the reality of the present law and the prospect of being forced to sign contracts. The operatives braced for this possibility by resolving en masse to refuse to sign away their rights.[29] When the measure became law on July 4, they were pleasantly surprised. Smaller manufacturers thought better of testing the operatives' will and announced they would comply with the ten-hour standard. But Joseph Ripka, the largest Manayunk manufacturer, employing about two-thirds of the hands, informed his workers that those who chose to work less than thirteen hours a day would be assessed proportionate wage reductions, ranging from 10 to 22 percent.[30] Ripka's response put revivalists on notice that this was not a moral struggle at all, but a conflict between classes whose resolution transcended moral persuading. Faced with Ripka's decision, the operatives rallied their forces and grudgingly vowed to resist with a strike. The standout, however, was confined to the cotton spinners, who, buoyed by their own sense of moral right and revivalist discipline, held out for three weeks, but then relented and returned to work on Ripka's terms.[31]

Manayunk operatives had achieved their goal of a ten-hour day with minimal employer resistance. But the contract clause was still intact, and the millhands, fearing it would be invoked at a more

opportune time, once again turned to the legislature. They were to be
sorely disappointed. Their allies among the lawmakers and in the
"Friends of Ten Hours," convinced that a stronger law stood no
chance of getting through the State House, lowered their sights and
pressed for a statute limiting the ten-hour day to women and
children.[32] But conservative legislators rejected even this concession.
The 1849 law, which superseded that of 1848, merely regulated the
labor of minors. It raised the minimum age—in cotton, woolen,
paper, silk, bagging, and flax mills—from twelve to thirteen, and
restricted the employment of those between thirteen and sixteen to
nine months a year and ten hours a day. Employers and their agents
who "knowingly or willfully" violated the law were subject to civil
suits and fines of $50 for each offense. The contract clause did not
reappear and adult operatives received nothing in return for its
deletion. They were probably better off under the old law, for the new
one held them liable to the same punishment as the owners for
violating the provisions for child labor.[33]

The operatives, once again, were responsible for enforcing the law.
They organized still another round of demonstrations, and these bore
the unmistakable hand of revivalist culture and politics. There was
music by the Sons of Temperance band and speeches by leaders who
beseeched followers to honor their ten-hour pledge without disrupting class harmony. Not one of them mentioned a strike in the
likely event of employer opposition. Their refusal to entertain the
idea of withholding their labor exposes the differences between the
ten-hour movements of 1835 and 1849. In the past, working-class
radicals broke down revivalist inhibitions with pealing republican
oratory and marched them out on strike.[34] But such radicals were as
rare as cornfields in Manayunk by the late 1840s, and their absence
left local revivalists to conduct the struggle in the only way they knew
how. To admit the necessity of a strike was tantamount to acknowl-
edging class polarities and to denying the social fluidity that was the
ideological keystone of revivalism. It was a step they had taken with
the greatest reluctance in 1848 and one they could not bring
themselves to repeat. Left to their own devices, revivalist operatives
drafted a resolution addressing their bosses not as employers but as
fellow Christians and citizens and describing observance of the ten-
hour law as the "imperative and religious duty, of every employer as a

citizen and a *philanthropist*."[35] Their last line of defense was the hope that the lords of the loom would heed their Christian consciences and lawabiding instincts.

As it turned out, the operatives came away with a victory partly by default and partly by virtue of their own solidarity. Their collective resolve to work ten hours only deterred some employers from reverting to the thirteen-hour day and the downturn of 1849 did the rest. No textile boss seriously considered extending the workday in slack times.[36]

Traditionalists

Quite apart from moral and ideological perspectives, revivalists were distinguished from other working-class cultures by their national homogeneity. They were, to be sure, English, German, and even Irish, but most were native-born Americans. This had been true of traditionalists as well, though it is probable that immigrants were more widely represented among them in the past. Such a configuration was the result of demographic trends. Immigrants were such a small fraction of the population in the 1830s (about 10 percent) that they could not dominate any subculture.

The massive influx of immigrants during the forties changed the ethnic base of traditionalism. Tens of thousands of Irish immigrants fleeing the Great Famine inundated Philadelphia in the second half of the decade, and by 1850 reached 70,000, or just about one-fifth of the population.[37] They displaced native-born Americans as the chief group of traditionalists.

The Irish differed from their predecessors in several respects. Previous waves of Irish newcomers included radical republicans and artisans who had practiced trades in the Auld Sod or had learned rudimentary skills as migrants in England. A minority of the famine generation were of the tradition of artisan radicalism, but the vast majority were unschooled in political dissent, though rabidly anti-British, and unacquainted with artisan skills or even wage labor. A diverse group of renters and laborers without fixed employment, they were a downtrodden peasantry whose brooding fatalism was equaled only by the depth of their misery. For them, life hinged on potato cultivation, and when the blight of the forties struck, those who managed to stay alive made their way to the nearest port and passage to the New World.[38] They came in the hundreds of thousands and no nineteenth-century immigrants were as ill-prepared for the industrializing city. The "first and pressing necessity," wrote a contemporary historian of Irish Philadelphia, "was employment," and while the diversified economy of the Quaker City offered a long roster of artisan work and industrial jobs, the debilitating legacy of peasant life consigned them to the lower end of the occupational hierarchy.[39] Lacking skills and industrial experience, most scavenged for work as casual laborers or put together crude carts and wheelbarrows in hopes of working as carters and teamsters. For every Irish laborer and carter there was a skilled worker, or at least an individual who identified himself as such. The bulk of these were actually semiskilled workers in the shoe and clothing trades and hand loom weavers whose vocations hardly qualified as skilled at all. Most such "artisans" worked at home as cottagers rather than in manufactories or factories. Factory workers were still in the minority among the Irish.[40]

Strangers in an unfamiliar environment, the Irish preferred to live in close proximity to family and friends. But Philadelphia's unique housing stock discouraged rigid ghettoization and ethnic clustering. Row homes spread across the face of the city and shanties tucked away behind thoroughfares awaited the famine Irish. Those unable to find housing in the old Irish districts settled in the western fringe of the city and in the suburbs, where the extension of row-house construction dispersed them in every direction, and mixed peoples of all nationalities, in uneasy togetherness.[41]

If integration and dispersal distinguished the settlement of the Irish, cohesion and segregation typified their religious and social life.[42] This, too, was a recent development. Prior to the forties, Catholic institutions were as anemic and remote in Philadelphia as they were in Ireland. As late as 1838, there was no Catholic hospital or parochial school system, only one asylum (St. Joseph's which had been built in 1797), and just six churches—five of them in the old port far from the newer Irish neighborhoods. Irish Catholics in the northern districts did not have a church until 1833, when St. Michael's opened its doors, and their counterparts in the south, one of the oldest Catholic communities in the county, had no parish at all. Catholic children who did seek an education used the public school system; the needy relied on public charity or the benefactions of Protestant philanthropists; orphans were placed in Protestant homes or in Protestant-dominated asylums; and the church itself exercised precious little influence until the 1840s—with the sudden immigrant influx and the nativism controversy. Both developments made Catholics, the hierarchy in particular, more aware of themselves as a religious minority with their own interests, and goaded the diocese into an ambitious effort at building institutions. In the twelve years following 1838, Catholics constructed three orphans' and widows' asylums, four hospitals, and no less than thirteen churches, ten of which were located in the industrial suburbs.[43]

The quick assembly of this diocesan network modified Catholic Philadelphia in two ways. It segregated Catholic from Protestant in a web of Catholicity, and lifted the clergy into new prominence. Parish priests, commanding the same status as the evangelical ministry, combined the roles of political, spiritual, and community leader into one. They presided over every rite and ritual from birth to death, distributed charity to the infirm and the needy, dispensed advice to the forlorn. They also reunited recent arrivals with kin and loved ones, read and wrote letters for the illiterate, and, by their very presence, provided a symbolic link between the Old World and the New. Never before did Catholic clerks enjoy such authority in America.[44]

Church officials employed their newly found authority to solidify the willful segregation reflected in the church's infrastructure. They used their pulpit and press to prod the laity into taking refuge from abusive Protestantism in the haven of diocesan institutions. Such clerics directed the sick and the homeless to Catholic hospitals and asylums. They implored parents to send their children to parish schools, and impressed them with the absolute necessity of instilling the faith in their offspring , even if this meant sacrificing readiness for the trades or for social improvement. One of them went so far as to condemn indenturing young boys to non-Catholic masters, for the paramount obligation of youths was to learn the "first principles of faith, religion . . . and then, if the condition of the poorer classes of youth is not bettered—if they do not continue attached to their faith . . . we have nothing to answer for in their regard."[45]

The fatalism intimated in such counsel suffused Catholic teaching.

Catholicism, it has been observed, gave "perfect expression" to the dejection that was the peasant experience and, one might add, to the insouciant morality of traditionalist culture. Church canon, firmly rooted in the notion of original sin and human depravity, underlined the hopelessness of redemption in this life and stressed "divine transcendence" in the next.[46] It favored ritualistic devotion over emotional displays of piety, and discounted moral probity and social betterment as conditions or signs of grace.[47] The few clerics who did advocate temperance denied any connection between self-perfection and salvation and the church itself raised its voice against prohibition, Sabbatarianism, and other coercive reforms favored by revivalists.[48]

Catholicism's growing conservatism on cultural affairs also began to color its view of political economy. Clerics and journalists had consumed an ocean of ink in the early forties denouncing the attempts of Repealer Daniel O'Connell and American abolitionists to fuse their causes and enlist the Catholic masses.[49] They succeeded in distancing themselves from abolitionist effusions and heading off the Repealer-Abolitionist marriage, but the specter of radicalism haunted church officials throughout the forties. It raised its ominous head in a dramatic way at the end of the decade, as revolution swept across Europe and threatened the temporal and spiritual power of Roman Catholicism. Such revolutionary spasms riveted the attention of American prelates on the Old World and ripened their inchoate political conservatism. Clerics and journalists, having fended off the romantic radicalism of abolitionism, now took up the cudgel against its secular and anticlerical counterparts. They tarred radical republicanism with the brush of "red revolution" and extrapolated the lessons of 1848 in Europe to the politics of their adopted city.[50] They took a dim view of any tinkering with the established order or any form of collective action in redress of social injustice. Clerics insisted that the aggrieved resolve class conflict through "moral suasion."[51]

Catholicism's crusade against radicalism and for the loyalty of its laity had begun in earnest by the mid-forties. It did not penetrate the masses overnight, nor did lay Catholics follow church guidance to the letter. But it did begin the transformation of a traditional culture without an inherent antiradical bias into a conservative one with a pronounced antiradical edge.

This emphasis upon religious segregation and group cohesion had a secular dimension. The leisure-time activities of working-class Irish Catholics continued to revolve around street corners, public markets, taverns, and fire houses, but the resurgence of Irish Catholic consciousness and the concurrent flaring of nativism altered such mainstays of traditionalism. Bars and fire companies integrating immigrants and native-born Americans, though still extant in some neighborhoods, gave way to ethnic homogeneity. In Moyamensing, for example, Irish Catholic and Irish Protestant volunteers set up separate fire companies (the Moyamensing and Franklin Hose, respectively) and Irish Catholics in integrated companies found themselves at odds with nativist factions.[52] At Southwark's Weccacoe Engine Company in 1842, a heated feud pushed the Irish and sympathetic Americans to secede and organize their own group, the Weccacoe Hose.[53] Four years later nativists in lower Southwark founded the Shiffler Hose, in honor of George Shiffler, the first native-born fatality of the Kensington riots.[54] The repetition of this pattern in other suburbs produced a hornet's nest of rival groups in a subculture already known for its social turbulence.

Traditionalist culture took an even more ominous turn with the emergence of street gangs. Age-segregated and ethnically cohesive, they had various origins. The youth gangs consisted of adolescents who escaped the discipline of schools and waning apprenticeship, and evolved out of friendship networks and fire company "runners."[55] The adult gangs had several beginnings. Irish history supplied ample precedent for such groups. Rural Eire was thick with gang-like bands that chastised ravenous landlords, disciplined villagers resisting boycotts, and other types of retaliation. Eighteenth-century bands, such as the Hearts of Oak and White Boys, were canonized in Irish lore and their exploits in the name of justice surely lived on in the memory of Irish immigrants.[56] But urban conditions also seem to have bred immigrant and native-born gangs. These developed out of bar and street-corner cliques, militia units returning from the Mexican War, and work groups that already involved gang labor on the waterfront and rivers. The originators of the ferocious Killers of Moyamensing, for example, were veterans of the Mexican fiasco, and the Schuylkill Rangers, a savage gang of boatmen, evidently grew out of crews on the Schuylkill.[57]

Gangs ran the gambit from loose groupings of companions to

tight-knit paramilitary organizations hierarchically arranged with discrete chains of command and definite division of labor. Youth gangs often were no more than ephemeral cliques. Adult gangs, especially Irish outifts, remained intact for decades and were highly structured.[58] A fictionalized account of the Killers tells of bizarre candlelight rituals and suggests a clear-cut internal hierarchy:

> They were divided into three classes—beardless apprentice boys who after a hard day's work were turned loose upon the street at night, by their masters and bosses. Young men of nineteen and twenty, who fond of excitement, had assumed the name and joined the gang for the mere fun of the thing, and who would either fight for a man or knock him down, just to keep their hand in; and fellows with countenances that reminded of the brute and devil well intermingled. These last were the smallest in number, but the most ferocious of the three.[59]

Highly organized and acutely aware of their cultural interests, nativist and Irish firemen and gang members constituted powerful voting blocs within their respective parties. On election day they would march to the polls and cast ballots for their favorite candidates. The rival groups supported different parties, but they were at one on some issues. Both, for example, opposed those urban reformers who had vainly sought to professionalize the fire department and who stepped up their law-and-order campaign following the bloodletting in Kensington. Largely in response to the Kensington riots and subsequent disorders, the reformers advanced a comprehensive reform platform. It included consolidation of the city and county into a single jurisdictional unit, professionalization of the police, and prohibitions on the production and marketing of liquor, in addition to replacing the volunteer firemen with paid workers.[60] Some American Republican and Democratic politicians endorsed all or part of this program, but they were ineffectual. Neither party, including the otherwise moralistic American Republicans, dared endorse such measures for fear of alienating their traditionalist wings. Rather, both accommodated to traditionalist demands. Democrats winked at violations in liquor and gambling laws, and American Republicans enforced such laws selectively, if at all, prosecuting Democratic violators only.[61]

More often than not traditionalists were at war with one another.

They created the wave of street crime that gripped the suburban districts after 1845, and turned streets into virtual battlegounds. As in the past, traditionalist violence was both expressive and purposive. Expressive acts included everything from youth gang skirmishes to full-scale riots between rival gangs and fire companies. These disorders differed from those of the past in their frequency and intensity. Firemen's fights occurred routinely in the late forties and lost their playful quality once the participants armed themselves and sniped at one another or resorted to arson simply to avenge an insult, impress youthful novitiates, or vent antiethnic anger. The heavily Irish Weccacoe Hose Company, for example, passionately hated the nativist Weccacoe Engine Company, from which it had seceded in 1842. Weccacoe Hose men provoked a rash of street fights with their rivals, and routinely embarrassed them with the help of the Bouncers, a gang of neighborhood toughs who ran with the Weccacoes and bolstered them in a crisis.

In June 1844, on the eve of the Southwark riots, the Weccacoes and Bouncers resolved to deliver the *coup de grace*, and stole to the engine house under cover of darkness. Someone tipped off the engine men, however, and they greeted the Weccacoes with a fussilade of musket shot. The astonished conspirators beat a ragged retreat, dragging their wounded to Diehl's tavern a few blocks away, and girded for another assault with firearms of their own. It was a frustrating evening. Watchmen aroused by the commotion of the first encounter followed the Weccacoes to the tavern, confiscated their weapons, and ordered them to disperse. The Weccacoes left for their homes wringing their hands in disappointment, and the engine men secured the protection of the Wayne Artillery, which stood guard outside their quarters for the next few evenings.[62]

The companies collided again and again in the following years, and on the night of February 4, 1850, the Weccacoes finally put the engine company out of commission. Four of them, led by shoemaker and company secretary Levi Fort, were completing the last leg of a weekend excursion to the neighborhood taverns. The drunken quartet first considered assaulting the nativist Shiffler Hose house, but settled on burning out their ancient enemies, the Weccacoe engine men. This time they executed their plan flawlessly. The arsonists divided into two groups. One pair broke into the engine house, tied the tender to a post to ensure its being conflagrated, and fled after igniting a pile of wood shavings. The other pilfered the spanner of the Southwark Fire Company, which had arrived to extinguish the blaze. Unable to open a plug, the Southwark had to wait for another company and by the time it appeared the fire consumed the first floor of the newly-erected, three-story building, causing over $2,000 in damages.[63]

Purposive or instrumental violence, which often shaded into expressive acts, resulted from the demographic patterns of the forties and from the desire of nativist and immigrant traditionalists to control the social composition of their neighborhoods. This contradiction between intense ethnic consciousness and heterogeneous settlement made these struggles exceptionally fierce, especially if they involved the Killers of Moyamensing.

One of the largest and most brutish gangs in Philadelphia County, the Killers had a following of at least three hundred.[64] They were also buttressed by the notorious Moyamensing Hose Company, which they had infiltrated and then taken over, and by local residents. They ruled over east Moyamensing, a growing Irish enclave adjacent to the Black ghetto and standing between an area claimed by the Irish Protestant Franklin Hose Company and the Stingers to the west, and by the Shiffler gang and Hose Company to the east. The Killers had beaten these enemies into submission by the late forties, and as one observer stated, established "perfect supremacy" over east Moyamensing.[65] Unwanted residents lived there in great peril and no gang or fire company thereafter ventured into this community. The calm of dominance bored the Killers and so they carried the fight to their enemies. Their favorite tactic was to set a fire in nearby Southwark to lure out and then ambush the Shifflers. Fighting escalated with each encounter and by the summer of 1849 both sides answered alarms equipped with pistols and rifles or duck guns.[66] Firearms were standard equipment in January 1850. The Killers torched a carpenter's shop near the Shiffler Hose house at Fifth and Wharton Streets, took cover behind a gravel heap in an adjacent storage yard, and opened fire on the unsuspecting nativists pulling their carriage to the blaze. The hail of shot repelled the Shifflers, but they were suddenly reinforced by late arrivals who returned the Killers' fire and wounded at least six of them.[67] Four months later the Killers ignited a rope walk in the same area, and left for Moyamensing to assemble additional allies. Their strategy backfired miserably. The Shifflers arrived first and planned a counterattack while flames enveloped the building. They hid in narrow alleys lining the Killers' route and fired on the advancing crowd, seriously injuring four, as well as two bystanders, and putting the rest to flight. These bloody encounters ended a five-year war of attrition.[68]

The Killers were just as active on their western flank. Here they confronted the Franklin Hose and the Stingers, Irish Protestant foes, and routed them in harrowing gang wars involving shoot-outs and hand-to-hand combat.[69] Their feud finally came to a head on the weekend of June 16, 1849, following successive ambushes on the part of the Killers, which inflicted heavy damages on the Franklins and pricked their manliness. The Franklins girded to square accounts and, it was said, they rallied the neighborhood with posters reading:

> Notice—The Millerites of Moyamensing, from ten years old and upwards, are requested to meet this evening, on business. The Western division will meet in the market house, in Eleventh Street, and the Eastern will meet at Eighth and Fitzwater Streets.
> Those having guns or pistols will bring them along; those not having these useful weapons are requested to bring as many brickbats and stones as they can carry. The police and watchmen will be on the ground to see fair play. Hurrah! Franklin! Go it, Moya![70]

The denoument was equal to its billing. The press referred to it as "one of the most terrific riots that has taken place in Philadelphia since the miserable riot of 1844."[71] There is no reason to doubt this assessment. The fighting began when the Killers and Moyamensings, victims of their own tactics, rushed to a blaze set by the Franklins in west Moyamensing and stepped into a trap. Armed Franklin men, gang members, and community partisans attacked, and the sides exchanged gunfire and missiles for nearly an hour. When the fighting stopped, one Franklin lay dead; and four, perhaps as many as ten, from both camps lay bleeding from gunshot wounds.[72]

The Killers' hostility transcended ethnic lines. Racial antagonism was renewed as traditional tensions between the Irish and neighboring Blacks heated up in the second half of the forties, and erupted into riots in 1849. In August the Killers marched to the California House, a popular Afro-American gambling room and tavern, and shot up its facade. The Blacks evidently expected the charge and drove off the assailants with a timely volley. Five Killers were wounded, but their comrades regrouped outside the ghetto and mounted another charge that was equally unsuccessful. It also alerted the authorities, who, in a rare display of rigor and equality, arrested rival leaders and confiscated the Blacks' arms. The watch occupied the area for the remainder of the week and thwarted still another foray of the indefatigable Killers.[73] A fragile calm prevailed. It would be shattered within two months.

October brought election day. Most wage earners passed this traditional holiday relaxing from work, some attending picnics and patriotic parades. The Killers decided to punish the Blacks. Setting fire to a barrel of tar mounted on a wagon, they crashed the mobile torch into the California House, stormed the tavern, and ripped out its gas fittings. The escaping gas triggered a raging fire that attracted two volunteer units, neither of which could reach the scene. A contingent of Killers, strategically stationed a few blocks away, intercepted the volunteers and fired on them, slaying two, wounding many more, and repulsing the remainder. Those at the California House fought off the watch and pommeled the Blacks, while the fire spread to adjacent homes and stores. By midnight, three hours after the fire was set, the area was chaotic—with the Killers fighting Blacks, watchmen, and still more firemen, who had fought their way through and hastened to douse the blaze. The flames and violence then trailed off, but peace was not restored or the fire brought under control until two o'clock, when four militia companies arrived to curb the remaining combatants and protect the volunteers. By this time over thirty buildings were burned out, at least four men (two Blacks and two firemen) lay dead, and over a dozen were seriously wounded.[74]

Like the interethnic strife between white traditionalists, the California House riots defy easy categorization. Racism, as we have seen, traditionally ran high in Irish Philadelphia and, clearly, set the Irish against the Blacks. In observing that the Irish swore revenge against the "nagurs" and targeted the California House because the proprietor, a Black man or mulatto, had recently married a white woman, presumably of Irish extraction, contemporaries recognized the racist and hense expressive feature of these brawls.[75] The classic fantasy of racists, the interracial marriage was, to the Irish, sufficient cause for riot.

Other evidence also points to continuity between this riot and previous race wars. The flood of Irish immigrants in the late forties could only aggravate the chronic competition for jobs and housing that lay behind the early clashes. This side of the race question occurred to an observer who wrote in the aftermath of the 1849 affair that "there may be and undoubtedly is, a direct competition between them as to labor we all know. The wharves and new buildings attest to this fact, in the person of our stevedores and hod carriers as does all places of labor; and when a few years ago we saw none but Blacks, we now see nothing but Irish."[76] Such a perception, as Theodore Hershberg has shown, is mirrored in the quantitative sources, which record a sharp decline in the number of Black hod carriers (98 to 28) and stevedores (58 to 27) in the three years preceding and following the California House riot.[77] This encounter, it would seem, served the instrumental end of further dislodging Blacks from unskilled jobs prized by the Irish.

Irish gangs not only drove Blacks out of jobs, they also served as surrogate unions. This phenomenon was not altogether new. Vigilance committees policed cottager communities in the strikes of the early forties. Such committees, however, were not gangs. Rather, they were cliques and work groups operating within the weavers' union and pressed into service during standouts. By the end of the forties, however, formal gangs apparently assumed functions previously assigned to unions. They controlled access to work, negotiated with employers, and enforced unity in strikes. River boatmen, for example, regulated admission into their ranks through the Schuylkill Rangers, and Port Richmond dockers protected their job rights with a gang.[78] The dockers' gang had negotiated a bargain with the coal merchants in the winter of 1850–1851 that raised wages to $1.25 a day and permitted the merchants to scale down the rate to $1.00 in slack times. But when the employers exercised this option in early February without consulting their workers, the coal heavers walked off their jobs on the docks, and got ready for the expected trouble with strikebreakers. They positioned themselves along the water-

front, a maneuver that frightened local property-owners into requesting police protection. Police Marshal Keyser raised a posse and
marched to the waterfront where he addressed a crowd of 600 to 800
snarling dockers and youths. He exhorted them to disperse, but drew
such jeers as "To hell with the Keyser" and, from a band of feisty
traditionalists, a suitable "Ye can't take us!"[79] Keyser then read the
riot act, gave the crowd a minute to break ranks and, seeing no
movement, ordered his men to move in. A melee followed in which
the posse, fighting with dockers struggling to protect their leaders,
managed to arrest a total of fourteen.

The arrests did not appreciably deflect the course of the strike.
Gang members patrolled the docks and the community for an entire
week. They harassed would-be scabs looking for work at the job site
or seeking quarters at local boarding houses. About fifty German
strikebreakers worked under police protection by the end of the
week, but they were a thin workforce, at best, and no substitue for
the hundreds of coal heavers that usually unloaded the barges at Port
Richmond. In the end, the gang seems to have overcome the police
and the merchants.[80]

Traditionalist consciousness and behavior thus displayed elements
of continuity and discontinuity with the past. One thread of
continuity was the intense race consciousness and antipathy to Blacks
that pitted Irish traditionalists against Afro-Americans in brutal
riots, just as it had done throughout the previous decades. Another
thread was class consciousness, the same "us-them, we-they" mentality that had set traditionalists against employers during the
thirties. In certain economic contexts their class consciousness could
align them with cultural foes in opposition to capital. Irish Catholic
textile operatives, for example, allied with the revivalist majority in
the ten-hour movement at Manayunk in the late forties, and this is
not really surprising. The grind of the mills was anathema to these
neophyte industrial workers fresh from precommercial society. As
one of them put it, Americans "work too hard"; the possibility of
easing mill drudgery outweighed Irish revivalist abominations.[81]

Yet comparatively few Irish immigrants sweated over machinery
in the dreary textile mills. The vast number toiled as unskilled
laborers and cottagers, and with the exception of the coal heavers,
little was heard from them in the second half of the forties. Even the

hand loom weavers, who had staged popular strikes a decade before, lapsed into quiescence. Moyamensing loom tenders tried to advance their rates in February 1846. They inaugurated a standout with great fanfare, marching through the district with banners flying and soliciting support along the way, but eventually had to concede defeat and call off the strike.[82] Their newly arrived countrymen refused to leave the looms, just as Irish tailors and shoemakers, as we shall see, turned a deaf ear to the strike clarion of radicals.

Irish stillness at the workplace was a departure from the past. It was a reflection in part of the singular experiences of the famine generation, the leading traditionalist group, in the Old World and in the New. As Stephan Thernstrom observes, the famine Irish had known the depths of destitution in Ireland and they arrived in the United States with woefully modest expectations that were satisfied with relative ease.[83] Their subsistence outlook took the bite out of the poverty they tasted in the Quaker City, and their concentrating in outwork insulated them from the regimen of modernizing production. In addition, these immigrants developed a new sense of ethnic identity as a result of militant nativism and the resurgence of Roman Catholicism in the second part of the forties. This emergent ethnic consciousness coincident with the nativist upsurge fueled the firemen's riots in which Irish Catholic traditionalists and their nativist foes took turns butchering one another in the city streets. More than this, it accented cultural issues and paved the way for new leadership within the Irish Catholic community. Church officials and ethnic politicians supplanted John Ferral and other radicals who had spoken out for the cultural and the economic interests of the Irish masses and had simultaneously agitated radicalism. The new leadership, drawn as it was from the church and from Irish middle class, specialized in the politics of ethnicity *and* economic conservatism. They held down class conflict and poisoned radicalism's rapport with their followers.

Ironically, both revivalists and traditionalists raised essentially the same demands at the workplace: they limited themselves to "bread and butter" issues. It was the radicals who called for more sweeping change, and they, too, did not wholly resemble their predecessors.

Varieties of Radicalism

8

Rationalist radicals felt profound discomfort when surveying the cultural landscape of the late forties. Their luminous years were behind them and their dream of rescuing labor from the incapacities of ignorance and bigotry came crashing down under the weight of intraclass discord. They helplessly watched the revivalist clerics, the ethnic politicians, and the fire company captains push them aside and—make a mockery of Philadelphia's renown as the "City of Brotherly Love." Every raucous gang war and malicious nativist diatribe came as a chilling reminder of their impotence and of the power of the merchants of hate.

Ethnic antagonism was disconcerting enough to old radicals. More troubling still was the condition of their own culture. Rationalist radicalism never recovered from the demographic changes and the cultural leavening that accompanied the depression years. Many radicals died or left Philadelphia; numerous others defected to revivalism and nativism, which thinned their number, making them a small minority. The few remaining were left with the onerous task of reviving their shattered organizations. None achieved much success. The indefatigable John Caney, perennial treasurer of the General

Material on nativism has been adapted from Bruce Laurie, "'Nothing on Compulsion': Life Styles of Philadelphia Artisans, 1820–1850," *Labor History* 15 (Summer 1974): 337–366, with permission of the publisher.

161

Trades' Union and leading light in the Society of Free Enquirers (S.F.E.), tried to reorganize the S.F.E. as the Liberal Union, but met with indifference and had to abandon his effort.[1]

Universalists fared somewhat better at first. Larger in number and socially more established than the deists, they had no difficulty surviving the depression and even underwent a fleeting rebirth during it, when their churches gained new members and two "preaching stations" were founded. By the mid-1840s, however, both stations had closed, the Kensington church was in disarray and on the verge of collapse, and the parent churches in Southwark and the Northern Liberties were on the wane.[2] Universalist auxiliaries, such as the Young Men's Institute and various scientific groups, fell apart, and the Universalist press, which had conducted an animated exchange with mainstream religion in the thirties, was not heard from in the forties.

A marked change in the social composition of Universalism attended its decline. Church discipline was lax and asked only that communicants pay nominal pew rents and reject the notion of the divinity of Christ (as stipulated in Article X). This article was never really enforced until the depression, when there were flagrant violations of both provisions by Universalists of all classes, who joined evangelical churches, and by the poor, who could not afford pew rents. The First Church then decided to clear its books of both groups and expelled no less than 170 members—on the grounds of violating Article X. Most of them were impoverished tradesmen and unskilled workers who evidently left Universalism for evangelicalism.[3] The desertion and subsequent expulsion of these workers virtually destroyed the working-class contingent of the church and assigned Universalism to the middle and upper-middle classes.

Trade unions were the sole institutional survivals of the old radicalism with emphatic working-class memberships. Even these were confined to the sweated trades and persisted only because of continuity in leadership. The tailors William Doores and Joseph D. Miller, and the cordwainers Solomon Demars and Frederick M. Rooke, whose trade-union careers extended back to the Mechanics' Union and the Trades' Union, continued to lead combinations in their respective vocations during the forties.[4] These worthy veterans kept radicalism in touch with unionism, but their societies hardly recovered at all from the ravages of lean times. They presided over tattered unions too weak to challenge capital and more effective as debating clubs and beneficial groups.

Just as the old radicalism teetered on the brink of extinction, it received an infusion of life from two streams of immigrants originating in England and Germany. Each flowed at its own pace. The English arrived in two flurries in the early and late forties, and the Germans came in a mounting wave that peaked in 1846–1847, and ebbed with the tumult of 1848.[5] By the end of the decade some 40,000 Germans and English aliens were deposited in Philadelphia, and they accounted for 6 and 4 percent of the population, respectively.[6]

Their backgrounds diverged sharply from the Irish. Both groups hailed from nations and states that were in the throes of the industrial revolution but provided different contexts for the unsettling transition from handicraft to mass production. As Mack Walker has shown, the typical unit of German settlement was not the sullen peasant village or the Dickens-like Coketown with satanic mills belching out soot but the small town with scores of artisans specializing in handicraft work. Such tradesmen governed the terms of recruitment, training, production, and merchandising through guilds whose rules and regulations had the force of law. Apprenticeship was still intact. Young trainees advanced to journeyman status under the strict supervision of masters. They graduated to master status providing their workmanship and character met the approval of guildsmen and market conditions warranted additional shops. This interlocking of guild law and practice, coupled with local tariff barriers, gave guildsmen virtual monopolies in their callings.[7] No European region boasted such a pervasive system of craft production and local autonomy.

Two groups tested the resiliency of the guilds in the first four decades of the nineteenth century. Cosmopolitan merchants, bankers, rising industrial capitalists, and nationalist intellectuals united around a program of economic growth and national unity, and strove to undermine the guilds and the political basis of localism. By the early 1820s they effectively qualified or abolished artisan law and rights in many states. The guildsmen answered with a campaign of their own. They restored and patched up protective law, but it was a phyrric victory. What the cosmopolitans lost in the states and principalities, they gained on the national level, both by organizing the Zollverein and erecting a transportation network, a tandem that broke down the defenses of localism and of the guilds.[8]

This unleashing of free market forces threatened masters from above, while journeymen began to challenge them and the industrialists from below. Young craftsmen who had completed their apprenticeship customarily did a stint as journeymen, and then spent a year tramping through western Europe. They returned home expecting to set up on their own in accordance with tradition. A privileged few fulfilled this time-worn dream, but many more ran up against the frustrations of modernization. Opportunities for advancement contracted and working conditions declined as foreign competition ruined many masters and the panicky survivors restricted access to their ranks and bore down on their workers. This created an expanding class of journeymen destined either to spend their lives in the employ of masters in degraded conditions or as industrial workers toiling in the mills of the burgeoning cities.[9] Neither course sat well with craft-proud journeymen, and they shook urban centers to the foundations with militant strikes and dramatic riots in the 1830s.[10]

New ideological and political forms took root in the labor unrest that wracked Germany. Republicanism and varieties of radicalism and pre-Marxian socialism, which would gain more currency as 1848 approached, enraptured disillusioned workers and disaffected middle-class intellectuals. Such ferment alarmed church and state alike. It led to the persecution and forced exile of thousands of political dissidents, who fled to London, Paris, and other metropolitan centers where they collected in intellectual communities that throbbed with radical discourse.[11] The repression of the thirties, endorsed as it was by the church, stimulated worker interest in the anticlericism then being fomented by European intellectuals. This blend of radicalism and anticlericist rationalism distinguished the culture of German leftists during the 1840s.[12]

Guilds had long passed out of existence in contemporary England. They were only dim memories by the time of the Reform Bill of 1834, and English workers now agitated for the equality of primitive socialism and not for the structural asymmetry of the guild system. Some English radicals embraced rationalism as they reclaimed the

"Rights of Freeborn Englishmen," first as Owenites and then as Chartists.[13]

Such rationalist radicals were among the thousands of German and English immigrants who made their way to Philadelphia during the course of the 1840s. There they reestablished Old World ties and transplanted the institutions of radicalism in the soil of the Quaker City. The most outspoken, if less numerous, of them was a group of Chartists, many of whom bolted from England at the point of a gun. In Philadelphia they may have relived the drama of the past over mugs of beer in Chartist inns and taverns, much like their comrades in New York, who gathered at Peter Bussey's boarding house. It is certain that John Campbell, David Johnston, Joseph Smith, and William Butterworth—to name just a few veterans of the Chartist uprising—were the inspirational forces behind several lyceums and debating clubs, including the Chartist League of Philadelphia, that appeared after 1845.[14]

Campbell was a key figure in the English radical community. Born in Ireland in 1810, he migrated to Manchester as a youth and spent his formative years manning a loom in the city's bleak mills. He was also schooled in radicalism in Manchester's vibrant workingmen's clubs. By the late thirties he was a confirmed radical and, by 1841, secretary of the National Charter Association, a position that made him fair game for the authorities. He fled England and a prison sentence, landing in Philadelphia in 1843, and here found ample opportunity to resume his trade. Instead, Campbell opened a small book shop in partnership with Edward Power, a part-time cabinetmaker with Chartist leanings. Lagging business kept Campbell poor and forced him into secondary employment as a writer and journalist. It also enabled him to pursue a busy schedule of political activism that included membership in the Chartist League and Friends of Ten Hours.[15] Campbell's most important organizational initiative was the Social Reform Society, which was a debating club that he started in the mid-forties, comprised of English and native-born radicals and loosely affiliated with George Henry Evans' National Reform Association.[16]

The language barrier closed groups like the Chartist League and Social Reform Society to German-speaking rationalists. They came together in separate organizations and meeting places that manifested larger German influences and the distinct character of German radicalism. Beer halls and singing societies, popular among non-evangelical Germans, were the social centers of community life, where lounging tradesmen discussed politics, recalled Old World experiences, and sang the old beer hall songs, foaming steins in hand.[17] Several Free Thought societies (and at least two radical newspapers) served the intellectual interests of deists and skeptics.[18] The societies exhibited the national penchant for order and structure. More formal than analogous English-language institutions, they hired "speakers" who read selections from popular radical tracts to their attentive listeners. Debate and discussion followed, and while familiar to English-speaking rationalists, it reflected the context of its rehabilitation in Europe.[19] American Free Thinkers, it will be recalled, equated the religious establishment with Presbyterianism and occasionally expressed sympathy with the victims of Presbyterian invective, both Catholic and Protestant. Since the Presbyterians were the cutting edge of the antiliquor forces in Philadelphia Germans shared this animus.[20] But the bitter entanglement with Continental Catholicism was seered in the German radical mind and the Catholic presence in the Quaker City rekindled this antipathy. Thus, German rationalists continued to be more anti-Catholic than their American cohorts.[21]

Though founded by immigrant radicals, Free Thought groups, debating clubs, and even trade unions should not be seen simply as cultural transplants existing independently of conditions in Philadelphia or sustained solely by the influx of radical émigrés. They were the cultural products of newcomers whose political inclinations originated in the Old World but would not have amounted to much were it not for the surroundings that greeted both radical activists and ordinary immigrants only casually acquainted with radicalism. Apart from the émigrés, most immigrants left for the New World in hopes of finding an environment more hospitable to social customs and laboring traditions. The German Auswanderer, writes Mack Walker, went to America less "to till new fields and find new customers [than] . . . to keep ways of life they were used to, which the new Europe seemed determined to destroy."[22] This was very much on the mind of an Esslingen wine gardener who requested the release of his foster son from military service because the lad had "(*a*)

. . . learned the saddlers' trade, but that trade has been seriously affected hereabouts in recent times by the railroad; (*b*) a brother and other relatives in America have invited him to join them; and (*c*) he will be better and sooner able to assure his future there."[23] Seventy-five Badenese villagers set out for America with similar intentions. "We have reached the decision," they reasoned, "since Capital so commands Labor in our Fatherland, to find a new home . . . where the reverse relationship prevails."[24] English immigrants also thought they were entering a workingman's paradise that promised independence to the industrious. Their correspondence, Charlotte Erickson concluded, indicates that the goals of English immigrants "were directed towards the non-material ends of independence and leisure, not so much towards the acquisition of a higher standard of living in material goods."[25]

The political and economic experiences of these Philadelphia immigrants were mixed. They deeply appreciated popular democratic attitudes and freedom from arbitrary rule, to say nothing of the right to vote. "We like this country very well," an English immigrant wrote home, "and I am glad to think that we are in a free country, free from the . . . tyrannies of Kings, Priests, and Lords."[26] But what of the current political climate and the tyrannies of nativists? Few English and German immigrants had much pity for Catholics, but fewer still savored the fulsome bigotry of American Republicansim, even through party orators singled out Catholics for abuse. This was small consolation, for the American Republican platform made no such distinction. It would disfranchise aliens of whatever religion and its program drove most English and Germans to the shelter of the Democratic party.

Some of the newcomers did well as employees. Wages were higher, jobs were plentiful, if more taxing than in the Old World, and the dream of establishing independence by purchasing a farm or opening a small shop was still possible. Unknown numbers did accumulate enough income to buy a modest farm or set up shop, but only after years of frugal living.[27] And they were probably exceptional; the great number concentrated in the sweated trades and in factory work.[28] The haven from industrial capitalism that they so eagerly sought in the New World eluded them in Philadelphia.

Antagonized by the exactions of sweatshop and factory, immigrant radicals might have lashed out in several directions. They could have turned against Irish immigrants crowding the sweated trades or they might have followed middle-class politicians contriving to contain worker frustration. There was precedent for both courses in the 1840s. Many native-born tradesmen imputed the decline of artisanship to immigration and to the plunder of accumulators, and fell in line behind radical politicians who, as we shall see, thought of themselves as producers and exploited popular suspicions of aliens and financiers. Yet neither course impelled foreign-born radicals. Such dissidents were simply not preoccupied by Catholics either as a cultural menace or as job competitors. They scorned the ethnic fulminations and class formulations of middle-class radicals because such politicians were incorrigibly nativistic. These radicals espoused a purer form of the producer ideology—one that posited their right to the full product of their labor. A minority of immigrant radicals, best represented by John Campbell and Edward Power, shied from the class confrontation prescribed by this version of the producer ideology and wandered off into utopian socialism.[29] Most English and German immigrants spurned the romantic radicalism of Campbell and the watery radicalism of middle-class nativists. They braced for conflict, forming their own combinations or enrolling in those of American radicals.

The New Radicalism
English and German political émigrés gave the old radicalism a new lease on life, but their numbers were insufficient to revive it from minority status within the radical community. It was eclipsed by a new radical subculture that consisted of the producer ideology and revivalist morality. This would become the dominant expression of American radicalism, or, more formally, radical revivalism.

Who were the radical revivalists? Their leaders liked to think of themselves as spokesmen for respectable mechanics—that is, skilled workers in the sweated trades, craftsmen in the prestigious pursuits, and the employers of both.[30] There is no direct way of identifying the social base of radical revivalism with certainty. Complete membership lists of radical revivalist groups are lacking and when they are available, it is difficult to differentiate the skilled from the semiskilled workers within most trades. The one group that did come closest to representing such mechanics was the American Republican party and, in this regard, it is helpful to compare the social profile of its activists with that of the Democrats, the party of old radicals and immigrant traditionalists.

Table 11 reveals several differences between the groups in Southwark. The most unsurprising of these is national origins: all American Republicans were native-born, while Democrats included sizable minorities of English, Irish, and German immigrants. Some foreign-born Protestants, presumably evangelical Protestants, may have voted American Republican, but did not figure in the party hierarchy. As other studies of nativism have shown, American Republicans were younger and perhaps not as politically experienced as their rivals.[31] Equal numbers in both groups, about 40 percent, owned real property in 1850, but Democratic holdings were larger and more unevenly distributed. Two Democratic stalwarts, Joseph Diamond and Dr. D. F. Condie, were among the wealthiest men in the district, which hints at another distinction between the parties. Both leaderships contained substantial representations of artisans, but twice as many Democrats, a third of the party chieftains, were involved in nonmanual work. Their party was a classic coalition of the very rich and the poor—gentlemen, merchants, and professionals, on the one hand, and propertyless wage earners, on the other. By way of contrast, American Republican leadership was the exclusive preserve of artisans and tradesmen of all callings, but drawn disproportionately from printing, construction, the shipbuilding trades, gun making, and other honorable occupations. Fully half of these mechanics were masters who ran small businesses. Having less than eight journeymen in his employ, the typical proprietor was either a custom producer or a subcontractor.[32] His business was as new as it was modest; he had been a journeyman who inched his way to master status after 1845, no mean achievement in a period of declining opportunity.[33]

This social configuration confirms the impressions of American Republicans themselves. Their party did include mechanics of the "better" trades but more important, it united journeymen and masters under the domination of the latter. Most nativist leaders, moreover, had been radical Democrats, such as the master mechanics Lamuel Paynter and Thomas Grover, or former Trades' Unionists, such as

Table 11
Democrats and American Republicans: Southwark

Characteristic	Democrats No.	Democrats %	American Republicans No.	American Republicans %
Age				
19–29	8	10.7	15	17.2
30–39	23	30.6	31	35.6
40–49	26	34.7	22	25.3
50–59	12	16.0	13	15.0
60–69	4	5.3	6	6.9
70+	2	2.7	0	0
Average		42.3		40.7
Total	75		87	
Place of Birth				
Pennsylvania	48	64.0	69	79.3
Other state	11	14.7	18	20.7
Europe	16	21.3	0	0
Distribution of Real Property				
With real property	30	40.0	36	41.3
Without real property	45	60.0	51	58.6
(Average holding of holders)	($6,431)		($5,022)	
$1–499	0	0	4	11.1
$500–2,999	16	53.5	11	30.6
$3,000–4,999	15	16.7	11	30.6
$5,000–9,999	4	13.3	6	16.6
$10,000+	5	16.7	4	11.1
Total	40		36	
Occupational Distribution				
Professional	3	4.0	0	0
Manufacturer	2	2.7	1	1.1
Gentleman	0	0	1	1.1
Merchant	8	10.6	1	1.1
Clerk	2	2.7	3	3.5
Public official	3	4.0	2	2.3
Retailer	8	10.7	5	5.8
Master craftsman*	24	32.0	42	48.3
Journeyman	25	33.3	31	35.6
Unskilled worker and street trade	0	0	1	1.1
Total†	75		87	

Table 11
(continued)

*See Table 5.

†There were 100 Democrats and 104 American Republicans on the original list. Seventy-five of the former, or 75 percent of the sample, were located in the directories and the census, and 87 of the latter, or 83.6 percent, were located in both sources.

Source: The names of party activists were collected from *Public Ledger* and *Daily Sun* for the years 1846 to 1848 and traced to the corresponding city directories, to the United States Census Office, *Census of the United States, Population Schedule, (Southwark), 1850,* (microfilm, MSS, National Archives, Washington. D.C.,); and to United States Census, *Industrial Schedule (Southwark), Philadelphia County, 1850.*

the bricklayer John Bottsford, the coachmaker Joshua Fletcher, and the printer Hector Orr. Their shift into American Republicanism left the Democracy with a narrow base in the artisan community and, at the same time, made American Republicanism the voice of native-born mechanics.

These one-time radicals followed various routes from the Democracy to American Republicanism, and from the old radicalism to the new. Some of them underwent conversion in the evangelical surge of the depression; others were attracted to the revivalist temperance movement, if not to the church itself.[34] Neither group, however, subscribed entirely to revivalism in quite the same way as Benjamin Sewell, the former vice president of the Trades' Union and then Methodist convert who became an apostle of revivalist culture. Like Sewell, they accepted the moral side of revivalism but unlike him, rebuffed its conservative thrust. The politics and morality of these radicals were distinct and separate.

Radical revivalist mechanics did not completely segregate themselves from revivalists or traditionalists. They commingled with both groups in the American Republican party, but none lazed about in fire houses or fraternized in pubs and few showed much interest in the life of the church. Although respecting Protestantism, they had a residual mistrust of the clergy and were revivalist constituents, rather than formal church members.[35] They reserved displays of piety for holidays, weddings, baptisms, and similar occasions that usually drew nonmembers to pews. Some of them consorted with revivalists in temperance-beneficial societies and other voluntary associations gotten up by the clergy, but they also organized parallel groups free of clerical influence and restricted to masters and journeymen.[36]

As evangelical Protestants, such mechanics expressed revivalism's cultural interests. They could be equally nativistic and, in a sense, even more so than the most avid revivalist. The latter, for example, welcomed immigrant converts into their churches during revivals, when the holy spirit crossed ethnic boundaries and brought Irish immigrants into American congregations. This integration of suburban churches occurred without raising tensions between native-born and immigrant; native-born evangelicals accepted their Irish coreligionists in the community of Christ, if nowhere else. Radical revivalists were not always so charitable. They spurned Protestant immigrants seeking nomination for office on the American Republican ticket and barred foreigners from fraternal orders under their control.[37] They constituted a militant brigade within the cold-water army, and, judging from the records of their social organizations, enforced the liquor ban as rigidly as any evangelical minister.[38] Here the consonance between radicals and revivalists ended.

Radical revivalists did not identify exclusively as Protestants or view the world through the myopic glass of evangelicalism. They conceived of themselves as Protestant mechanics and workingmen. They remained loyal to the radical faith of their youth, the labor theory of value, and grafted the new morality onto this venerable creed. The result was that they perceived social phenomena through the dual lens of evangelical morality *and* class, as they understood the term, and passed judgment on the basis of both. Such radicals never disguised their low opinion of nonproducers of whatever nationality. They defamed the Irish, for example, not only because of their national origin and thirst for liquor, but also because they refrained from productive labor. "Three-fourths of the grocery stores and nine-tenths of the liquor stores," wrote one radical, "seem to be kept by Irishmen. These are not productive occupations."[39] Another divided the foreign-born into two groups, the Irish and everyone else, and confessed to grudging respect for the resourceful Swiss and Germans who settled in the west and worked the land. The Irish, however, lingered in the city and shunned "honest industry and economy" for the "mean [and] squalid" life.[40] Then there were the urban commercial and financial elites. They basked in extravagance on incomes accumulated through "speculation," "robbery," and means as unproductive as Irish occupations. Both the elites and the immigrants were drones subsisting on wealth produced by honest mechanics and their very existence led a radical to ask "Whether a country is most benefitted by a community of farmers and workingmen, or a community of loafers, agents, idlers and gamblers?"[41]

Revivalist radicals were preeminently concerned with the causes of inequality and poverty. Why, they asked, must worthy mechanics struggle to provide for their families, while merchants and bankers lived in affluence? They rejected the revivalist contention that the hardship of producers resulted from faulty character traits alone. Diligence and pluck, industry and sobriety, in their view, carried one only so far—and normally not far enough. Mechanics suffered chiefly because of the pressures exerted by immigrants and by accumulators. Foreign-born workers, it was argued, depressed wages and displaced skilled journeymen and endowed their unscrupulous employers with a cheap labor pool that gave them a competitive edge over the honest master craftsman who "pays fair wages, and charges fair prices."[42] Such masters, and all but the most craven entrepreneurs, insisted radical revivalist spokesmen, qualified as producers and as the friends of journeymen. They were the mere "agents of capital," captives of the iron laws of supply and demand, for when capital was abundant and cheap, they and their employees reaped the fruits of prosperity. But when denied credit, they had to slash wages or cut employment rolls in order to survive.[43] The real culprits were accumulators who regulated the money supply. They had the "leisure to combine, . . . scheme and make enormous profits, sometimes without investing a cent" and "the power to elevate or depress the market, . . . make money plenty [sic] or scarce, gamble with impunity, even control, by combination and monopoly, the very circulating medium."[44] Nor were they alone in villany. Corrupt legislators, who chartered banks and corporations, were inseparable from the accumulators.[45]

Thus, master and journeyman had common foes in the upper and lower reaches of society. This community-of-interest—the equivalent of what Lewis Levin had in mind when he called for "knitting up the sympathies" between the classes—became a central theme of American Republicanism and radical revivalism. Party orators cultivated it by acting as champions of productive labor and of moral and material improvement, independence, and respectability. In this effort they secured the aid of self-made proprietors who considered their careers to be models of emulation, or they praised those who had achieved public recognition without abandoning the mechanical arts. H. H. K. Elliot thus exhorted a gathering of nativist artisans: "Look around . . . and . . . discover in your own city, among those who now have high places, great wealth, and much respect, very many who started in life as, and who continue [to be], mechanics."[46]

Outside the party no radical revivalist group better illustrated the community-of-interest ideal than the Order of United American Mechanics (U.A.M.). Founded in 1845, appropriately in Jefferson Temperance Hall, it spread like wildfire through artisan neighborhoods, and five years later could claim over one hundred lodges in the county, with memberships ranging from ten to a hundred.[47] Twenty-three charter members, both masters and journeymen, came from such skilled occupations as carpentry and printing, but the Order, much like the American Republican party, also had a following of workmen in the baser crafts.[48] Leaders belonged to kindred nativist groups. Founding member and journeyman carpenter George F. Turner was an American Republican party activist; so, too, were journeyman bricklayer John Bottsford and journeyman bookbinder James Bayne. Bottsford, Bayne, and Joseph Hollenbeck, a shoemaker by trade, were temperance advocates as well as officials of trade-based teetotal clubs and temperance-beneficial societies.[49] Master craftsmen included such nativist darlings as Oliver P. Cornman, a journeyman house painter turned newspaper editor, and H. H. K. Elliot, the publisher.

Radical revivalist morality and politics supplied the cement of this union of masters and journeymen within the U.A.M. The Order barred nonproducers—merchants, bankers, and professionals—and immigrants. It was so nativist, in fact, that the Executive Council once turned down an applicant "born on the seas."[50] And upon learning of a Vatican bequest of a block of marble for the proposed

Washington Monument, the Council moved to withdraw its own donation "in solemn protest against foreignism in all its forms."[51] Those who did gain entry displayed an abiding respect for the new morality. They pledged loyalty to the motto "Honesty, Industry, Sobriety" as individuals and as members of an enterprise instilled with evangelical purpose. Members not only swore off drink and other libertine habits, they also policed one another's behavior and reported incidents of swearing, profanation of the Sabbath, whoring, and, of course, drinking. Backsliders were fined, suspended, expelled, or refused welfare benefits.[52]

The U.A.M. also offered a program of economic improvement. A fraternal order and beneficial society rather than a union, it nonetheless proposed to pursue "every honorable means to obtain 'a fair day's wage for a fair day's work'" so that fellows could "support themselves and their families in comfort and respectability" and could "accumulate a sufficient sum . . . to . . . sustain them through the mischances and mishaps of a rainy day."[53] But the Order recoiled from setting worker against employer. On the contrary, its followers were encouraged to behave as mechanics with mutual needs rather than employers and employees with conflicting interests. They attended seminars on "How to Accumulate Property" and set up shop, and they heard lectures on the producer ideology, which reviled commercial and financial capital.[54] Those in financial straits, owing to joblessness, irregular work, or bad luck, were urged to sign an unemployment register which was circulated among appropriate employers.[55] Members were also advised to patronize American mechanics only in the hope of providing more business and employment for fellow artisans.[56] Such measures, in conjunction with the political program of the American Republican party, would, it was thought, harmonize class relations and bring independence and respectability.

This rendition of radicalism represented a subtle change in emphasis within the radical tradition. Working-class rationalist radicals of the thirties and forties consorted with Philadelphians of middling status in debating clubs, lyceums, and political organizations, but they also had maintained some distance and independence from employers through the medium of trade unionism. Revivalist radicals sacrificed such independence. They were allied with master craftsmen in the American Republican party, the Order of United American Mechanics and temperance organizations, and they had little use for unions or for battling employers.

This change in the temper of radicalism owed to three factors. The uneven course of capitalist development sundered employers into a class of large entrepreneurs and a class of small subcontractors and master craftsmen. The petty producers far outnumbered the entrepreneurs, and they dominated the leadership of the American Republican party, the United American Mechanics, and other nativist groups, and controlled the nativist press. Such employers were one-time journeymen with modest accumulations whose social practice was more consonant with the workers who joined their organizations and staffed their shops than with the large producers. They shunned fashionable dress and other markings of social status for the plebian garb of their crafts; they worked with their hands at the same benches as those in their employ; and many still boarded their own journeymen.

The petty producers also boasted of paying "good" or "fair" wages, and they were not far from the truth, if one substitutes "better" for fair and makes the entrepreneur the standard of comparison. Statistical evidence shows that masters did offer better wages, and journeymen were probably aware of this.[57] Such structural arrangements laid the groundwork for the mutual respect and fraternal feeling that united small producer and journeymen and received organizational expression in the U.A.M. and the American Republican party.

Secondly, the resurgence of revivalism and temperance built a cultural bridge between the petite bourgeoisie and radical workers— one that was nonexistent a decade earlier, when skepticism and Free Thought were handmaidens of radical culture. Radicals who turned to revivalist morality during the depression moved closer to the middle class and left themselves vulnerable to the oratory of politicians adept at manipulating the symbols of the new morality and exploiting popular anxieties. Every nativist politician understood the political capital to be gained from cloaking himself in the mantle of the new morality and agitating the "foreign question" among recruits to the temperance crusade. These recruits, after all, had known the insecurity and horror of unemployment, and feared for their jobs in the wake of the immigrant influx during good times.

Third, the producer ideology was so flexible that it accommodated masters and small producers as well as journeymen. The struggling small producer who worked with his hands and depended upon money markets was difficult to place. No radical theoretican, not even William Heighton, settled the question. Heighton, it will be recalled, discussed exploitative master craftsmen and excused them on the grounds that they were obligated to bargain with "accumulators more powerful than themselves" or merchants and financiers. This ideological loophole gave master craftsmen access to the producer class and allowed them to enter it on their own terms. Those in the American Republican party, picking up where Heighton left off, read themselves into the producing class and vented their spleen against merchants, bankers, and "monopolistic legislation," the standard *bette noire* of radicalism. In so doing they deflected worker animus from themselves and onto those who extracted profit through exchange.

They also paid homage to mechanics and artisans at every opportunity. National holidays, such as Independence Day, were turned into nativist spectacles in which tradesmen wore the dress of their crafts and marched according to trade. Thousands of admirers turned out to pay their respects, and speakers waxed rhapsodic in addresses identifying nativistic mechanics as the keepers of true republicanism.[58] Party organs published and reprinted poems, songs, and sentimental short stories in praise of mechanics. Politicians listed their occupations in campaign propaganda in order to enlist mechanic support. Political slogans proclaimed "Native agriculture we cherish first—native industry first and last, in every branch of trade—art—ingenuity—mechanics—and invention."[59] No political organization of the period, with the possible exception of the Working Men, made such a point of identifying with the producing classes.

Yet this master and journeyman connection was fragile. It depended on the capacity of the market economy and the measures of nativism to fulfill the mechanics' dream of independence—a dream nurtured by the producer ideology itself. By the mid-1840s cracks were already discernible.

Toward Unity
Old radicals wasted no time in rebuilding their ragged combinations.

On two occasions, in 1843–1844 and in 1847, radical shoemakers and tailors staged vigorous organizing drives in preparation for strikes to recoup the wage reductions of the depression. Their struggles conformed to a pattern. Radical orators lectured on the "condition of the craft," in an attempt to renew interest in unionism; committees drafted lists of prices for presentation to employers; and organizing teams fanned out through the county, visiting homes and workshops, just as they had done a decade before.[60]

The organizers confronted imposing obstacles. Shoe and clothing workers were dispersed among manufactories, garrets, and sweatshops in the downtown and in distant suburbs, and many still worked at home, which made communication and coordination difficult. The workers themselves were a heterogeneous lot. Radicals constituted a distinct minority in the trades which had become cultural mosaics under the impact of immigration and revivalism. There were traditionalists, revivalists, and radical revivalists of both sexes and all nationalities; and their cooperation was vital. Radicals had no difficulty obtaining the support of the German radicals, who formed separate unions and joined together with their American counterparts in both standouts.[61] They were frustrated, however, in the effort to reach those in other subcultures.

The organizing committee of the Journeymen Tailors' Association, for example, could not mobilize the many outworkers of the trade. Strike committees, which intercepted cottagers carrying raw materials and finished goods to and from shops, succeeded only in strengthening the resolve of the strikebreakers. Scabbing outworkers so resented such harassment that they pressed charges against their antagonists and landed them in jail during both standouts. The second legal ensnarement (and perhaps the first as well) resulted in the conviction of several Association members for conspiracy.[62]

The cultural identities of the scabs is difficult to determine. Strikers did not refer to them in cultural terms, but there is reason to believe that they were revivalists and traditionalists. Evangelized workers, after all, were singularly timid and usually refrained from confronting employers except over the hours issue. They were also imbued with nativist feeling and the presence of immigrant leadership in the Journeymen Tailors' Association and Union Beneficial Society of Journeymen Cordwainers, Men's Branch, further tainted the unions. Traditionalists stood aloof because they brought minimal expectations to the workplace and had a low standard of what constituted a fair wage. Or, at least, this is the impression left by radical organizers who constantly bemoaned the refusal of lowly and uninitiated workers to join unions or participate in strikes. "Don't stay away because you are poor," implored the radical tailors in an appeal to scabs. "If you continue to work as you do, you will be even poorer, if it were possible for you to be so."[63] Striking cordwainers betrayed the same exasperation in an even more pointed reference to the immigrants—the Irish in this instance. In a circular letter addressed to the famine generation, they observed that Irish immigrants had belonged to the Union Beneficial Society in the thirties and called upon "those who in the past have done honor to our trade, but now refuse to join our society, the majority of whom are strangers in our city . . . and are consequently ignorant of the things of which . . . [we] complain."[64]

Radical revivalists, on the other hand, were caught in cross pressures of their own culture and economic change. The first of these was the combination of nativism and the entrepreneurial rendition of the producer ideology, which bound them to employers in the organizational matrix of radical revivalism. They believed it futile to assail bosses, if, as their spokesmen insisted, avaricious financiers and ignorant immigrants lurked behind the degradation of craftsmanship and the erosion of earnings. This formula was convincing enough at first, but less so with the growing domination of entrepreneurs in shoe and clothing production and the attendant worsening of conditions. Radical revivalism had reached a crisis. It was unequal to the task of arresting the ravages of growth or mollifying its working-class adherents with protestations against foreigner and financier. Entrepreneurs were accountable to the money changers, just as radical revivalist leaders argued, but this was small comfort to restive workers. Such employers and not bankers or merchants turned down even the modest wage demands of old radicals. Their behavior belied the community-of-interest ideal and now estranged new radicals.

These new radicals thus parted company with their employers. On the eve of the tailors' strike in 1847, for example, U.A.M. member and nativist activist William Green organized the United Brotherhood of Tailors, an independent union of journeymen, and his group collaborated with unions of English and German-speaking trades-men.[65] Green's radical revivalist colleagues in shoe production evidently filed into the Union Beneficial Society and both groups manned the pickets in the 1847 standouts. Their numbers bolstered the ranks of the strikers, but shoe and clothing manufacturers still turned back the journeymen for the second time in four years.

United but unable to improve conditions through strikes, old and new radicals scheduled a meeting in 1847 to discuss "certain measures which would tend materially to their happiness and prosperity."[66] The ensuing Trades' Convention brought out many delegates who had just gone through the disastrous strikes and were determined to find an alternative. They shelved standouts but not their radicalism and mused over several schemes that would guarantee workers the full product of their labor. There was virtual unanimity in favor of cooperation, and several resolutions outlining alternative methods of collective endeavor were put forth. After some debate, the delegates opted for protective unions, which were then being formed in other urban centers.[67] Such unions began with consumer cooperatives that raised the capital for productive ventures in light consumer goods. The Convention thus sponsored a grocery store in the winter of 1848–1849, and then branched out into cooperative workshops specializing in shoes, clothing, and hats. But this cooperationist scheme was cut short. Financial difficulties, deepened by the recession of 1849, destroyed two stores and eventually claimed the rest.[68]

The Convention is noteworthy because of the occupations and cultural identities of its delegates. Organizers looked forward to uniting workers in all trades and subcultures. Advertisements in the press beckoned "operatives in the different mechanical arts" and included a special invitation to the hand loom weavers.[69] Old radicals of all nationalities responded to the call. Germans in the Northern Liberties, who had recently come together under the German Workingmen's Union, resolved to "act in concert" with the "Ameri-can Laboring classes" and sent several deputies, among them the boot and shoemakers T. C. Liebrich and Lewis Mahlke.[70] Yorkshire-born tailor John Shedden, an ardent cooperationist who would turn up in the International Workingmen's Association in the late 1860s, attended along with Irish radicals (and presumably ex-

Chartists) James McShane and Peter McIlroy. Native-born delegates included Joseph D. Miller, longtime leader of the Association of Journeymen Tailors, and William Hunter, current president of the United Brotherhood of Tailors.[71] The Convention thus cast a fairly narrow net. Traditionalist and loom weavers, indifferent to unionism in general and increasingly circumspect of radicalism, were conspicuous by their absence. So were radical revivalists outside the sweated trades. New radical printers and building craftsmen persisted in looking upon immigrants and financiers as greater threats to their well being than employers.

Indeed, as the Trades' Convention took shape, new radicals planned a rally at Independence Square in June 1847. A publicity committee of nine, dominated by construction workers and small entrepreneurs closely identified with the American Republican party and the United American Mechanics, flooded the press with advertisements and plastered fences with broadsides welcoming "Honest" American workingmen to attend and register their opposition to the growing tide of immigration.[72] Their nativistic comrades made a beeline to the State House yard. A great crowd had already assembled when American Republican favorite Peter Sken Smith rose to speak. As he began, an even larger contingent of suburban workingmen marched into the Square, in step to the rhythm of a fife and drum. Their dramatic arrival elicited a reception of nine cheers and made this one of the largest demonstrations of mechanics since the antibank rallies of the late thirties. Speakers hammered away at the central themes of radical revivalism. Sken Smith, the temperance orator and newspaper publisher, was followed by master carpenter Jacob Beck and journeyman bricklayer John Bottsford. All lambasted unproductive labor in the parlance of producerism, arraigning "professional politicians" and singling out the immigrants. Lax immigration laws were the root of the problem, Beck asserted: ease of naturalization lured immigrants who "depressed and is [sic] depressing with perpetually increasing rapidity, the rewards of American Labor by glutting the market with laborers beyond all possible demand . . . sinking at the same time the boasted respectability and moral standing of the American Mechanic and Workingman."[73] This motif ran through a set of resolutions that would compel candidates in the upcoming elections to endorse the principle that "American labor is entitled to legal protection against the labor of imported laborers by duty, capitation tax, and sanitary regulations."[74] These radicals still perceived immigrants as the bane of American labor and employers as honorable allies in the campaign to turn back Europe's hordes. The wage earners among them were not yet inclined to cohere with foreigners, radicals or not, in a workers' movement.

But what of those employers who were absorbing a larger share of the labor market in the respectable trades and who increasingly resembled accumulators? They were holding down wages and making tidy profits on the labor of those in their employ, like their counterparts in the sweated industries. Such developments were beginning to antagonize new radicals with expectations of a fair compensation for honest endeavor and a life of dignity. They aired their grievances in letters to the local press at the twilight of the forties. Journeyman carpenter George F. Turner, a noted temperance advocate, American Republican official, and founder of the U.A.M., vividly captured the aspirations and disappointments of the respectable radical revivalist. The "worthy mechanic," he wrote, was fully entitled to a "house . . . on a front street, three stories high, bath room, hydrant, good yard, cellar . . . house furniture, bedding, amusements," but was barely able to provide the basic necessities for his family.[75] Fellow carpenter and U.A.M. comrade Matthew W. Robinson, writing to "further add to the example so nobly set for us by . . . Turner," had no objection to an individual who purchased luxuries, but continued,

> here is where I [do] object. The Carpenters or any other trade, shall be compelled to toil for low wages, themselves not able to procure the necessaries, much less the comforts, while the luxuries must not be drempt of; while on the other hand, those who "toil not neither do they spin," are in full possession of every article which can and does make a paradise of this world of ours. The Carpenters look around them, and they behold that the palaces built in part by their labor, in possession of—not themselves—but of others.[76]

This blend of Christian imagery, worldly aspiration, and class consciousness also cropped up in a letter of journeyman printer George W. Heilig. "In earlier times," he wrote, man was content simply to "eat and clothe himself," but the "sciences and arts have at this day disclosed an *artificial, intellectual, moral,* and *social life,* which . . . is as essential to maintain as the merely natural; and, as it is more refined and exalted, so also does it require a freer and more liberal nourishment." Workingmen had to

> meet the demands of this more elevated life, which . . . is the religious as well as the political duty of every American to seek and maintain. The *true light* now lighteth every man that cometh into the world, and *it will be received.* We must, therefore, also be in a condition that will enable us to contribute to the support of churches and other associations that will afford us the opportunity of engaging in such religious exercises and social duties as may tend to bring into genial activity our religious feelings and moral affections.[77]

Radical revivalists in the better trades found themselves pursuing the illusory goal of a life of respectability, while earning little better than subsistence wages. Awareness of this contradiction spread with the realization that the program of the American Republican party failed to relieve the maldistribution of wealth or improve the lot of wage earners. Middle-class leaders might condemn bankers, but, as Matthew W. Robinson observed, it was the employers who could afford "pianos and music books, ottomans and plate, carriage horses, or livery and servants" because of the toil of workers. "By what process," he inquired, "is it that wealth producers are generally in indigence, if not in absolute want, while the classes who do not produce, are at the summit of society? The carpenters are making these inquiries; and in due time satisfactory answers will be evolved."[78]

Such introspection was part of a larger process in which new radicals in the prestigious crafts despaired of the community-of-interest ideal and gradually arrived at the same conclusions as old radicals. Most likely, some of them took part in strikes (if not in unions) headed by rationalist building tradesmen in 1847 and 1848.[79] Most assuredly, they became the dominant trade-union force in such vocations by the close of the decade. The very same George F. Turner and Matthew W. Robinson, whose angry letters appeared in the local press, became leaders in the newly formed Association of Journeymen House Carpenters in 1850. William G. Russell, another member of the U.A.M., was secretary.[80] But the union transcended the community of new radicals. Robert Mansure, an old radical and president of the Trades' Union in 1837 who withdrew from unionism in the forties, now lent his experienced voice to the Association.[81] Other old radicals undoubtedly followed Mansure, duplicating in his union the coalition that had emerged during the mid-1840s within the tailors' and shoemakers' societies.

United in the Association, old and new radicals drafted a list of wage and nonwage demands for presentation to masters and contractors. But their timing was poor. Builders, locked into contracts signed several months earlier, were in no mood to compromise. They flatly refused to consider the issues and thus precipitated a strike that dragged into late summer. By early September demoralized radicals began to return to work, but vowed to resume the struggle the following spring.[82] They spent the winter of 1850–1851 girding for a resumption of the strike, and this time achieved a qualified success: about half the masters and contractors agreed to advance wages $.25 per day and to recognize worker control over recruitment of apprentices and work loads. But the rest were as tenacious as ever, and wore down the journeymen by mid-summer.[83]

Such frustrating strikes further shook radical revivalist faith in the community-of-interest ideal. They also helped turn worker thinking toward cooperative production. Thus, during the 1851 strike, George F. Turner opined that carpenters "ought" to be "producing for themselves" and should "unite to work fewer hours." He advised an inquiry "into that system of acquisition and distribution" that assured workers the full proceeds of their labor, and he struck a resonant chord among his strike-weary followers.[84] They discussed the virtues of cooperation in the midst of their standout and then organized several cooperative firms in the summer of 1851.[85]

Radical revivalist printers followed the same path to class conflict and cooperation as the carpenters. They differed only in their prompt recognition of the need for unionization. By 1843 a group of them organized the Franklin Typographical Association, which originated as a union but never conducted a strike, not even in the mid-forties, when fellow radicals in the sweated trades broke with employers over wages.[86] Nor is this surprising. No trade society boasted such a solid phalanx of radical revivalists as the Franklin. Virtually all of its executive officers belonged to the American Republican party or the U.A.M., and usually both. Financial secretary Henry L. Walter was an American Republican ward leader, as was his successor, Robert Phillips, who served as secretary of the American Republican Association of the Second Ward in Moyamensing and headed that district's rabidly nativistic John Hancock Temperance Beneficial Society. John Henderson, corresponding secretary and then president, sat on the executive board of the U.A.M. and William Sharpless, holder of several offices in the Franklin, was a founder of the U.A.M.[87] Under their direction, the Franklin lost sight of its purpose and was metamorphosed from a trade union into a nativistic fraternal lodge.

This transformation worked to the detriment of the printers. Preoccupied with the immigrant menace, they stood idly by as their trade underwent a boom marked by expansion and modernization, as well as by mushrooming small book and job shops. Printers who had once worked their trade in the casual setting of the small shop now faced the choice of doing increasingly specialized tasks in large factories or sweatshops. They saw their work traditions assaulted as employers divided up skills and hired "half-trained" men and women, many of whom had their hours extended to eleven and twelve a day. On top of this, wages hardly improved in the course of the decade, and journeymen printers, still the best paid of all artisans, were beginning to grow restless.

This degradation of workers fractured the accord between radical revivalist printers and their employers. Preliminary indications of stress were there in the summer of 1849, when the Franklin's leadership, alarmed over the decline of the trade, ordered a union committee to survey its calling in Philadelphia County. The committee reported what the membership had already suspected. There was a decided worsening of conditions, mirrored in the changed distribution of the labor force. A fourth of the 728 workers, read the report, were apprentices and minors doing routinized jobs and over half the trade found employment in the book and job shops, the industry's answer to garrets, where conditions were especially harsh.[88] The committee did not note that the proprietors of such establishments were among the devotées of the community-of-interest ideal, but the lesson was not lost on the membership.

Resolved to rescue their trade from the perils of industrialization, the Franklin men pursued a new strategy—one that conformed closely to that of the carpenters. They dissolved the outmoded Franklin Association in the winter of 1849–1850 and reconstituted themselves as a trade union, which would later affiliate with the International Typographical Union (I.T.U.) as I.T.U. No. 2.[89] They also sought to broaden their base with an inspired organizing campaign geared to rearch all practitioners of the craft, native-born and foreign-born alike. It proved a mixed success, in spite of a series of shop meetings and mass rallies aimed at bona fide journeymen and marginal workers. Many specialized workers rejected the union, while the journeymen signed up by the score. Old radicals, such as William Wellington, who had been inactive for the greater part of the decade, joined the I.T.U., along with those Germans who spoke English.[90] Though German-speaking immigrants were organized separately, they purposed to stand together with the I.T.U. in the event of a strike.

A strike was precisely what the newly unionized printers had in mind. As organizing committees met in shops and public places, tradesmen employed by publishers and jobbers drew up a laundry list of demands that included a rate advance, a ten-hour day where it was not acknowledged, a limitation on the apprentice-journeyman ratio, a closed shop, and the maintenance of traditional work practices.[91] The employers received this package in early August and within a month all but two of the publishers and two-thirds of the jobbers conceded.[92] The resisters triggered a protracted standout that extended for two long months and posed a severe test for the journeymen. Internal discord occurred when nonradicals, who had joined the strike in order to reduce working hours, refused to hold out from other nonwage issues and pressed for acceptance of an employer compromise. Their moderation sent the new radicals to their quills in an attempt to sustain militancy and resolution. Radical polemics appealed for solidarity, in language clearly aimed at the sensibilities of revivalists. "Cultivated and mature minds," one of them affirmed, "cannot be bound in chains; circumstances for a time may oppress them, but they will eventually burst the bands that are wrapped around them, and stand forth as exemplars of what God intended man to be."[93] The radicalism of the leaders also became more pronounced in the course of the strike, as debate turned toward cooperation. Such ideas further repelled the acquisitive and individualistic revivalists who censured the "ultra agrarian sentiments" of the leadership and returned to work.[94] Their abandonment of the strike brought it to a halt, but did not arrest the ideological ferment building among the radicals. Instead of manning the presses and composition rooms of boss printers, they organized cooperatives.[95]

The spirit of independence shown by the carpenters and printers simultaneously began to make itself evident in other trades dominated by radical revivalists. Stone cutters, plasterers, and related building tradesmen as well as bookbinders and cabinetmakers unionized in violation of the community-of-interest ideal.[96] This union movement reawakened the interest of old radicals in building a council of trades, and in October 1850—during the printers' strike the Germans proposed a convention of mechanics. No one knows precisely who attended the October German-American Workingmen's Congress, which convened in Philadelphia, but it probably did not evoke much interest in radical revivalist circles. Most delegates represented trades identified with German workers and, we may believe, German radicals dominated. The proceedings also suggest the prominence of immigrants. Resolutions openly attacked nativism and indirectly attacked revivalism by condemning Sabbatarian laws.[97]

Nothing came of this convention. Proposals for labor exchanges linked to producer and consumer cooperatives were warmly endorsed but never implemented, at least not in Philadelphia. But the gathering did have catalytic value. Six members of the I.T.U. called a meeting of the local workingmen that would settle upon a plan to "free each individual from the oppressive hand of capital."[98]

Part Five:
Epilogue

Radicalism United and Divided

9

News of the printers' proposal rippled through working-class Philadelphia, breaking the lethargic chill of the late fall. Workers preparing for the rigors of the cold months suddenly brimmed with anticipation over the prospect of a collective effort in the name of radicalism. Unionized artisans called emergency meetings to elect representatives, and activists in unorganized trades initiated unions and choose delegates. Representatives of both groups met in November and December, and coincident with the new year, launched the Assembly of Associated Mechanics and Workingmen.[1] The Assembly consisted of thirty trades at its acme in early 1851, a decided improvement over the Mechanics' Union's eighteen affiliates but far below the fifty-one societies that comprised the mighty General Trades' Union. It represented everyone from the relatively privileged printers to the humble shoemakers, but reached no deeper into the ranks of manual labor. Textile operatives, hand loom weavers, and unskilled workers fell outside the Assembly's compass, which left it to the artisans alone.[2]

This constellation makes sense. The Assembly crystallized the class and cultural currents within the better and the sweated trades during the forties. Revivalists and traditionalists inside and outside such crafts shunned the Assembly just as they had eschewed unionism or had organized largely on the spur of the moment to redress immediate grievances. Old and new radicals on the other hand, allied within several occupations, and they coalesced under the broad aegis

191

of the Assembly. Thus, the revivalist radicals, George W. Heilig (printer), A. H. Russell (house carpenter), and John Bottsford (bricklayer) were in league with Solomon Demars and James Mc-Shane (ladies' shoemakers), John Shedden and Peter McIlroy (tailors), and Adolph Zabiensky (litographic printer)—to name just a few of the more visible representatives of each subculture.[3]

A brief review of the past dramatizes the extraordinary cultural thaw of the early fifties. A scant three years before most revivalist radicals spurned the rationalist (and immigrant) inspired Trades' Convention and ostentaciously denounced cooperation with the foreign-born at a huge nativist rally. John Bottsford was one of immigration's detractors on that hot summer afternoon. Now he joined hands with foreign-born workingmen, not out of love or in a sudden fit of compassion, but in recognition of their mutual commitment to radicalism.

New radicals also remained wary of middle-class radicals. In the fall of 1850, for example, radical revivalist house carpenters held a strike meeting during their standout against contractors. Their conclaves were restricted to tradesmen, but they unwillingly agreed to hear out John Campbell and Edward Power who persistently sought out working-class audiences in order to peddle a blueprint for utopian socialism. They had exaggerated views of their persuasive powers and despite the topic on the floor, ridiculed strikes as a waste of time and resources which could be better spent furthering utopianism. Their untimely and condescending lecture so disturbed union secretary A. H. Russell that he railed against nonproducers and insisted upon expelling the two in attendance. Campbell barked back that he in fact was a producer, as was anyone who turned out "thought for the good of society."[4] But he convinced no one and the carpenters had the last word. Russell moved that they be shown the door and the interlopers were ordered out. The same actors rehearsed this scene at the opening session of the Assembly a few months later. Undaunted, Campbell and Power showed up prepared to make yet another pitch for their panacea, but their chances of speaking were remote since their nemesis, Russell, was in attendance and his comrades were no more enamored of middle-class reformers, nativist or not, than he. One of them resolved to bar all but "journeymen mechanics" and the motion passed without a dissenting vote.[5]

Radical revivalist workingmen not only kept reformers at arm's length, they also rejected the current petty-bourgeois, nativistic prescription for the attainment of a competency. They did not necessarily sour on the new morality or suspend their repugnance of financiers, but they did refrain from airing these in the forum of the Assembly. None of them spoke of temperance or the Protestant work ethic, nor did they lapse into the customary assault on merchants and bankers or obligatory adoration of entrepreneurs. Such matters were the forte of American Republican politicians and they faded away without the advocacy of their promoters.

Unfettered by the moral and ideological fixations of middle-class nativists, radical revivalists aligned themselves with old radicals in articulating the pristine form of the producer ideology. They reaffirmed the worker's right to the "full product" of his toil and reviled both "wage slavery" and competition on the floor of the Assembly, and this antiwage sentiment found its way into policy. Early meetings established a fund "for the accomplishment of such ends as may be determined upon" by a majority vote.[6] The precise course of the deliberations is somewhat unclear, but there appears to have been minimal if any friction between the proponents of strikes, or class-conscious workers, and supporters of cooperation, or labor reformists. Recent historians have laid the myth of this polarity to rest. No such distinction existed in contemporary Lynn, Massachusetts or in Philadelphia.[7] The same workers who endorsed strikes pressed for cooperation and even land reform, a scheme that had been on the radical agenda since the 1820s but assumed new urgency with the advancing capitalism's ominous threat to worker autonomy. It was a forgone conclusion that the Assembly would reach concensus on cooperation and land reform and both causes won a ringing endorsement by the spring 1851.[8]

Having settled their ideological direction, Assembly spokesmen addressed the unorganized of the suburban districts at open-air meetings that recalled the agitation of the thirties. A typical demonstration heard speeches by John Shedden (tailor) and Eugene Ahearn (bookbinder) who ably demonstrated how labor reformism, or cooperation, suited both the immediate and long range interests of workers. They "earnestly recommend[ed]" cooperative production for "the purpose of securing to ourselves shorter hours of labor, and more of the products of our own industry," as well as equalizing the distribution of wealth. These fiery orators also declared the worker's right to "labor for himself," and with this in mind, proposed that the government hold the public domain in trust and then parcel it out in 160-acre homesteads to "each actual settler."[9]

By the spring 1851, then, new and old radicals concurred on two fundamental points. They tacitly agreed to avoid the divisive cultural issues of immigration, moral reform, and the like, which had kept them at odds throughout the forties. They coalesced, too, around economic matters. They rejected the rampant acquisitiveness and individualism of emergent capitalism for the mutualism of cooperative production.

Yet radicals never did advance their program beyond the stage of fleeting agitation. Instead of tending to their brittle cooperatives and proselytizing noncompetitive labor, they chose the treacherous path of independent politics. Just why they elected such a course at this juncture, and with such haste, is difficult to fathom. Perhaps it was another indication of labor's mounting dissatisfaction with the conventional parties, which were headed for self-destruction and realignment. For whatever reason, the Assembly sponsored a political convention in August 1851 that gave birth to the Workingmen's Republican party, the second independent workers' party to vie for office in twenty years. Workers themselves initiated this political expedition, but typical of such organizations, it proved a beacon for master craftsmen, entrepreneurs, petty professionals, and adventurers alienated from mainstream parties and in search of an alternative.[10] It put forth a platform encompassing municipal reform and labor reform with such planks as consolidation of the city and suburban districts into a single jurisdiction and strengthened ten-hour legislation.[11] There was virtual unanimity on these issues, or at least no significant dissent. The workingmen took their lead from the Assembly, and steered clear of the troubled waters of culture and ethnicity—but not for long.

The first indication of dissidence actually predated the founding of the party. Many Assembly delegates were loyal Democrats and American Republicans and they sat out the Workingmen's nominating convention or declined positions on its ticket. Such partisans stumped for their chosen parties or ran on rival tickets. Solomon

Demars, for one, captured the Democratic nomination for the state Assembly and wound up challenging both American Republicans and Workingmen.[12] The loss of such leaders stripped the Workingmen of their most articulate and popular figures.

They sustained an even more devastating setback during the campaign. Ethnic dissonance still punctuated local politics and in entering the 1851 race, the Workingmen unwittingly but inexorably walked into a maddening political imbroglio that even the most judicious voices could not contain. The occasion was a new statute that changed local judgships from appointive to elective offices.[13] There was a surfeit of aspirants to the bench and all parties, including the Workingmen, planned to enter slates. Judge William D. Kelley, favorite of radical Democrats, would have secured one of the Democracy's slots, but he had recently affronted the party's Irish wing by ruling against it in a case involving election fraud in Moyamensing.[14] Irish blood was still boiling at convention time, and the Irish not only blocked Kelley's nomination, but embarrassed him by throwing the vote to his arch enemy, Vincent Bradford.[15]

This left one of Philadelphia's most colorful and promising politicians without a party, and there was no dearth of suitors. The most persistent of these were the Whigs, who were on the verge of collapse and desperate for a good showing at the polls, as well as most American Republicans, who nervously watched their majorities decline and relished the thought of fusion with the Whigs. The flagging fortunes of both parties produced a marriage of convenience in which the Whigs agreed to endorse American Republican nominees. But Kelley's availability was too much to resist. The Whigs drafted him without consulting the nativists—a rash maneuver that disturbed but did not estrange American Republican fusionists. Such nativists valued victory above protocol and they went with Kelley, salvaging the alliance.[16]

This unexpected turn of events ripped apart the American Republicans and evoked a torrent of anti-immigrant hysteria as virulent as that of the mid-forties. A minority of American Republicans, styled Independents, condemned fusion on the grounds that the Whigs were inadequately nativistic and too elitist. They were even more critical of their party's nominating Kelley, an outspoken American Republican detractor who had reviled nativist "fanaticism" and had stigmatized the party faithful as "church burners," and they barraged the press with letters of invective against the fusionists and Kelley himself.[17] They delighted in reminding nativists of his Irish origins, his prominence in the hated Repeal movement, and his unkindly characterizations of their party. The most ambitious slanderers researched Kelley's past, sniffing for scandal, and their labors were rewarded. They learned that he had once been seen drinking at a social gathering while holding a key position in the Sons of Temperance and they took great relish in recounting the incident. Kelley's defenders retorted that the Sons had looked into the matter and their investigation had cleared him of any wrongdoing.[18] Their rejoinder helped correct the public record and may have humiliated Independents, but it failed to still the purple pens. It might have encouraged Independents to shift ground and raise even more heated issues—issues designed to stir popular fears and apprehensions. They first depicted Kelley as an abolitionist plotting to usher hordes of freed Blacks into northern labor markets and then fell back on the standby of nativism—anti-immigrant hysteria. They correctly identified Kelley's most avid working-class supporters as English and German immigrants, and made the most of this connection. "Red, White, and Blue, U.S.A.," writing in the *Public Ledger,* observed that John Shedden and other "unnaturalized foreigners" electioneered for the judge and admonished "American Mechanics" not to "suffer yourselves to be lead blindfolded into the toils of your worst enemies."[19]

In the midst of such political tumult the Workingmen met to choose candidates for the judgships. Three positions were to be filled, two of which went to Joel Jones and Vincent Bradford. Immigrant radicals believed that the third position was reserved for Kelley, but the mere mention of his name produced such acrimony that it was kept in nomination by virtue of convention chairman William J. Mullen's casting a vote that created a tie between him and an unknown candidate. Mullen then averted a bolt of one of the sides by adjourning the meeting and rescheduling it in two weeks, ample time for emotions to cool, or so he believed.[20] He inadvertently gave Kelley loyalists the space to regroup and plan a counterattack that included nominating their hero and punishing his enemies by dumping Bradford. They accomplished both objectives by means that remain unclear, though one observer was probably close to the mark in charging that they stacked the convention with pro-Kelley Democrats and American Republicans.[21] Their heavy-handed politics also caused an irreparable rift within the party. Anti-Kelley men stormed out in disgust, formed a separate ticket headed by Bradford, and ran a bitterly nativistic campaign.[22]

That Kelley won handily on election day was no consolation. Republican Workingmen stumped vigorously on his behalf, so vigorously that their radical spirit got lost in the flurry of ethnic and personalistic politics.[23] Voters went to the polls ignorant of their program and unaware that their ticket included candidates for the state Senate and Assembly. Kelley's candidacy and nativism overshadowed all else, and the Workingmen's State House hopefuls ran poorly, collecting an average of 220 votes each.[24]

And what of the Assembly, parent of the ill-fated Workingmen's party? Much like the Mechanics' Union of the late 1820s, it was forgotten in the commotion of the campaign and died a quiet death amid the chaotic infighting. With its demise went the last hope of harmonizing secular and religious radicalism. Those with visions of uniting them had cause for optimism as the American Republican party, font of divisiveness, faded away in 1852–1853. But just as it expired, Know Nothingism burst on the scene—an arresting reminder of nativist resilience.

Mobility, Ethnicity, Ideology

Another political pilgrimage, another dead end. The pattern has a familiar ring to historians of the nineteenth-century American working class. This pattern recurred throughout the century in the port cities with diversified economies and in the single-industry towns of the interior. Time and again radicals broke with mainstream parties and agitated their politics free from fetters of party orthodoxy only to go down to defeat with frustrating regularity.[25] Such lost opportunities raise two questions that have long preoccupied labor historians: why American workers resisted acting as a collective entity, or a class, and why they were not more receptive to capitalist alternatives. The two are causally related and while there are several schools of thought, we shall explore those which are most germane to the Philadelphia case, the "mobility thesis" and the "ethnic thesis."

The mobility thesis speaks to geographical and social movement. The geographic dimension is the extraordinarily high rate of population turnover that characterized nineteenth-century cities. Few workers stayed in one town or even in a single neighborhood very long and their volatility is proffered as an impediment to solidarities and bonds of trust which are presumed to be essential ingredients in the making of class consciousness and maintenance of worker organizations.[26] Philadelphia's manual laborers were rather footloose, but as other writers have observed, we should not make too much of this.[27] Population volatility and class consciousness were not necessarily incompatable and might even have been quite consonant.[28] The ebb and flow of population, on the other hand, could have upset the process of building confidence among workers and undermined their social organizations. Logic would endorse this proposition, but logic does not always make good history. Every imaginable kind of institution and association took root and flourished in spite of population fluidity and this renaissance led a historian of the Jackson period to dub it, *"par excellence* the era of the urban parish church, the lodge, the benefit association, the social and political club, the fire company, and the gang."[29] He might have added trade unions and worker lyceums to this roster. Both survived in Philadelphia and elsewhere for the same reason as other organizations. Small groups of activists remained in their communities amid the population flow and these pillars of stability provided leadership and continuity.[30] If unions and debating clubs showed less resiliency than, say, churches and fire companies it was less the result of population turnover than of the resources of the membership and sponsors. Unions, after all, were not accorded the financial support of the middle class or the wealthy. Workers and workers alone foot the bill of unions and radical lyceums; meager resources and hard times, not unstable memberships, seem to have been the bane of such working-class associations.

Social mobility consists of both occupational improvement and / or property ownership. The argument is that success in either or both of these and the promise of self-improvement give workers a stake in the status quo, dampening radicalism's attraction.[31] As we have seen, some Philadelphia workers did rise out of their class and accumulate modest holdings. More than this, they accepted the

growing national faith in social advancement and its corollaries—
that diligence yielded success and that individuals rose or fell on their
own merits. Such workers, however, were exceptional in an age of
receding opportunities for men of humble origins and it is doubtful
that their less fortunate brothers subscribed to the mobility ethic.
Traditionalists and rationalists expressed no interest in occupational
improvement; Catholic traditionalists of the forties valued survival
above all else and were a decade or two away from endorsing the idea
of accumulating the income for a house—the goal that they achieved
with such frequency in the post-Civil War period. Radical revivalists
felt themselves entitled to a house equipped with indoor plumbing
and furnished with modern fixtures, such as an organ or piano, and
other comforts and symbols of status, but they recoiled from the
thought of sacrificing manual labor to this standard of living. They
hoped to achieve these badges of respectability on the wages of a
journeyman instead of rising up the social ladder beyond the rung of
their class. Revivalists were alone in paying homage to the mobility
ethic and they were but a single cultural group in a larger
aggregate. The mobility thesis thus has limited explanatory power.

The ethnic thesis stresses class fragmentation rather than loyalty to
the established order. It posits that the steady arrival of European
immigrants converted the manual labor force into a patchwork quilt
of different and often hostile groups whose national loyalties and
suspicions of one another doomed the working class to internal
discord.[32] There is something to this argument. Gilded Age and
Progressive period historians focusing on the so-called "new immigrants" have marshalled an impressive corpus of evidence in its
support, but it is wanting in two respects. It does not give one insights
into predepression Philadelphia or into any other locale whose
working class consisted largely of native-born Americans. Its view of
national consciousness, moreover, is simple-minded and profoundly
ahistorical, for it envisions national identity or ethnic consciousness
as a given that assumes cultural and political salience at all points in
time. It may well apply to immigrants with homogeneous values and
experiences. The famine Irish, uniformly peasant in origin and
overwhelmingly Catholic, immediately come to mind. The com-
monality of their experiences and the political context that greeted
them in Philadelphia enforced both group cohesion and a strong

sense of ethnicity. But one hesitates to lump the Irish immigrants who had artisan backgrounds and radical politics with the famine generation, or to regard English and German newcomers as homogeneous groupings bonded together around an awareness of nationality to the exclusion of other sources of identity. The English and the German populations contained subgroups of nonsectarian radicals, revivalists, and perhaps even Catholic and non-Catholic traditionalists who had more in common with one another than with their fellow countrymen.[33] Thus the ethnic thesis has its limitations as well.

Divisiveness there was, but it did not derive strictly from nationalistic particularisms. Working-class Philadelphians were balkanized long before immigration made much of an impact. Prior to the panic of 1837 they sorted themselves out along cultural lines and such groupings subsumed the small nationality groups in the city. This cultural fragmentation itself had less to do with immigration than with the uneven development of capitalism and the prior experiences of the workforce in rural and urban America and Europe. Not until the forties, with its nativist effusions and massive influx of Irish immigrants, did nationalistic divisions count for much. Even then, ethnicity did not always confound cross-cultural alliances against capital. Deteriorating working conditions or the arbitrary exercise of employer authority sometimes dissolved cultural animosities and encouraged unity between rival groups. Catholic traditionalists and revivalist millhands buried their differences during the ten-hour movement of 1848–1849, just as they had done in 1835, and old and new radicals gradually constructed a promising, if fleeting, union as the 1840s drew to a close.

When workers heeled to the will of the boss, it was not simply because they despised one another. Nor was it because they reflected the political behaviorists' "negative reference group theory" in which one group expresses its animus for another by siding with its enemy— in this instance revivalists currying favor with capital as a way of thumbing their nose either at radicals or traditionalists.[34] Instead, worker deference is better understood as the result of their conceptions of class and their attitudes toward work. Revivalists resisted confronting their employers not because of their suspicion of those who did but because of the respect for individualism and reverence for employers and entrepreneurs emitted by evangelical

Protestantism. Such workers blamed themselves for their travail. Traditionalist views, quite frankly, are more difficult to pin down. We know that they did not tolerate individualism and that they had modest expectations, but traditionalists may have been far more sophisticated than appears at first. The traditionalist bailiwick of hand loom weaving, for example, persisted partly because of low labor costs, which enabled employers to withstand the competition of modern mills fitted with power looms.[35] Traditionalist frame tenders may have understood this, as well, and may have concluded that to demand excessively high rates was to doom their industry and force themselves into the factories they did so much to avoid. Holding down wages below a certain threshold might have been a calculated strategy, a means of preserving the casual style of life that was so much a part of outwork. But this is conjecture. The point is that culture and nationality were not simply sources of dissension and should not been seen solely as such. Historians would do better to probe the social and economic understandings conveyed by such constructs.

This matter gets us closer to the reasons behind radicalism's failure. It was not for lack of effort on the part of radicals themselves. Unlike the urban socialists of the Progressive period, they did not assume that capitalism would collapse under its own weight or that economic deterioration would swell the socialist throng. These socialists set the table in anticipation of celebrating capitalism's demise, but did very little to bring out the guests in the belief that the economy would send out its own invitations. Rationalist radicals had no use for such vulgar economism. They had a true feeling for the political limitations of nonradicals and well understood the imperative to cultivate dissident consciousness. They made some headway among traditionalists (and perhaps among a fraction of revivalists) during the thirties, by means of the educative apparatus of the Trades' Union and informal agitation. They were deterred, however, by the antiradical fulminations of revivalist leaders, and were stopped in their tracks by the depression of 1837, which wrecked their organizations and stimulated the penultimate events of the Second Great Awakening. (The last would come in the panic of 1857.)

The revivalist upsurge of the depression gave radicalism an

entirely different cast. Revivalism gave birth to the new radicalism that became the ruling expression of worker insurgency. The nativistic strain of the new radicalism distinguished it from its rationalist predecessor and made its partisans less willing to proselytize among the uninitiated, especially if they were Catholic or foreign born. As it turned out, many nonradicals were in fact immigrants, and the Catholics among them were being incorporated into their church for the first time and barraged with antiradical prejudice. The convergence of these developments produced a cultural standoff, an ebb in radical agitation, on the one hand, and a new resistance to radicalism, on the other. But again, one should be wary of accenting intergroup discord. New radicals, after all, were still of the radical camp, and their rejection of Catholic immigrants stemmed not only from nativism but also from the producer ideology. They simply refused to believe that Catholic workers, many of whom were unskilled, qualified as producers.

Radicalism's grounding in the producer ideology and the labor theory of value holds the final key to its unhappy fate. This ideology proved both a blessing and a curse to a forceful critique of capitalism for old and new radicals. In affirming the worker's right to the full proceeds of his labor, it propelled him against employers and provided the most important ideological impetus for reorganizing production along cooperative lines. At the same time, its fuzzy conception of class and exploitation left the worker vulnerable to the appeals of middle-class radicals, whose translation of the producer ideology deflected attention from employers to financiers, and lured him into fighting rear-guard battles against the money changers.

The producer ideology also prescribed political action against accumulators. This was not in itself a liability, but in the context of American politics it shackled radicals with the labors of Sisyphus. As Alan Dawley has argued, the establishment of white universal suffrage in the United States before workers felt "the worst effects of the industrial revolution" tied them closer to the political system than their European comrades, who had to struggle as a class for the ballot.[36] This took some of the punch out of the class struggle in the United States and all but guaranteed that parties would not be firmly rooted in class differences, as they were on the Continent. Workers gave their votes to all parties, as noted above, and partisanships were fairly resilient. Parties were also remarkably accessible to articulate pleabians who routinely ran for office and served as functionaries at the local level—and often for different standards. Thus radicals had it difficult whichever way they turned. They were either drawn off into existing parties, their voices muted amid the moderate majorities, or when fielding independent tickets, could not easily entice workers from the parties of their choice.

Notes
Bibliography
and
Index

Notes

Abbreviations

A.B.	*American Banner*
C.H.	*Catholic Herald*
D.A.B.	*Dictionary of American Biography*, 20 vols. (New York: Charles Scribner's Sons, 1937).
D.S.	*Daily Sun*
E.B.	*Evening Bulletin*
Fellow-laborer, *Address*	*An Address to the Members of Trade Societies, and to the Working Classes Generally: Being an Exposition on the Relative Situation, Condition, and Future Prospects of Working People in the United States of America. Together with a Suggestion and Outlines of a Plan, by which They May Gradually and Indefinitely Improve their Condition. By a Fellow-laborer* (Philadelphia: Young, 1827).
F.T.R.	*Fincher's Trades Review*
G.T.	*Germantown Telegraph*
Lib.	*Liberalist*
M.C.	*Manayunk Courier*
M.F.P.	*Mechanics' Free Press*
N.Y.D.T.	*New York Daily Tribune*
Operative, *Principles*	*The Principles of Aristocratic Legislation, Developed in an Address, Delivered to the Working People of the District of Southwark, and Townships of Moyamensing and Passyunk. In the Commissioners' Hall, August 14, 1828, By an Operative Citizen* (Philadelphia: J. Coates, Jr., 1828).

Penn.	*Pennsylvanian*
Penn. Senate, *Peltz Committee*	Pennsylvania Senate, *Report of the Select Committee Appointed to Visit the Manufacturing Districts of the Commonwealth, for the Purpose of Investigating the Employment of Children in Manufactories, Mr. Peltz, Chairman* (Harrisburg: Thompson and Clark, 1838).
P.L.	*Public Ledger*
S.T.	*Spirit of the Times*
T.A.	*Temperance Advocate and Literary Repository*
T.R.	*Temple of Reason*
Unlettered Mechanic, *Address*	*An Address, Delivered Before the Mechanics and Working Classes Generally of the City and County, of Philadelphia. At the Universalist Church in Callowhill Street, on Wednesday Evening, November 21, 1827. By the "Unlettered Mechanic"* (Philadelphia: Mechanics' Delegation, 1827).
U.S. Census, *Industrial Schedule, Southwark*	United States Census Office, *Census of the United States, Industrial Schedule, Philadelphia County (Southwark), 1850* (microfilm, MSS, National Archives, Washington, D.C.).
U.S. Census, *Population Schedule, Manayunk*	United States Census Office, *Census of the United States, Population Schedule, Philadelphia County (Manayunk), 1850* (microfilm, MSS, National Archives, Washington, D.C.).
U.S. Census, *Population Schedule, Moyamensing*	United States Census Office, *Census of the United States, Population Schedule, Philadelphia County (Moyamensing), 1850* (microfilm, MSS, National Archives, Washington, D.C.).
U.S. Census, *Population Schedule, Philadelphia County*	United States Census Office, *Census of the United States, Population Schedule, Philadelphia County, 1850* (microfilm, MSS, National Archives, Washington, D.C.).
U.S. Census, *Population Schedule, Southwark*	United States Census Office, *Census of the United States, Population Schedule, Philadelphia County (Southwark), 1850* (microfilm, MSS, National Archives, Washington, D.C.).
U.S.G.	*United States Gazette*

Introduction

1. For reviews of such works see Paul Faler, "Working-class Historiography," *Radical America* 3 (March-April, 1969): 56–68; Thomas Krueger, "American Labor Historiography, Old and New: A Review Essay," *Journal of Social History* 4 (Spring, 1971): 277–85; Robert Zieger, "Workers and Scholars: Recent Trends in American Labor Historiography," *Labor History* 13 (Spring, 1972): 245–66; and David Brody, "The Old Labor History and the New: In Search of an American Working Class," *Labor History* 20 (Winter, 1979): 111–26.

2. E. P. Thompson, *The Making of the English Working Class* (pbk. ed.; New York: Vintage, 1966), p. 10. For a richer theoretical discussion of culture and ideology see Raymond Williams, *Marxism and Literature* (New York: Oxford University Press, 1977), esp. pp. 75–144.

3. See, for example, David Montgomery, *Beyond Equality: Labor and the Radical Republicans, 1862–1872* (New York: Alfred A. Knopf, 1967); Herbert G. Gutman, "Work, Culture, and Society in Industrializing America, 1815–1919," *American Historical Review* 78 (June, 1973): 531–87; Alan Dawley, *Class and Community: The Industrial Revolution in Lynn* (Cambridge: Harvard University Press, 1976); Paul Faler, "Workingmen, Mechanics, and Social Change: Lynn, Massachusetts, 1800–1860" (unpub. Ph.D. diss., University of Wisconsin, 1971); Faler, "Cultural Aspects of the Industrial Revolution: Lynn, Massachusetts Shoemakers and Industrial Morality, 1826–1860," *Labor History* 15 (Summer, 1974): 367–94; Dawley and Faler, "Workingclass Culture and Politics in the Industrial Revolution: Sources of Loyalism and Rebellion," *Journal of Social History* 9 (June, 1976): 466–80; Bruce Laurie, "'Nothing on Compulsion': Life Styles of Philadelphia Artisans, 1820–1850," *Labor History* 15 (Summer, 1974): 377–66; and Gary Kulik, "Pawtucket Village and the Strike of 1824: The Origins of Class Conflict in Rhode Island," *Radical History Review* 17 (Spring, 1978): 5–38. See also Daniel J. Walkowitz, *Worker City, Company Town: Iron and Cotton-Worker Protest in Troy and Cohoes, New York, 1855–1884* (Urbana: University of Illinois Press, 1978); and Leon Fink, "Workingmen's Democracy: The Knights of Labor in Local Politics, 1886–1896" (unpub. Ph.D. diss., University of Rochester, 1977).

4. See fn. 3, especially their "Workingclass Culture and Politics."

5. See, for example, Lee Benson, *The Concept of Jacksonian Democracy: New York as a Test Case* (pbk. ed.; Princeton: Princeton University Press, 1961); Paul J. Kleppner, *The Cross of Culture: A Social Analysis of Midwestern Politics, 1850–1900* (New York: Free Press, 1970); and Ronald P. Formisano, *The Birth of Mass Political Parties: Michigan, 1827–1861* (Princeton: Princeton University Press, 1971). I might add that one can find

value in these works without accepting their structural-functionalist assumptions or their conservative politics.

Chapter 1

1. Eric Foner, *Tom Paine and Revolutionary America* (New York: Oxford University Press, 1976), pp. 206–7. For a complete account of the procession see "Account of the Grand Federal Procession in Philadelphia," *American Museum* 4 (July, 1788): 57–75.

2. Foner, *Tom Paine,* pp. 19–69 and esp. n. 22, p. 280. See also Jacob M. Price, "Economic Function and the Growth of American Port Towns in the Eighteenth Century," *Perspectives in American History* 8 (1974): 139.

3. David Montgomery, "The Working Classes of the Pre-industrial City, 1780–1830," *Labor History* 9 (Winter, 1968): 5.

4. See, for example, John R. Commons, "American Shoemakers, 1648–1895: A Sketch of Industrial Evolution," *Quarterly Journal of Economics* 24 (Nov., 1909): 39–84; Carl Bridenbaugh, *The Colonial Craftsman* (pbk ed.; Chicago: University of Chicago Press, 1961), pp. 125–54; Sam Bass Warner, Jr., *The Private City: Philadelphia in Three Periods of Its Growth* (Philadelphia: University of Pennsylvania Press, 1968), pp. 7–9; and Foner, *Tom Paine,* pp. 37–45.

5. John Fanning Watson, *Annals of Philadelphia,* 3 vols. (Philadelphia: Edwin S. Stuart, 1887), 1: 220–21.

6. See, for example, John R. Commons, et al., *Documentary History of American Industrial Society,* 10 vols. (rpt. New York: Russell and Russell, 1958), 3: 77–78 and 99–103; J. Thomas Scharf and Thompson Westcott, *History of Philadelphia, 1609–1884,* 3 vols. (Philadelphia: L. H. Everts, 1884), 3: 2231–32; and Foner, *Tom Paine,* pp. 41–45.

7. Ian M. G. Quimby, "Apprenticeship in Colonial Philadelphia," (M.A. thesis, University of Delaware, 1963), pp. 60–63.

8. Foner, *Tom Paine,* n. 24, p. 280.

9. Montgomery, "Working Classes," p. 6.

10. Allan R. Pred, *Urban Growth and the Circulation of Information: The United States System of Cities, 1790–1840* (Cambridge: Harvard University Press, 1973), pp. 189–90.

11. Commons, *Documentary History,* 3: 100.

12. Ibid., pp. 99–101.

13. Lewis Hartz, *Economic Policy and Democratic Thought: Pennsylvania, 1776–1860* (pbk. ed.; Chicago: Quadrangle Books, 1968), pp. 129–42.

14. George R. Taylor, *The Transportation Revolution, 1815–1860* (pbk. ed.; New York: Harper and Row, 1968), p. 107.

15. Hartz, *Economic Policy,* pp. 148–60.

16. Taylor, *Transportation Revolution,* pp. 38–42 and 43–45.

17. Ibid., pp. 77–80.

18. Ibid., pp. 135–40 and 442.

19. *P. L.* December 28, 1836.

20. James T. Lemon, *The Best Poor Man's Country: A Geographical Study of Early Southeastern Pennsylvania* (Baltimore: The Johns Hopkins University Press, 1972), pp. 73–92.

21. Ibid. See also John Modell, "A Regional Approach to Urban Growth: The Philadelphia Region in the Early Ninetcenth Century" (paper delivered at the Fall Regional Economic History Conference, Eleutherian Mills–Hagley Foundation, Wilmington, Del., 1968). Modell has found similar migration patterns for the Reading, Pennsylvania hinterland. See Modell, "The Peupling of a Working-class Ward: Reading, Pennsylvania, 1850," *Journal of Social History* 5 (Fall, 1971): 71–95.

22. See also Modell, "Regional Approach." Diane Lindstrom, *Economic Growth in the Philadelphia Region, 1810–1850* (New York: Columbia University Press, 1978), pp. 24–25; and Warner, *Private City,* pp. 56–57.

23. Douglass C. North, *The Economic Growth of the United States, 1790–1860* (New York: Norton, 1966), p. 168.

24. See, for example, Edward Pessen, *Riches, Class, and Power before the Civil War* (Lexington, Mass., D. C. Heath, 1973), pp. 183–89.

25. Stuart M. Blumin, "Mobility in a Nineteenth-century American City: Philadelphia, 1820–1860" (Ph.D. diss., University of Pennsylvania, 1968), pp. 110–37.

26. On the concentration of industrial jobs in the core see Richard Greenfield, "Industrial Location in Philadelphia, 1850–1880" (working paper, Philadelphia Social History Project, University of Pennsylvania, 1978); and Warner, *Private City,* pp. 59–60.

27. See, for example, Charles V. Hagner, *Early History of the Falls of Schuylkill, Manayunk, Schuylkill and Lehigh Navagation Companies, Fairmount Water Works, etc.* (Philadelphia: Claxton, Remsen, and Haffelfinger, 1869); "Address of Dr. John Elkinton," *M.F.P.,* July 26 and Aug. 2, 1828; and *M.C.,* Mar. 11, 1848.

28. For descriptions of the suburbs see David Montgomery, "The Shuttle and the Cross: Weavers and Artisans in the Kensington Riots of 1844," *Journal of Social History* 5 (Summer, 1972): 411–47; Sam Bass Warner, "If All the World Were Philadelphia: A Scaffolding for Urban History, 1774–1930," *American Historical Review* 74 (Oct., 1968): 26–43; and Bruce Laurie, "Fire Companies and Gangs in Southwark: The 1840s," in Allen F. Davis and Mark H. Haller, eds., *The Peoples of Philadelphia: A History of Ethnic Groups and Lower-class Life 1790–1940* (Philadelphia: Temple University Press, 1973), pp. 71–86.

29. Foner, *Tom Paine,* p. 23. See also Richard G. Miller, "Gentry and Entrepreneurs: A Socioeconomic Analysis of Philadelphia in the 1790s," *Rocky Mountain Social Science Journal* 12 (Jan., 1975): 71–84.

30. Blumin, "Mobility in a Nineteenth-century City," pp. 45–50; and Pessen, *Riches, Class, and Power,* p. 40.

31. Pessen, *Riches, Class, and Power,* pp. 46–75, esp. pp. 50, 120–28, and 327–31.

32. Taylor, *Transportation Revolution,* pp. 294–95.

33. Ibid., pp. 296–97. For Campbell's budget see *N. Y.D.T.,* May 27, 1851.

34. The average yearly earnings of male artisans and industrial workers are estimated in Bruce Laurie, et al., "Immigrants and Industry: The Philadelphia Experience, 1850–1880," *Journal of Social History* 9 (Winter, 1975): 229.

35. For an overview of the factors affecting women's employment see Susan J. Kleinberg, "The Systematic Study of Urban Women," *Historical Methods Newsletter* 9 (Dec., 1975): 14–25.

36. The best and perhaps only study of the frequency of women's involvement in outwork during the antebellum period is Carol Groneman, "'She Earns as a Child, She Pays as a Man': Women Workers in a Mid-nineteenth-century New York City Community," in Milton Cantor and Bruce Laurie, eds., *Class, Sex, and the Woman Worker* (Westport, Conn.: Greenwood Press, 1977), pp. 83–100. Quantitative data on this is unavailable for Philadelphia, but the testimony of artisans suggests a goodly number of their wives were employed in the home under the putting-out system. See, for example, the letters of journeymen cordwainers, *Penn.,* April 1, 1836; and journeymen house carpenters, *D.S.,* Aug. 9, 1850.

37. For the occupational distribution of women in 1850 see Bruce Laurie and Mark Schmitz, "Manufacture and Productivity: The Making of an Industrial Base, 1850–1880" in Theodore Hershberg, ed., *Toward an Interdisciplinary History of the City: Work, Space, Family and Group Experience in Nineteenth-century Philadelphia* (New York: Oxford University Press, 1980), table 2.

38. Blumin, "Mobility in a Nineteenth-century City," p. 20. For a biographical sketch of Evans see *D.A.B.,* 6. 208–10.

39. Hagner, *Early History of Manayunk.* The best description of textile production and machinery is Anthony F. C. Wallace, *Rockdale: The Growth of an American Village in the Early Industrial Revolution* (New York: Alfred A. Knopf, 1978), pp. 125–239.

40. Samuel Hazard, ed., *Register of Pennsylvania* 1 (Jan., 1828): 28; and Montgomery, "Shuttle and the Cross," pp. 416–17.

41. U.S. Census, *Population Schedule, Manayunk.*

42. Hagner, *Early History of Manayunk,* p. 75; and *M.C.,* March 11, 1848.

43. *Manayunk Star,* March 29, 1862.

44. See, for example, letter signed "A Jeffersonian American Working-Man," *G. T.,* Sept. 18, 1833. The local press is sprinkled with news of mill shutdowns due to fires, freshets, and, of course, slack times. See letter signed "A Looker-on in Manayunk," *P.L.,* May 2, 1846. See also ibid., Jan. 30, 1851; and *G.T.,* April 3 and July 31, 1839, Nov. 29, 1843, Dec. 27, 1847, and Jan.1, 1851.

45. See, for example, Merritt Roe Smith, *Harpers Ferry Armory and the New Technology: The Challenge of Change* (Ithaca: Cornell University Press, 1977); and David Montgomery, "Workers' Control of Machine Production in the Nineteenth Century," *Labor History* 17 (Fall, 1976): 485–509.

46. On the millhands' struggles for a ten-hour day, see below, pp. 91 and 143–47.

47. See letter signed *"A Jeffersonian American Working-Man," G.T.,* Sept. 18, 1833.

48. Robert Baird, *The American Cotton Spinner, and Manager's and Carder's Guide: A Practical Treatise on Cotton Spinning, Compiled from the Papers of the late Robert Baird* (Philadelphia: A Hart, 1851), p. 203.

49. See the testimony of Philadelphia textile hands in Penn. Senate, *Peltz Committee,* esp. pp. 25–26, 49, and 75–76.

50. Penn. Senate, *Peltz Committee,* p. 58.

51. *G.T.,* Nov. 6, 1833.

52. See letters signed "A Jeffersonian American Working-Man," ibid., Sept. 18, 1833; and "J.F.," ibid., Nov. 13, 1833.

53. Ibid., Nov. 6, 1833.

54. Laurie, et al., "Immigrants and Industry," p. 229.

55. Rona Weiss, "The Transition to Industrial Capitalism: Workers and Entrepreneurs in Randolph, Massachusetts, 1800–1870" (seminar paper, University of Massachusetts at Amherst, 1974).

56. The names of the largest shoe manufacturers in 1850 were selected out of the manuscripts of the industrial census and traced backwards in the city directories each year for twenty-five years.

57. *Penn.,* April 4, 1834. See also letter signed "Sherman," *U.S.G.,* April 2, 1836.

58. See letter signed "A Reflecting Operative," *S. T.,* Oct. 9, 1849.

59. See, for example, ibid., June 21, 1847.

60. Edwin T. Freedley, *Philadelphia and Its Manufactures: A Hand-*

book *Exhibiting the Development, Variety, and Statistics of the Manufacturing Industry of Philadelphia in 1857, together with Sketches of Remarkable Manufactories, and a List of Articles Now Made in Philadelphia* (Philadelphia: Edward Young, 1858), p. 223. See also the advertisement of Bennett and Company, *P.L.*, Aug. 14, 1847.

61. See Freedley, *Philadelphia and Its Manufactures*, pp. 186–88; *Penn.*, April 1 and 4, 1836; and *D.S.*, Feb. 14, 1845.

62. *U.S.G.*, July 6, 1834; and Freedley, *Philadelphia and Its Manufactures*, p. 173.

63. Adam Smith and then Karl Marx, of course, placed great emphasis on the division of labor. One of the first scholars to analyze this process in the American setting was John R. Commons in his classic article published in 1909, "American Shoemakers." Since then many American writers have investigated the division of labor in one-industry towns and cities with diversified economies, the most recent of which are Alan Dawley, *Class and Community: The Industrial Revolution in Lynn* (Cambridge: Harvard University Press, 1976), esp. pp. 42–50; and Susan E. Hirsch, *Roots of the American Working Class: The Industrialization of the Crafts in Newark, 1800–1860* (Philadelphia: University of Pennsylvania Press, 1978), esp. pp. 21–36. It should be added that Prof. Hirsch also draws attention to the unevenness of this process within the crafts.

64. The best analysis of the persistence of hand techniques in Raphael Samuel, "The Workshop of the World: Steam Power and Hand Technology in Mid-victorian Britain," *History Workshop Journal* 3 (Spring, 1977): 6–72. Though Samuel claims that American industry mechanized much faster than British manufacturers, the evidence presented here and in Hirsch's *Roots of the American Working Class* suggests that the gap was not as great as Samuel believes.

65. Sweatshops necessarily overlap with what will be described as artisan shops since both were quite small and are not easily distinguished from one another in the census manuscripts. There is reason to believe, however, that sweatshops or garrets were larger than artisan shops in this period. Freedley observes that they had as many as twelve workers and one can easily imagine the largest of them as twice that size. Thus it was decided to treat such operations as shops with six to twenty-five workers. See Freedley, *Philadelphia and Its Manufactures*, p. 188.

66. See, for example, ibid.; the letter of a garret boss in *P.L.*, Oct. 10, 1846; Elva Tooker, *Nathan Trotter, Philadelphia Merchant, 1783–1853* (rpt. New York: Arno Press, 1972), esp. p. 115; Commons, "American Shoemakers"; and letters of "sweated" workers in *F.T.R.*, May 14, 1864, and Feb. 11, 1865.

67. On the fitful pace of work in the needle trades see *P.L.*, Sept. 21, 1837. That many small producers did repair work is indicated in the manuscripts of the industrial census.

68. There is no easy way of estimating the proportion of outworkers in the various trades. Evidence from antebellum New York and Philadelphia indicates, however, that with the notable exception of Alan Dawley (see *Class and Community*) historians have vastly underestimated the role of outwork in the early period of industrialization. Thus, the largest clothing producers in New York and Philadelphia in 1849 and 1869, respectively, hired the overwhelming majority of their female employees at home under the putting-out system. See *Hunt's Merchants' Magazine* 20 (March, 1849): 347–48; and Isaac Vansant, ed., *Royal Road to Wealth: An Illustrated History of the Successful Business Houses of Philadelphia* (Philadelphia: Samuel Loage, n.d.), p. 144. On the frame tenders in the county see Hazard, *Register of Pennsylvania* 1 (January, 1828): 28; and Freedley, *Philadelphia and Its Manufactures*, pp. 239–49.

69. They earned less than $1.00 a day throughout this period. See Montgomery, "Shuttle and the Cross," p. 417.

70. Ibid., pp. 414–18.

71. Freedley, *Philadelphia and Its Manufactures*, p. 241–42.

72. See, for example, *P.L.*, March 2, 1846.

73. That workers in the smallest shops usually earned the best wages is disclosed in Laurie, et al., "Immigrants and Industry," table 8, p. 228.

74. Tabulated from U.S. Census, *Population Schedule, Philadelphia County.*

75. See, for example, Herbert G. Gutman, "Work, Culture, and Society in Industrializing America, 1815–1919," *American History Review* 78 (June, 1973): 531–87; and Montgomery, "Workers' Control."

76. *Penn.*, April 4, 1835.

77. *P.L.*, Oct. 10, 1846.

78. U.S. Census, *Population Schedule, Philadelphia County.* For the occupational distribution of nationality groups see Laurie, et al, "Immigrants and Industry," tables 12 and 13, pp. 235–38.

79. Warner, *Private City*, p. 71 also makes this point.

Chapter 2

1. J. Thomas Scharf and Thompson Westcott, *History of Philadelphia 1609–1884*, 3 vols. (Philadelphia: L. H. Evarts, 1884), 1. 623. See also *U.S.G.*, Aug. 13–14 and Dec. 8, 1828; *Poulson's Daily American Advertiser*, Aug. 14, 1828; and *Democratic Press*, Aug. 13, 1828.

2. Robert Adair, *Memoir of Rev. James Patterson, Late Pastor of the*

First Presbyterian Church, Northern Liberties, Philadelphia (Philadelphia: Henry Perkins, 1840), pp. 170–76.

3. On the origins of the Mechanics' Union see Lewis H. Arky, "The Mechanics' Union of Trade Associations and the Formation of the Philadelphia Working-men's Movement," *Pennsylvania Magazine of History and Biography* 76 (April, 1952): 142–76. The speech Heighton delivered on this occasion is *Operative, Principles*. The other speeches are: Fellow-laborer, *Address* and Unlettered Mechanic, *Address*.

4. These terms are obviously adapted from Alan Dawley and Paul Faler, "Workingclass Culture and Politics in the Industrial Revolutions: Sources of Royalism and Rebellion," *Journal of Social History* 9 (1976): 466–80.

5. See, for example, Adair, *Memoir of Rev. James Patterson*, pp. 100–01; Alfred P. Smith, *In Memorium, Abraham Oothout Halsey, D.D., 1798–1868: First Pastor of Eleventh, Now West-Arch Presbyterian Church* (Philadelphia: n.pub., 1897); and Rev. William Ramsey, Diary, 1822–1849, 23 vols., Presbyterian Historical Society, Philadelphia vol. 6, Aug. 25, 1826, and passim. (Since Rev. Ramsey neglected to number the volumes of his diary after vol. 10, the citations to such volumes will include the date only.)

6. Robert W. Doherty, "Social Basis of the Presbyterian Schism, 1837–1838: The Philadelphia Case," *Journal of Social History* 2 (Fall, 1968): 69–79; and George M. Marsden, *The Evangelical Mind and the New School Experience* (New Haven: Yale University Press, 1970).

7. The most recent and clearly superior study of the Second Great Awakening is Paul E. Johnson, *A Shopkeeper's Millenium: Society and Revivals in Rochester, New York, 1815–1837* (New York: Hill and Wang, 1978). See also Whitney R. Cross, *The Burned–over District: A Social and Intellectual History of Enthusiastic Religion in Western New York, 1800–1850* (Ithaca: Cornell University Press, 1950); T. Scott Miyakawa, *Protestants and Pioneers: Individualism and Conformity on the American Frontier* (Chicago: University of Chicago Press, 1964); and Donald G. Mathews, "The Second Great Awakening as an Organizing Process, 1780–1830: An Hypothesis," *American Quarterly* 21 (Spring, 1969): 23–43.

8. Quoted in Marsden, *Evangelical Mind*, p. 52.

9. On Barnes's career see Edward B. Davis, "Albert Barnes, 1798–1870: An Exponent of New School Presbyterianism" (Ph.D. diss., Princeton Theological Seminary, 1961).

10. Albert Barnes, *The Choice of a Profession: An Address Delivered before the Society of Inquiry in Amherst College, August 21, 1838* (Amherst, J.S. and C. Adams, 1838), p. 18.

11. Doherty, "Presbyterian Schism," p. 78.

12. See, for example, Barnes, *Choice of a Profession*, p. 11 and passim; and Barnes, *The Desire of Reputation: An Address before the Mercantile*

Library Company of Philadelphia, December 8, 1841 (Philadelphia: Henry Perkins, 1841).

13. Albert Barnes, *The Connexion of Temperance with Republican Freedom: An Oration Delivered on the 4th of July, 1835 before the Mechanics and Workingmens Temperance Society of the City and County of Philadelphia* (Philadelphia: Boyles and Benedict, 1835), p. 17.

14. Faler, "Cultural Aspects of the Industrial Revolution," pp. 367–68.

15. Doherty, "Presbyterian Schism"; and Marsden, *Evangelical Mind,* pp. 59–87.

16. Charles W. Ferguson, *Organizing to Beat the Devil: Methodists and the Making of America* (Garden City, N.Y.: Doubleday, 1971), pp. 355–56; Philip W. Ott, "The Mind of Early Methodism, 1800–1844" (Ph.D. diss., University of Pennsylvania, 1968); and Othniel O. Pendleton, Jr., "Temperance and the Evangelical Churches," *Journal of the Presbyterian Historical Society* 25 (March, 1947): 20–21.

17. Centennial Publishing Committee, *History of Ebenezer Methodist Church, Southwark* (Philadelphia: J.B. Lippincott, 1892), pp. 27–28.

18. Ferguson, *Organizing to Beat the Devil,* p. 357.

19. *Minutes of the Philadelphia Conference of the Methodist Episcopal Church, 1833–1846* (Philadelphia; n.pub., n.d.), p. 27.

20. *Minutes of the Philadelphia Conference of the Methodist Episcopal Church, Held at Philadelphia, March 30, 1836* (Philadelphia: James Harmsted, 1836), p. 16.

21. John Allen Krout, *Origins of Prohibition* (New York. Alfred A. Knopf, 1925), pp. 112–13.

22. Ferguson, *Organizing to Beat the Devil,* p. 359.

23. Rev. J. Kennady, *Sermon Delivered before the Sunday School Teachers' Union of the Methodist Episcopal Church of Philadelphia, September 29, 1839* (Philadelphia: Thomas U. Baker, 1839), p. 9.

24. Rev. Fitch Reed, "The Influence of Moral Principle, Secured by Early Culture, Essential to National Prosperity," in Shipley W. Willson and Ebenezer Ireson, eds., *The Methodist Preacher: Or, Monthly Sermons from Living Ministers* (Boston: J. Putnam, 1832), pp. 355–73. The quotation is on p. 367.

25. Compiled from *Minutes of the General Assembly of the Presbyterian Church in the United States of America from its Organization in A.D. 1798 to A.D. 1820* (Philadelphia: Presbyterian Board of Publication, 1847); *Minutes of the General Assembly of the Presbyterian Church, 1821–1835, 1836–1841, 1842–1847, 1848–1849* (Philadelphia: By the Stated Clerk of the Assembly, n.d.); *Minutes of the General Assembly of the Presbyterian Church in the United States of America (New School), 1838–1851* (New York: By the Stated Clerk of the Assembly, n.d.); *Minutes Taken at*

the Several Annual Conferences of the Methodist Episcopal Church, 1810–1820, 1821–1829 (Philadelphia: n.pub., n.d.); and *Minutes of the Philadelphia Conference of the Methodist Episcopal Church, 1833–1846, 1847–1864* (Philadelphia: n.pub., n.d.).

26. Pendleton, "Temperance and the Evangelical Churches," pp. 26–33. See also Pendleton, "The Influence of Evangelical Churches upon Humanitarian Reform: A Case Study Giving Particular Attention to Philadelphia, 1790–1840" (Ph.D. diss., University of Pennsylvania, 1945). The most recent works on temperance are Joseph R. Gusfield, *Symbolic Crusade: Status Politics and the American Temperance Movement* (Urbana: University of Illinois Press, 1963); and Norman Clark, *Deliver Us from Evil: An Interpretation of American Prohibition.* (New York: Norton, 1976).

27. On Hopkins see Marsden, *Evangelical Mind,* pp. 34–38 and 40–41.

28. See, for example, Clifford S. Griffin, "Religious Benevolence as Social Control, 1815–1860," *Mississippi Valley Historical Review* 44 (Dec., 1957): 423–44; and Griffin, *Their Brothers' Keepers: Moral Stewardship in the United States, 1800–1865* (New Brunswick, N.J.: Rutgers University Press, 1960).

29. Doherty, "Presbyterian Schism," pp. 76–78.

30. Hazard, *Register of Pennsylvania* 2 (Aug. 1828): 65–69. See also Benjamin Klebaner, "The Home Relief Controversy in Philadelphia, 1782–1861," *Pennsylvania Magazine of History and Biography* 76 (Oct., 1954): 413–23.

31. Quoted in Montgomery, "Shuttle and the Cross," p. 424.

32. On the Pennsylvania Society see Pendleton, "Influence of the Evangelical Churches," pp. 35–40. See also Barnes, *Connexion of Temperance with Republican Freedom:* and John J. Rumbarger. "The Social Origins of the Political Temperance Movement in the Reconstruction of American Society" (Ph.D. diss., University of Pennsylvania, 1968).

33. See Michael B. Katz, "Four Propositions about Social and Family Structure in Pre-industrial Society" (paper delivered before the Comparative Social Mobility Conference, Institute for Advanced Study, Princeton, N.J., July 15–17, 1972), esp. pp. 7–8.

34. See letter signed "Obediah," *M.F.P.,* Oct. 31, 1829, and editorials, July 10 and 24, 1830.

35. Rev. Thomas P. Hunt, *Life and Thoughts of Rev. Thomas P. Hunt* (Wilkes-Barre, Pa.: Robert Baur and Son, 1901), p. 300.

36. Benjamin T. Sewell, *Sorrow's Circuit, or Five Years' Experience in the Bedford Street Mission, Philadelphia* (Philadelphia: n.pub., 1859), p. 274.

37. American Temperance Union, *Report of the Executive Committee* (Philadelphia: L. Johnson, 1838), p. 5.

38. Sewell, *Sorrow's Circuit,* pp. 275–76. Nor was this an isolated incident of a worker's committing suicide in frustration over his inability to refrain from drink, unemployment, or more likely, a combination of both. See *D.S.,* Jan. 3, 1845, June 3 and 15, 1845, and March 29, 1848.

39. On the enrollment in the local temperance movement see Pendleton, "Temperance and the Evangelical Churches," p. 35.

40. The names of the officers of the Pennsylvania Society were collected from Pendleton, "Influence of the Evangelical Churches upon Humanitarian Reform" and Rumbarger, "Social Origins of the Political Temperance Movement," and traced to the city directories. The leadership included six ministers, twelve physicians, and twenty-four merchants, manufacturers, and lawyers. The Mechanics' and Workingmen's Society did not boast the names of wealthy merchants or professionals, but it did have a healthy representation of rising industrialists in addition to Baldwin and Vaughan. See Barnes, *Connexion of Temperance with Republican Freedom.*

41. Johnson, *Shopkeeper's Millenium,* p. 119, finds the same pattern in Rochester where "A full 42 percent of the men who joined churches between 1832 and 1837 were journeymen craftsmen."

42. On Patterson see Adair, *Memoir of Rev. James Patterson,* pp. 25–44. See also ibid., pp. 321–34, for a sketch of Rev. Albert Judson. On Halsey see Smith, *Alfred O. Halsey;* on Ramsey see Ramsey, Diary, vol. 1, passim.

43. See Ramsey, Diary, vol. 5, Nov. 3, 1826; and A. O. Halsey to John Johnson, March 11, 1828, Miscellaneous Papers, Presbyterian Historical Society, Philadelphia. See also Adair, *Memoir of Rev. James Patterson,* p. 105.

44. Z. Smith to Halsey, Jan. 9, 1827, Miscellaneous Papers; Ramsey, Diary, vol. 5, Jan. 23, 1826, and vol. 6, July 29, 1829; and Young Men's Association of the First Presbyterian Church, *Annual Report* (Philadelphia: I. Ashmead, 1839).

45. Adair, *Memoir of Rev. James Patterson,* p. 158.

46. A. O. Halsey to John Johnston, March 11, 1828, Miscellaneous Papers.

47. Ramsey, Diary, vol. 6, July 25, 1826.

48. Adair, *Memoir of Rev. James Patterson,* p. 134.

49. Ibid., pp. 59–61, 105–06, and 170–76.

50. Ibid., p. xi.

51. Ramsey, Diary, vol. 3, April 11, 1824.

52. Ibid., vol. 7, July 13, 1828.

53. Adair, *Memoir of Rev. James Patterson,* pp. 126–47. The quotation is on p. 143. See also Ramsey, Diary, vol. 6, Feb. 2, 1828; vol. 8, Sept. 8, 1828; and vol. 9, May 4, 1830.

54. Adair, *Memoir of Rev. James Patterson,* p. 143.

55. Ramsey, Diary, vol. 7, Sept. 7, 1828.

56. Adair, *Memoir of Rev. James Patterson,* pp. 66–67.

57. See, for example, First Presbyterian Congregation of Kensington, Session Books, 1814–1845, 1843–1859, Presbyterian Historical Society, Philadelphia, June 2, 1821, June 2, 1827, June 23, 1828, and passim; Ramsey, Diary, vol. 8, Nov. 19, 1829, and passim; and Central Presbyterian Church in Northern Liberties, Minutes of the Session, 1832–1852, Presbyterian Historical Society, Philadelphia, Nov. 28, 1832, Nov. 7 and 21, 1832, June 8, 1836, and May 3, 1838.

58. Adair, *Memoir of Rev. James Patterson,* p. 146.

59. Stuart M. Blumin, "Mobility in a Nineteenth-century American City: Philadelphia, 1820–1860" (unpub. Ph.D. diss., University of Pennsylvania, 1968), pp. 103–9.

60. Paul Johnson finds that a comparable percentage of evangelical journeymen in Rochester improved their social standing, though his study terminates in 1837. See Johnson, *Shopkeeper's Millenium,* pp. 123–24.

61. Doherty, "Presbyterian Schism," p. 75.

62. U.S. Census, *Industrial Schedule, Southwark.*

63. Ramsey complained that he was "frequently sent for by those who attended no place of worship and perhaps think of me only when ill" (Diary, vol. 6, Aug. 24, 1826). For instances of conversion encouraged by illness, the death of loved ones, and the like see ibid., vol. 7, June 13–14, 1828; vol. 8, Sept. 12, 1829; and vol. 9, June 12, 1830. See also Adair, *Memoir of Rev. James Patterson,* pp. 63 and 93.

64. Ramsey, Diary, vol. 6, Nov. 26–27, 1826.

65. See, for example, Adair, *Memoir of Rev. James Patterson,* pp. 45–49 and 105–06; and Ramsey, Diary, vol. 4, Jan. 26, 1825; vol. 7, Feb. 11, 1829; and vol. 9, April 4, 1830. For an intimate portrait of upper-class evangelical women see Wallace, *Rockdale,* pp. 22–32, 312–17, and 459–67. For the revivalist efforts of middle-class women see Carol Smith Rosenberg, *Religion and the Rise of the American City: The New York City Mission Movement: 1812–1870* (Ithaca: Cornell University Press, 1971), pp. 97–124; and Barbara Welter, "The Feminization of American Religion, 1800–1860," in Mary Hartman and Lois Banner, eds., *Clio's Consciousness Raised: New Perspectives on the History of Women* (New York: Harper and Row, 1974), pp. 137–57.

66. See, for example, First Presbyterian Church in Southwark Minutes, 1830–1840; and Cedar Street Presbyterian Church, Records of the Session, 1838–1870, Presbyterian Historical Society, Philadelphia.

67. Johnson, *Shopkeeper's Millenium,* pp. 33–34 finds that evangelical converts were more residentially stable than nonchurch members between

1830 and 1834, and thus deemphasizes the connection between rural-urban migration and evangelical instincts. A close reading of his evidence suggests, however, that the persistence rates of revivalist converts (79) and nonchurch members (67) are not strikingly different. My argument is not that in-migration alone predisposed an individual to evangelicalism, but that it was one of three interacting factors, the others being career mobility and the nature of work.

68. *G.T.,* May 20, 1835.

69. Johnson, *Shopkeeper's Millenium,* pp. 104–06, notes that employers in the more advanced work settings were more likely to become evangelized than those who ran traditional workshops. I have extended this argument to the workers in the employ of such owners.

70. Johnson's remarkably thorough research on Rochester led him to play down the possibility that evangelized workers succeeded because they internalized the Protestant work ethic and to emphasize the material ties between journeymen and employers of the same congregation. He finds that such employers "sponsored" the careers of workingmen in their congregations by hiring them over nonchurch workers, bringing them into their firms as partners, and lending money in hard times to those who achieved employer status, as well as publicly endorsing their products. See ibid., pp. 124–28. Sources do not disclose whether wealthier evangelicals in Philadelphia's suburban churches assisted their humbler brothers in similar ways, but it is unlikely that they did much beyond hiring them since there were very few prestigious members of these churches. That is, the churches under analysis here were not as class integrated as those studied by Johnson.

71. See, for example, Adair, *Memoir of Rev. James Patterson,* pp. 49–51, 66–69, and 105–06; Ramsey, Diary, vol. 7, June 13–14, 1828, and Feb. 10, 1829, and passim; and First Presbyterian church in Southwark, Trustees Minutes, 1818–1832, Presbyterian Historical Society, Philadelphia.

72. See letter signed "True American," *U.S.G.,* Oct. 8, 1836. See also letter signed "Pater Familias," ibid., March 5, 1836.

Chapter 3

1. James W. Alexander [Charles Quill], *The American Mechanic* (Philadelphia: Henry Perkins, 1838), pp.. 66–67. See also Alexander, *The Working Man* (Philadelphia: Perkins and Purvis, 1843).

2. Alexander, *American Mechanic,* pp. 63–68. For examples of working-class recreation in this period see *U.S.G.,* August 14, 1828; letter signed "I Am, Gentlemen, with Great Respect, a Working Man," *M.F.P.,* April 8, 1831; *Fountain,* Feb. 24, 1838; and *P.L.,* June 6, 1843. See also R. Sean Wilentz, "Ritual, Republicanism, and the Artisans of Jacksonian New York

City" (paper delivered at the Annual Meeting of the Organization of American Historians, New York, April 14, 1978).

3. Alexander, *American Mechanic,* p. 87. See also William Cobbett, *A Year's Residence in the United States of America* 1819 (rpt., Cardondale: Southern Illinois University Press, 1964), pp. 205–06.

4. See, for example, J. Thomas Scharf and Thompson Westcott, *History of Philadelphia, 1609–1884,* 3 vols. (Philadelphia: L. H. Everts, 1884), 2: 748–58; *P.L.,* Aug. 14, 1837; and *D.S.,* June 6, 1846.

5. For an amusing but generally accurate analysis of the drinking habits of elites and workers see *Fountain,* Feb. 24, 1838. See also Rev. Thomas P. Hunt, *Jesse Jackson and His Times* (Philadelphia: Griffith and Simon, 1845), pp. 20–21; and *P.L.,* April 17,1839. For an overview of traditional attitudes toward drink see Joseph R. Gusfield, *Symbolic Crusade: Status Politics and the American Temperance Movement* (Urbana: University of Illinois Press, 1963), pp. 36–39.

6. Scharf and Westcott, *History of Philadelphia,* 2: 987.

7. Ibid., 2: 986.

8. *P.L.,* Nov. 24, 1851. See also Scharf and Westcott, *History of Philadelphia* 2: 941; and *D.S.,* March 5, 1846.

9. Society of Friends, *Statistical Inquiry into the Condition of the People of Colour, of the City and Districts of Philadelphia* (Philadelphia: Kite and Walton, 1849), p. 39. See also *P.L.,* June 23, 1848, and Nov. 9, 1849.

10. Scharf and Westcott, *History of Philadelphia,* 2: 941–42. See also *P.L.,* May 4, 1836, and March 29, 1838.

11. Alexander, *American Mechanic,* pp. 12–15, 21–22, and 61–67. See also *P.L.,* April 17, 1839; and *D.S.,* Sept. 21, 1849.

12. Pennsylvania Society for Discouraging the Use of Ardent Spirits, *Anniversary Report of the Board of Managers* (Philadelphia: n.pub., 1831), pp. 22–23.

13. Benjamin J. Sewell, *Sorrow's Circuit, or Five Years' Experience in the Bedford Street Mission, Philadelphia* (Philadelphia: n.pub. 1859), p. 273.

14. For an overview of the Old School's social perspective see Doherty, "Social Basis of the Presbyterian Schism, 1837–1838: The Philadelphia Case," *Journal of Social History* 2 (Fall, 1968): 79. See also "Report of the General Assembly of the Presbyterian Church" in *D.S.,* June 7, 1848.

15. See Herbert G. Gutman, "Work, Culture, and Society in Industrializing America, 1815–1919," *American Historical Review* 78 (June, 1973): esp. 543–46 and 563–64. See also *A Full and Accurate Report of the Trial for Riot before the Mayor's Court of Philadelphia . . . Arising Out of a Protestant Procession* (Philadelphia: Jesper Harding, 1831); and *E. B.,* June 11, 1855.

16. See, for example, *U.S.G.,* Aug. 14, 1828; and *P.L.,* June 6, 1843.

17. *Report of the Trial,* p. 44.

18. Hunt, *Jesse Jackson,* p. 11.

19. See *Fountain,* Feb. 24, 1838.

20. Bruce Laurie, "Fire Companies and Gangs in Southwark: The 1840s," in Allen F. Davis and Mark H. Haller, eds., *The Peoples of Philadelphia: A History of Ethnic Groups and Lower-class Life, 1790–1940* (Philadelphia: Temple University Press, 1973), p. 76; Nicholas B. Wainwright, ed., *A Philadelphia Perspective: The Diary of Sidney George Fisher, 1834–1871* (Philadelphia: Historical Society of Pennsylvania, 1967), p. 122; Ellis P. Oberholtzer, *Philadelphia: A History of the City and Its People,* 4 vols. (Philadelphia: S. J. Clark, 1911) 2: 89–90; and Andrew Neilly, "The Violent Volunteers: A History of the Philadelphia Volunteer Fire Department, 1736–1871" (Ph.D. diss., University of Pennsylvania, 1959), p. 20.

21. Scharf and Westcott, *History of Philadelphia,* 3: 1912. See also Elizabeth M. Geffen, "Violence in Philadelphia in the 1840s and 1850s," *Pennsylvania History* 36 (October, 1969): 406.

22. For example, fully 85 percent of the members of Southwark's Niagara Hose Company who were found in the census of 1850 were journeymen without real property. The remaining 15 percent were master craftsmen, grocers, and tavern owners, and most of them were officers. See Niagara Hose Company, Minute Books, 1833–1848, 1848–1864 Historical Society of Pennsylvania, Philadelphia; city directories; and U.S. Census, *Population Schedule, Southwark.* The social profiles of several other Southwark companies closely resembled that of the Niagara. See Laurie, "Fire Companies and Gangs," n. 29, pp. 85–86. It would be interesting to plot the occupational mobility and property holdings of such traditionalists from the 1830s to 1850, but this is not possible. Membership lists for the 1830s are rare and those that are available pertain to companies situated in suburban areas which were either covered poorly or ignored entirely in the city directories. Still, it should be obvious that in 1850, and probably in the 1830s, these traditionalists were not as prestigious as the revivalists or the radicals.

23. Borough of Manayunk, Council Minutes, 1840–1852, 1852–1854 2 vols., Historical Society of Pennsylvania, Philadelphia vol. 1, April 23, and Sept. 5, 1843, and vol. 2, June 28, 1854.

24. For the locations of the companies see Scharf and Westcott, *History of Philadelphia,* 3: 1911–12.

25. Frank H. Schell, "Old Volunteer Fire Laddies, the Famous, Fast, Faithful, Fistic, Fire Fighters of Bygone Days," Frank H. Schell Papers, Historical Society of Pennsylvania, Philadelphia, ch. 4, p. 2.

26. Ibid. See also a retrospective on the county fire department in *P.L.* Sept. 13, 1903; and Neilly, "Violent Volunteers," ch. 9.

27. *P.L.,* Jan. 14, 1853.

28. Ibid.

29. Quoted in Oberholtzer, *Philadelphia,* 2: 89.

30. There is some evidence, however, that women did drink in the grog shops of the city's "skid row." See Sewell, *Sorrow's Circuit,* passim.

31. Schell, "Old Volunteer Fire Laddies," ch. 2, p. 3.

32. See the collection of firemen's memorabilia in the Atwater-Kent Museum, Philadelphia.

33. See Mark H. Haller, "Recurring Themes," in Davis and Haller, eds., *Peoples of Philadelphia,* p. 286.

34. The following account is based on coverage in Hazard, *Register of Pennsylvania* 14 (Aug. 23, 1834) and 14 (Sept. 27, 1834). Both editions reprinted items published in other local newspapers.

35. See, for example, Leonard L. Richards, *"Gentlemen of Property and Standing": Anti-abolitionist Mobs in Jacksonian America* (New York: Oxford University Press, 1970).

36. Hazard, *Register of Pennsylvania* 14 (Aug. 23, 1834).

37. Ibid. Lists and names and addresses of 17 men who were arrested in the early stage of the riot. Eight of them were located in the city directories and of these three were weavers, two were laborers, and the remaining three were listed as cabinetmaker, limeburner, and house painter.

38. Ibid.

39. "The Diving Bell," for example, was an integrated tavern, and the houses of two employers who evidently hired Blacks were attacked with singular fury.

40. Theodore Hershberg, "Free Blacks in Antebellum Philadelphia: A Study of Ex-slaves, Freeborn, and Socioeconomic Decline," *Journal of Social History* 5 (Winter, 1971–72): 183–209, and esp. 191–92.

41. Hazard, *Register of Pennsylvania* 14 (Aug. 23, 1834).

42. Ibid., (Sept. 27, 1834).

Chapter 4

1. Robert Adair, *Memoir of Rev. James Patterson, Late Pastor of the First Presbyterian Church, Northern Liberties, Philadelphia* (Philadelphia: Henry Perkins, 1840), pp. 177–81. The best study of cholera is still Charles E. Rosenberg, *The Cholera Years: The United States in 1832, 1849, and 1866* (Chicago: University of Chicago Press, 1962).

2. *Lib.,* July 14, 1832.

3. Ibid.

4. Eric Foner, *Tom Paine and Revolutionary America* (New York: Oxford University Press, 1976), p. 261. See also Edward Pessen, *Most*

Uncommon Jacksonians: The Radical Leaders of the Early Labor Movement (Albany: State University of New York Press, 1967), p. 111.

5. Anthony F. C. Wallace, *Rockdale: The Growth of an American Village in the Early Industrial Revolution* (New York: Alfred A. Knopf, 1978), pp. 243–95. Only three pages, 289–92, of this lengthy section are dedicated to worker rationalists.

6. See Sidney Ahlstrom, *A Religious History of the American People* (New Haven: Yale University Press, 1972), pp. 356–58, 391–93, and 481–83; John H. Gihon, *A Review of the Sermon against Universal Salvation* (Philadelphia: By the author, 1841); Abel Thomas, *A Century of Universalism in Philadelphia and New York: With Sketches of Its History in Reading, Hightstown, Brooklyn, and Elsewhere* (Philadelphia: Collins, 1872), esp. pp. 162–66 and 176–86; and *Lib.,* Aug. 17, 1833.

7. Letter signed "A.M.," *Lib.,* July 7, 1832.

8. J. Thomas Scharf and Thompson Westcott, *History of Philadelphia, 1609–1884,* 3 vols. (Philadelphia: L. H. Everts, 1884), 2: 1445.

9. See, for example, *T.R.,* Aug. 29 and Sept. 1 and 29, 1835; see also July 11, 1835.

10. Scharf and Westcott, *History of Philadelphia,* 2: 1442–48; and Thomas, *Century of Universalism,* pp. 63–64 and 104–05.

11. On the Society of Liberal Friends see letter signed "A Liberal Friend," *M.F.P.,* June 7, 1828; and *Lib.,* March 22, 1834. On the Society of Free Enquirers see *T.R.,* Feb. 6 and Sept. 3, 1836. On the Liberal Union which was either an independent group or the Society of Free Enquirers under another name see *P.L.,* Dec. 13, 1838. In addition to these groups there was one or more German-speaking organizations. See ch. 8, pp. 165–66. Another Free Thought newspaper, *The Correspondent,* appeared during this period, but copies have not survived.

12. These figures are based on projections of membership in churches and groups that left no records, and on estimates of the membership of some organizations that did leave records as reflected in First Universalist Church, Minute Book, 1820–1842, Historical Society of Pennsylvania, Philadelphia; and Second Universalist Church, Minute Book, 1820–1854, Historical Society of Pennsylvania, Philadelphia; Edward Thompson, *Oration on the Ninety-eight Anniversary of the Birth Day of Thomas Paine, at the Military Hall, before the Society of Free Enquirers, January 29, 1834* (Philadelphia: Thomas Clark, 1834); and *T.R.,* Feb. 6, 1837, and Feb. 18, 1837.

13. See, for example, *Lib.,* Oct. 18 and Nov. 22, 1834, and May 6 and 15, 1835.

14. *T.R.,* Feb. 6, 1836. See also Feb. 18, 1837; and Thompson, *Oration.*

15. See letters signed "Scrutator," *T.R.,* Sept. 1 and 29, 1835.

16. Ibid., May 28, 1836; and Thomas, *Century of Universalism*, p. 121.

17. Quoted in Pessen, *Most Uncommon Jacksonians*, p. 86.

18. See, for example, Gihon, *Sermon against Universal Salvation*, pp. 23–24; *Gazetteer*, Nov. 22, 1824; and letter signed "Paul," *M.F.P.*, May 24, 1828.

19. Compare the list of incorporators in *The Charter, Articles of Faith, Constitution, and By-laws of the First Universalist Church* (Philadelphia: Gihon, Fairchild, 1842) with the names on the register of First Universalist Church, Minute Book.

20. Most leaders of the General Trades' Union, for example, were rationalists, and one of their number answered a critic who accused his organization of being a foreign import with a roster of the officers showing that all but one, John Ferral, an Irish immigrant, were native-born Americans. See letter signed "Sherman," *U.S.G.*, April 6, 1836.

21. See, for example, R. S. Neale, *Class and Ideology in the Nineteenth Century* (London: Routledge and Kegan Paul, 1972), pp. 15–40; William H. Sewell, Jr., "The Working Class of Marseille Under the Second Republic: Social Structure and Political Behavior," in Peter N. Stearns and Daniel J. Walkowitz, eds., *Workers in the Industrial Revolution* (New Brunswick: Transaction Books, 1974), pp. 75–116; and Joan W. Scott, *The Glassworkers of Carmaux: French Craftsmen and Political Action in a Nineteenty-century City* (Cambridge: Harvard University Press, 1974).

22. Louis H. Arky, "The Mechanics' Union of Trade Associations and the Formation of the Philadelphia Working-men's Movement," *Pennsylvania Magazine of History and Biography* 76 (April, 1952): 144.

23. On Heighton's English counterparts see E. P. Thompson, *Making of the English Working Class* (pbk. ed; New York: Vintage, 1966), pp. 17–103; and Trygve Tholfsen, *Working-class Radicalism in Mid-victorian Britain* (New York: Columbia University Press, 1977), pp. 25–82.

24. Quoted in Wallace, *Rockdale*, p. 290.

25. See Chapter 2.

26. Unlettered Mechanic, *Address*, p. 4. Most contemporary radicals, of course, did not consider unskilled laborers to be producers.

27. Ibid.

28. Fellow-labourer, *Address*, p. 14.

29. Ibid., p. 15.

30. Ibid.

31. Unlettered Mechanic, *Address*, p. 5.

32. Letter signed "Sherman," *U.S.G.*, April 6, 1836.

33. *T.R.*, July 11, 1835. See also Fellow-labourer, *Address*, pp. 14–25.

34. *M.F.P.*, Aug. 23, 1828.

35. See, for example, ibid., Jan. 24 and May 5, 1829; *Lib.,* May 23 and June 20, 1835; and *T.R.,* June 9, 1832, and Feb. 13, 1835.

36. *Lib.,* Dec. 8, 1832. See also *T.R.,* July 11, 1835.

37. Letter signed "J.P.," *Lib.,* March 9, 1833.

38. *Gazetteer,* Nov. 24, 1824. See also Aug. 8, 1824; letter signed *"Equity," M.F.P.,* Dec. 20, 1828; letter signed "An Operative," *M.F.P.,* June 27, 1829; and *T.R.,* July 11, 1835.

39. *Lib.,* June 14, 1834.

40. Gihon, *Sermon against Universal Salvation,* p. 27.

41. *Lib.,* May 18, 1833.

42. See letter signed "Edward," *M.F.P.,* July 23, 1828. See also letter signed "J.A.M.C.," April 26, 1828, and letter signed "Rational Recreation," July 30, 1828.

43. Gihon, *Serman against Universal Salvation,* p. 27.

44. *T.R.,* August 15, 1835. See also May 9, 1835; *Lib.,* Jan. 26, 1833, and July 29, 1835.

45. Letter signed "Edward," *M.F.P.,* Aug. 16, 1828.

46. Ibid., Jan. 9, 1830.

47. See Wilentz, "Ritual, Republicanism, and the Artisans of Jacksonian New York City" (paper delivered at the Annual Meeting of the Organization of American Historians, New York, April 14, 1978). For an example of a mechanics' patriotic procession in Philadelphia see *U.S.G.,* July 18 and 24, 1843.

48. See, for example, *Radical Reformer and Working Man's Advocate,* July 4, 1835.

49. Compare the letters written by "Franklin" and "Sherman" in *U.S.G.,* March and April, 1836.

50. Wilentz, "Ritual, Republicanism, and the Artisans of Jacksonian New York City," esp. pp. 14–16, interprets republicanism in this light, but emphasizes the consensus view of it. He also regards it as an ambiguous ideology that propelled workers against employers while it limited the character of their protest, a point which we shall return to in assessing the political importance of the labor theory of value. See also Dawley, *Class and Community: The Industrial Revolution in Lynn* (Cambridge: Harvard University Press, 1976), pp. 1–3, 9–10, 191–93, and 226–27, for a discussion of the economic import of "equal rights," the Lynn shoemakers' rendition of republicanism.

Chapter 5

1. See Edward Pessen, *Most Uncommon Jacksonians; The Radical Leaders of the Early Labor Movement* (Albany: State University of New

York Press, 1967), pp. 3–51; Lewis H. Arky, "The Mechanics' Union of Trade Associations and the Formation of the Philadelphia Working-men's Movement," *Pennsylvania Magazine of History and Biography* 76 (1952): 142–76; John R. Commons, et al., *History of Labour in the United States,* 4 vols. (New York: Macmillan, 1918–1935), 1: 374–80 and 384–93; William A. Sullivan, *The Industrial Worker in Pennsylvania, 1800–1840* (Harrisburg: Pennsylvania Historical and Museum Commission, 1955) pp. 142–76 and 181–93; Sullivan, "Did Labor Support Andrew Jackson?" *Political Science Quarterly* 62 (Dec. 1947): 569–80; Sullivan, "Philadelphia Labor during the Jackson Era," *Pennsylvania History* 15 (Oct. 1948): 305–320; and Leonard Bernstein, "The Working People of Philadelphia from Colonial Times to the General Strike of 1835," *Pennsylvania Magazine of History and Biography* 74 (July 1950): 322–39.

2. *Constitution and By-laws of the Association of Journeymen Hatters of the City and County of Philadelphia, Instituted in 1824* (Philadelphia: William P. Finn, 1834), pp. 15–16.

3. Marcus T. C. Gould [recorder], *Trial of Twenty-four Journeymen Tailors, Charged with a Conspiracy: Before the Mayor's Court of the City of Philadelphia, September Sessions, 1827* (Philadelphia: n.pub., 1827), pp. 235–6.

4. *M.F.P.,* Dec. 20–27, 1828.

5. The most important veterans of the 1820s were William English and Edward Penniman. For their attitudes towards mixing politics with trade unionism see John R. Commons, et al., *Documentary History of American Industrial Society,* 10 vols. (rpt., New York: Russell and Rusell, 1958), 6: 214–15.

6. Commons, et al., *History of Labour,* 1: 373–80; Commons, *Documentary History,* 5: 325–28, 375, and 387–88; and letter signed "Sherman," *U.S.G.,* April 2, 1836.

7. Commons, et al., *Documentary History,* 5: 345–47. The quotation is on p. 346.

8. Letter signed "J.C.," *Penn.,* Feb. 9, 1836.

9. Letter signed "Sherman," *U.S.G.,* April 4, 1836.

10. Bruce Laurie, "The Working People of Philadelphia, 1827–1853" (Ph.D. diss., University of Pittsburgh, 1971), app. A.

11. Commons, et al., *Documentary History,* 5: 355, 360–61, 371–73, 379–80, and 390.

12. *U.S.G.,* June 4, 1835.

13. Committee of Boston Mechanics, *Proceedings of the Government and Citizens of Philadelphia, on the Reduction of the Hours of Labor, and Increase of Wages* (Boston: Committee of Boston Mechanics, 1835).

14. See, for example, *U.S.G.,* Oct. 2, 1835; and *Penn.,* April 4, 1835.

15. See, Commons, et al., *Documentary History*, 5: 351–52, 354, 356 and 383.

16. *U.S.G.*, Sept. 24, 1836.

17. Albert Barnes, *The Connexion of Temperance with Republican Freedom: An Oration Delivered on the 4th of July, 1835, before the Mechanics and Workingmens Temperance Society of the City and County of Philadelphia* (Philadelphia: Boyles and Benedict, 1835), p. 27.

18. *Penn.*, June 4, 1835.

19. See ibid., June 4, 5, 8, and 9, 1835; Committee of Boston Mechanics, *Proceedings of the Government and Citizens of Philadelphia;* Leonard Bernstein, "Working People of Philadelphia," pp. 366–69; and Sullivan, *The Industrial Worker in Pennsylvania*, pp. 134–37.

20. J. Thomas Scharf and Thompson Westcott, *History of Philadelphia, 1609–1884*, 3 vols. (Philadelphia: L. H. Everts, 1884), 1: 641.

21. Quoted in Commons, et al., *History of Labour*, 1: 391.

22. Cited in Sullivan, *Industrial Worker in Pennsylvania*, p. 135.

23. *Penn.*, June 18, 24, Aug. 4, and Oct. 17, 1835.

24. Ibid., June 6, 8, and 9, 1835.

25. Commons, et al., *Documentary History*, 6: 41.

26. Quoted in Commons, et al., *History of Labour*, 1: 362.

27. *M.F.P.*, Dec. 17, 1829.

28. Commons, et al., *Documentary History*, 5: 391.

29. Letter signed "Sherman," *U.S.G.*, April 6, 1836.

30. *Penn.*, May 15, 1834. See also *Penn.*, March 19, 1834; and Sullivan, *Industrial Worker in Pennsylvania*, p. 148.

31. *Penn.*, July 26, 1834.

32. The Democrats polled between 55 and 65 percent of the vote in these districts. Spring Garden and Northern Liberties returned slight Whig majorities in the early thirties, but shifted to the Democratic fold by the end of the decade.

33. Commons, et al. *Documentary History*, 5: 355.

34. Ibid., 6: 252–53. See also 6: 281–91.

35. See, for example, Barbara Welter, "The Cult of True Womanhood, 1820–1860," *American Quarterly* 18 (Summer, 1966): 151–74. See also Nancy F. Cott, *The Bonds of Womanhood: "Woman's Sphere" in New England, 1780–1835* (New Haven: Yale University Press, 1977), pp. 197–206.

36. See, for example, *Lib.*, March 22 and April 19, 1834; and *T.R.*, Sept. 10, 1836, and Jan. 28, 1837.

37. *T.R.*, Feb. 18, 1837.

38. *Penn.*, March 19 and May 15, 1834; and Commons, et al., *Documentary History*, 5: 355.

39. *Penn.*, March 23, 1836. See also Sept. 24 and Dec. 31, 1835.

40. Committee of Boston Mechanics, *Proceedings of the Government and Citizens of Philadelphia*, p. 9.

41. *U.S.G.,* Aug. 3, 1835. For additional testimony on the oratorical skills of radical workingmen see *Democratic Press,* July 12, 1828; and James W. Alexander [Charles Quill], *The American Mechanic* (Philadelphia: Henry Perkins, 1838), pp. 225–26.

42. *P.L.,* June 10, 1836.

43. Letter signed "Sherman," *U.S.G.,* April 6, 1836.

44. Letter signed "A Perceiver," *G.T.,* Oct. 30, 1833.

45. E. P. Thompson, *The Making of the English Working Class* (pbk. ed.; New York: Vintage, 1966), pp. 102–85.

46. Commons, et al., *Documentary History,* 5: 373. For other such disputes see 5: 371–73; and Sullivan, *Industrial Worker in Pennsylvania,* pp. 109–10.

47. *An Address to the Workingmen of the City and County of Philadelphia* (Philadelphia: Mifflin and Perry, 1839).

48. *U.S.G.,* April 5, 1836.

49. Commons, et al., *Documentary History,* 5: 383.

50. *U.S.G.,* April 5, 1836.

51. *Penn.,* Jan. 15, Feb. 12, and March 12, 1836. See also Sullivan, *Industrial Worker in Pennsylvania,* pp. 138–39.

52. *Penn.,* Feb. 5, 1836.

53. Commons, et al., *Documentary History,* 5: 377 and 384.

54. *Penn.,* Nov. 2, 1836.

55. Sullivan, *Industrial Worker in Pennsylvania,* p. 156.

56. Letter signed "J.C.," *U.S.G.,* Sept. 1, 1836.

57. Commons, et al., *History of Labour,* 1: 377–79.

58. *Penn.,* Feb. 9, 1836.

59. See letters signed "Sherman," *U.S.G.,* April 1 and 4, 1836. See also *P.L.,* Sept. 26, Oct. 19, and Nov. 17, 1837.

60. Letter signed "An Observer," *G.T.,* Nov. 27, 1833.

61. See, for example, Alexander, *American Mechanic,* pp. 225–26.

62. See, for example, *Penn.,* March 17 and 28, 1836; and Sullivan, *Industrial Worker in Pennsylvania,* p. 142.

63. Letter signed "Sherman," *U.S.G.,* April 2, 1836; and Commons, *Documentary History,* 5: 375 and 377–78.

64. See, for example, *U.S.G.,* March 3, April 2, 8, 9, and 20, and Oct. 11, 1836.

65. Ibid., Oct. 8, 1836.

66. Letter signed "Sherman," *U.S.G.,* April 4, 1836.

67. On the cordwainers see *P.L.,* June 10, 1836; on the saddlers see

Commons, et al., *Documentary History,* 5: 386; on the tailors and other tradesmen see 6: 58–62; on the weavers see *P.L.,* Nov. 25, 1836.

68. Commons, et al., *Documentary History,* 5: 357–58.

69. Ibid., 6: 60.

70. *P.L.,* Dec. 20, 1838.

71. See, for example, ibid., Feb. 14, March 6 and 25, April 5, Oct. 21, and Nov. 7, 1837. See also Commons, et al., *Documentary History,* 6: 58–65; and Commons, et al., *History of Labour,* 1: 468–69.

72. *P.L.,* May 17, 1837.

73. Ibid., Aug. 12, 1837.

74. Ibid., April 29, Sept. 29, and Nov. 28, 1837.

75. Ibid., Jan. 7, 1839. See also Jan. 25, 1839. Aug. 14, 1841, Feb. 21, 1842, and June 6, 1842.

76. Letter signed "A Workingman," Dec. 1, 1838.

Chapter 6

1. Ogden W. Niles, ed., *Niles' National Register,* 5th ser., vols. 4–14 (Washington, D.C.: By the editor, 1837–1843), vol. 5 (Sept. 22, 1838), p. 51.

2. Nicholas B. Wainwright, ed., *A Philadelphia Perspective: The Diary of Sidney George Fisher, 1834–1871* (Philadelphia: Historical Society of Pennsylvania, 1967), pp. 134–35.

3. *P.L.,* July 12, 1842. See also Jan. 14, 1842.

4. See, for example, Richard A. McLeod, "The Philadelphia Artisan, 1828–1850" (Ph.D. diss., University of Missouri, 1971), table 1, p. 43.

5. *P.L.,* Jan. 6, 1843.

6. *Penn.,* May 26, 1837.

7. *U.S.G.,* May 16 and 19, 1837. See also *Penn.,* May 4, 17, and 21, 1838; and *P.L.,* Oct. 16, 1839.

8. *U.S.G.,* May 19, 1837.

9. *Ibid.,* Sept. 1, 1836.

10. John R. Commons, et al., *Documentary History of American Industrial Society,* 10 vols. (rpt., New York: Russell and Russell, 1958), 6: 216.

11. For biographical sketches of the G.T.U. leadership see Bruce Laurie, "The Working People of Philadelphia, 1827–1853" (Ph.D. diss., University of Pittsburgh, 1971), app. A.

12. In this respect the Pennsylvania Democracy resembled its counterpart in other northern states. See Lee Benson, *The Concept of Jacksonian Democracy: New York as a Test Case* (Princeton: Princeton Univerity Press, 1961), esp. pp. 216–53; and Ronald P. Formisano, *The Birth of Mass Political Parties: Michigan, 1827–1861* (Princeton: Princeton University

Press, 1971), esp. pp. 56–80. On Pennsylvania politics in this period see Lewis Hartz, *Economic Policy and Democratic Thought: Pennsylvania 1776–1860* (pbk. ed., Chicago: Quadrangle Books, 1968). On the Democracy's support for "freedom of conscience" and opposition to evangelical extremism see *S.T.,* June 23 and 29, 1843.

13. See Charles M. Snyder, *The Jacksonian Heritage: Pennsylvania Politics, 1833–1848* (Harrisburg: Pennsylvania Historical and Museum Commission, 1958), pp. 75–95; and Hartz, *Economic Policy,* pp. 51–81.

14. Snyder, *Jacksonian Heritage,* pp. 50–67 and 82–95; and Hartz, *Economic Policy,* pp. 69–81 and 187–204.

15. Snyder, *Jacksonian Heritage,* pp. 120–21.

16. See, for example, *Penn.,* June 8 and 9, 1835, Nov. 17, 1836, and Jan. 17, 1837.

17. Laurie, "Working People of Philadelphia," app. A.

18. See *Penn.,* June 11, Aug. 16, 1835; and April 7, 8, 12, July 23, 26, Aug. 22, and Sept. 21, 24, 1836. Sam Bass Warner, Jr., *The Private City; Philadelphia in Three Periods of Its Growth* (Philadelphia: University of Pennsylvania Press, 1968), pp. 85–91, leaves the erroneous impression that Sutherland left his party voluntarily.

19. John Ferral to James Buchanan, February 19, 1838, James Buchanan Papers, Historical Society of Pennsylvania, Philadelphia.

20. See, for example, *Penn.,* June 13, 1838. See also *P.L.,* Feb. 12, 1839.

21. *P.L.,* Jan. 26, Feb. 2, 7, 11, and 18, 1839. The occupations of the delegates were: shoemakers (8), carpenters (4), tailors (3), brushmakers (2), coachmakers (2), and one each, jeweller, currier, cabinetmaker, bricklayer, oak cooper, house painter, laborer. The occupations of five delegates could not be identified.

22. The active Democrats were Solomon Demars, Joshua Fletcher, William Gilmore, Edward Penniman, Henry Scott, Samuel Thompson, and Israel Young.

23. *P.L.,* Jan. 4, 1839.

24. Ibid., Jan. 10, 1839.

25. *An Address to the Workingmen of the City and County of Philadelphia* (Philadelphia: Mifflin and Perry, 1839).

26. *Penn.,* Aug. 28, 1838.

27. Laurie, "Working People of Philadelphia," app. A.

28. *P.L.,* Aug. 1, 8, 13, Sept. 16, and Oct. 19, 24, 1842.

29. U.S. Census, *Population Schedule, Moyamensing.*

30. Cedar Street Presbyterian Church, Minutes of the Session, 1838–1870, Presbyterian Historical Society, Philadelphia, passim. See also Rev. William Ramsey, Diary, 1822–1849, 23 vols., Presbyterian Historical

Society, Philadelphia, Nov. 26, Dec. 27 and 28, 1837, Jan. 19, 1838, and Feb. 23, 1839. (Since Rev. Ramsey neglected to number the volumes of his diary after vol. 10, the citations will include the date only.)

31. William Ramsey, *Ebenezer: A Sermon Embracing the History of the Cedar Street Presbyterian Church, at the Close of the Year 1844* (Philadelphia: Christian Observer, 1845), p. 16.

32. Cedar Street Presbyterian Church, Records of the Session, 1838–1870, Presbyterian Historical Society, Philadelphia, passim.

33. See, for example, Margaret Byington, *Homestead: The Households of a Mill Town* (rpt., Pittsburgh: University of Pittsburgh Press, 1974), pp. 172–73.

34. Ramsey, Diary, Feb. 18, 1845, May 5, 1847, May 1, 1851, Nov. 1, 1852, and March 22, 1855.

35. See, for example, Robert Adair, *Memoir of Rev. James Patterson, Late Pastor of the First Presbyterian Church, Northern Liberties, Philadelphia* (Philadelphia: Henry Perkins, 1840), p. 231; First Presbyterian Congregation Church of Kensington, Session Books, 1814–1845, 1843–1859, Presbyterian Historical Society, Philadelphia, Nov. 9, 1842, and passim; and Centennial Publishing Committee, *History of Ebenezer Methodist Church, Southwark* (Philadelphia: J. B. Lippincott, 1892), pp. 109–16.

36. Centennial Publishing Committee, *History of Ebenezer Methodist Church*, pp. 113–14.

37. John C. Hunterson, *Echoes of Fifty Years: Memorial Record of Wharton Street Methodist Episcopal Church* (Philadelphia: William H. Pile's Sons, 1892), pp. 42–43.

38. Computed from the *Minutes of the Annual Conferences of the Methodist Episcopal Church, 1833–1846, 1847–1864,* (Philadelphia: n.pub., n.d.).

39. Computed from *Minutes of the General Assembly of the Presbyterian Church, 1836–1841* (Philadelphia: By the Stated Clerk of the Assembly, n.d.); and *Minutes of the General Assembly of the Presbyterian Church (New School), 1838–1851* (New York: By the Stated Clerk of the Assembly, n.d.).

40. John Allen Krout, *Origins of Prohibition* (New York: Alfred A. Knopf, 1925), p. 239; Robert W. Doherty, "Social Basis of the Presbyterian Schism, 1837–1838: The Philadelphia Case," *Journal of Social History* 2 (Fall, 1968): 79; and Ramsey, Diary, March 3, 1840.

41. *Minutes of the Philadelphia Conference of the Methodist Episcopal Church held at Philadelphia, April 7, 1841* (Philadelphia: James Harmstead), p. 11.

42. Rev. James W. Porter, *Revivals of Religion: Their Theory, Means, Obstructions, Uses and Importance, with the Duty of Christians in Regard to Them* (5th ed.; New York: Lane and Scott, 1850), p. 139. For the secular version of this argument see letter signed "M, A Member of the Jefferson Temperance Society," *T.A.,* Feb. 12, 1842.

43. *P.L.,* May 11, 1843.

44. *Fountain,* Dec., 1837.

45. Ibid., Jan. 20, 1838. See also, *T.A.,* Sept. 11, 1841, Feb. 12, 1842, and letter signed "A Reformed Jeffersonian," Dec. 3, 1842; and *D.S.,* Jan. 28, 1845.

46. *P.L.,* March 20, 1841.

47. On Levin see *D.A.B.,* 11: 200–01.

48. Letter signed "Old Jeffersonian," *T.A.,* June 17, 1843.

49. Ibid., March 11, 1843.

50. Ibid., Sept. 25, 1841.

51. Warner, *Private City,* pp. 140–41; Ogden, ed., *Niles' Register* 12 Aug. 6, 1842; and *P.L.,* Aug. 2, 3, 6, and 11, 1842.

52. David Montgomery, "The Shuttle and the Cross: Weavers and Artisans in the Kensington Riots of 1844," *Journal of Social History* 5 (Summer, 1972): 417–19; and Michael Feldberg, *The Philadelphia Riots of 1844: A Study of Ethnic Conflict* (Westport, Conn.: Greenwood Press, 1975), pp. 35–38.

53. Feldberg, *Philadelphia Riots of 1844,* p. 36.

54. See, for example, *P.L.,* Jan. 10, Sept. 7, and Nov. 9 and 11, 1843. See also *S.T.,* Sept. 9 and Aug. 26, 1843.

55. *P.L.,* Jan. 12–14, 1843.

56. Montgomery, "Shuttle and the Cross," pp. 425–26.

57. Ibid., p. 416.

58. *P.L.,* June 10, 1842.

59. Ibid., Aug. 22, 1842. See also Warner, *Private City,* p. 141.

60. *P.L.,* June 10, 1842.

61. Ibid., Aug. 15, 1842.

62. Ibid., Aug. 11, 1842.

63. Vincent P. Lannie and Bernard C. Diethorn, "For the Honor and Glory of God: The Philadelphia Bible Riots of 1844," *History of Education Quarterly* 8 (1968): 47–48.

64. Ibid., p. 48.

65. Ibid., pp. 57–58.

66. Elizabeth M. Geffen, "Philadelphia Protestantism Reacts to Social Reform Movements before the Civil War," *Pennsylvania History* 30 (April, 1963): 208.

67. See, for example, *P.L.,* Feb. 25, 1843. See also Feldberg, *Philadelphia Riots of 1844,* pp. 93–96.

68. John Hancock Lee, *Origin and Progress of the American Party in Politics; Embracing a Complete History of the Philadelphia Riots in May and July of 1844 and a Refutation of the Arguments Founded on the Charges of Religious Proscription and Secret Combinations* (Philadelphia: Elliot and Gihon, 1855), pp. 1–135.

69. *S. T.,* March 4, 1844. See also Lannie and Diethorn, "For the Honor and Glory of God," p. 65.

70. See the election returns in *P. L.,* March 16 and 18, 1844.

71. Feldberg, *Philadelphia Riots of 1844,* pp. 99–116.

72. Lee, *Origin and Progress of the American Party,* pp. 136–61; and *P. L.,* July 6, 1844.

73. Sister M. Theopane Geary, *History of Third Parties in Pennsylvania 1840–1860* (Washington, D.C.: The Catholic University Press, 1938), pp. 117–25, 136, and 141.

Chapter 7

1. See letter signed "A Reflecting Operative," *S. T.,* Oct. 9, 1849.

2. On the store order system see ibid., March 5, 1844, and letter signed "One Who Knows, and a Weaver," Sept. 9, 1848. See also *P. L.,* July 31, 1850.

3. Douglass C. North, *The Economic Growth of the United States, 1790–1860* (pbk. ed., New York: Norton, 1966) p. 260.

4. See, for example, *P. L.,* Oct. 15, and Nov. 18, 1847. See also March 15, 1844, and March 25, 1850.

5. Ibid., July 30, 1849.

6. Sam Bass Warner, Jr., *The Private City: Philadelphia in Three Periods of Its Growth* (Philadelphia: University of Pennsylvania Press, 1968), p. 52; *D. S.,* April 11, 1845; and *F. T. R.,* Jan. 28, 1865.

7. Stuart M. Blumin, "Mobility in a Nineteenth-century City: Philadelphia, 1820–1860" (Ph.D. diss., University of Pennsylvania, 1968), pp. 83–109.

8. The figure for the 1840 is based on a review of strike notices in *P. L.,* 1843 to 1853. The figure for 1836 is based on William A. Sullivan, *The Industrial Worker in Pennsylvania, 1800–1840* (Harrisburg: Pennsylvania Historical and Museum Commission, 1955), pp. 221–30.

9. See, for example, American Protestant Association, *First Annual Report of the American Protestant Association. Together with a Sketch of the Address at the First Anniversary, November 18, 1843* (Philadelphia: n.pub., 1844); and American Protestant Association, *Address of the Board of Managers of the American Protestant Association; with the Constitution and Organization of the Association* (Philadelphia: n.pub., 1843). See also Rev. Gideon P. Perry, "Of a Lecture to the Young," in *D. S.,* Jan. 6, 1845;

Rev. J.F. Berg, "The Papal Church and not a Church of Jesus Christ," Jan. 13, 1845; and letter signed "Sojourner," Feb. 13, 1845.

10. Rev. John Hersey, *Advice to Christian Parents* (Baltimore: Armstrong and Berry, n.d.), pp. 106–07.

11. Ibid., p. 107.

12. See, for example, *D.S.*, April 3, 1845, and March 25, 1848; Thomas Hunt, *Life and Thoughts of Rev. Thomas P. Hunt* (Wilkes-Barre, Pa.: Robert Baur and Son, 1901), pp. 167–169; Benjamin T. Sewell, *Sorrow's Circuit, or Five Years' Experience in the Bedford Street Mission, Philadelphia* (Philadelphia: n.pub., 1859), pp. 269–70.

13. Hersey, *Advice to Christian Parents,* pp. 106–07.

14. Rev. William Ramsey, Diary, 1822–1849, 23 vols., Presbyterian Historical Society, Philadelphia, vol. 1, March 1, 1824, vol. 6, Dec. 16, 1826, and passim. (Since Rev. Ramsey neglected to number the volumes of his diary after vol. 10, the citations to such volumes will include the date only.)

15. Sewell, *Sorrow's Circuit,* pp. 268–69.

16. Ramsey, Diary, March 31, 1848.

17. Ibid., May 4, 1840. See also Sewell, *Sorrow's Circuit,* pp. 269–70.

18. Ramsey, Diary, Aug. 20, 1841, March 2, 1842, and June 28, 1843. See also Sewell, *Sorrow's Circuit,* pp. 214–15; and *First Presbyterian Congregation of Kensington, Sessions Books, 1814–1845, 1843–1859,* June 24, 1845, and passim.

19. See, for example, Ramsey, Diary, Sept. 22, 1828, March 3, 1830, Nov. 17, 1837, and passim.

20. Alexander Fulton, for example, was a member of the Odd Fellows and many followers of local temperance-beneficial societies in Southwark and Moyamensing were on the rolls of New School Presbyterian and Methodist churches.

21. Sewell, *Sorrow's Circuit,* p. 270.

22. Anthony F. C. Wallace, *Rockdale: The Growth of An American Village in the Early Industrial Revolution* (New York: Alfred A. Knopf, 1978), pp. 296–317, esp. 316–17.

23. For the names and religious identities of Manayunk strike leaders see *P.L.*, October 15, and November 18, 1847 and Mt. Zion Methodist Episcopal Church, Members, Green Lane Methodist Episcopal Church Manayunk, Philadelphia. For the Manayunk Sons of Temperance see *P.L.*, Aug. 26, 1845.

24. These petitions are available in Pennsylvania State Archives, Harrisburg, Pa. box 26, folder 80, Senate File.

25. *S.T.*, Nov.12, 1847.

26. Ibid.

27. James L. Barnard, *Factory Legislation of Pennsylvania: Its History and Administration* (Philadelphia: Publications of the University of Pennsylvania Ser. in Political Economy and Public Law, no. 17, 1907), pp. 18–21. See also *Laws of the General Assembly of the Commonwealth of Pennsylvania* (Harrisburg: J. M. G. Lescue, 1848), pp. 278–79.

28. *Penn.,* May 30, 1848; and *P.L.,* June 17,1848.

29. Ibid.

30. Letter signed "An Observer," *S.T.,* July 4, 1848.

31. Ibid., July 29, and Aug. 10, 1848.

32. See, for example, ibid., June 30, 1848; and *P.L.,* October 2, 1848.

33. Barnard, *Factory Legislation of Pennsylvania,* pp. 21–23. See also *Laws of the General Assembly of the Commonwealth of Pennsylvania* (Harrisburg, J. M. S. Lescue, 1849), pp. 671–72.

34. This was true at Rockdale as well. Hiram McConnell, leader of the 1842 strike was clearly a radical, despite Prof. Wallace's claims to the contrary. See McConnell's speech in Wallace, *Rockdale,* p. 369.

35. *S.T.,* March 11, 1849, emphasis added. See also, March 15, 1849.

36. It should be noted that local manufacturers reimposed the twelve- and thirteen-hour day in the early 1850s as prosperity returned and the ten-hour movement fell apart. See *Penn.,* Aug. 20, 1852; and *P.L.,* Dec. 6, 1853.

37. U.S. Census, *Population Schedule, Philadelphia County.*

38. See, for example, William F. Adams, *Ireland and the Irish Emigration to the New World from 1815 to the Famine* (New Haven: Yale University Press, 1932); and Oliver Macdonaugh, "The Irish Famine Emigration to the United States," *Perspectives in American History* 10 (1976): 357–448.

39. John F. Maguire, *The Irish in America* (rpt., New York: Arno Press, 1969), p. 215.

40. U.S. Census, *Population Schedule, Philadelphia County.*

41. Michael Feldberg, *The Philadelphia Riots of 1844: A Study of Ethnic Conflict* (Westport, Conn.: Greenwood Press, 1975), pp. 24–25.

42. Ibid., pp. 19–38.

43. The foregoing data was compiled for me by Ms. Joann Weeks of the University of Pennsylvania. See also Dennis Clark "A Pattern of Urban Growth: Residential Development and Church Location in Philadelphia," *Records of the American Catholic Historical Society* 82 (Sept., 1971): 159–70.

44. Feldberg, *Philadelphia Riots of 1844,* pp. 26–27. See also T. Thomas McAvoy, "The Formation of the Catholic Minority in the United States, 1820–1860," *Review of Politics* 10 (Jan., 1948): 13–34.

45. *C.H.,* July 1, 1841.

46. Feldberg, *Philadelphia Riots of 1844,* p. 22. See also Oscar Handlin, *Boston's Immigrants: A Study in Acculturation* (2nd ed., rev. and enl.; New York: Antheneum, 1968), pp. 124–30.

47. See, for example, Paul J. Kleppner, *Cross of Culture: A Social Analysis of Midwestern Politics, 1850–1900* (New York: Free Press, 1970). pp. 76–79.

48. Dennis Clark, *The Irish in Philadelphia: Ten Generations of Urban Experience* (Philadelphia: Temple University Press, 1973), pp. 101–05: Feldberg, *Philadelphia Riots of 1844,* pp. 26–27; *C.H.,* Feb. 18, 1841.

49. Gilbert Osofsky, "Abolitionists, Irish Immigrants, and the Dilemmas of Romantic Nationalism," *American Historical Review* 80 (Oct., 1975): 889-912.

50. See *C.H.,* Jan. 6 and July 20, 1848.

51. Ibid., Aug. 15, 1850.

52. Frank H. Schell, "Old Volunteer Fire Laddies, The Famous, Fast, Faithful, Fistic, Fire Fighters of Bygone Days," Frank H. Schell Papers, Historical Society of Pennsylvania, Philadelphia. ch. 2, p. 4.

53. *P.L.,* Jan. 21, 1842.

54. Schell, "Old Volunteer Fire Laddies," ch. 2, p. 4.

55. Bruce Laurie, "Fire Companies and Gangs in Southwark: The 1840s", in Allen F. Davis and Mark H. Haller, eds., *The Peoples of Philadelphia: A History of Ethnic Groups and Lower-class Life, 1790–1940* (Philadelphia: Temple University Press, 1973), p. 78.

56. See, for example, Wayne G. Broehl, Jr., *The Molly Maguires* (New York: Vintage, 1964), pp. 1–40.

57. On the Killers see *Life and Adventurers of Charles Anderson Chester, the Notorious Leader of the Philadelphia "Killers"* (Philadelphia: Yates and Smith, 1850); and *P.L.,* April 1, 1901. On the Schuylkill Rangers see *P.L.,* June 23, 1849.

58. See David R. Johnson, "Crime Patterns in Philadelphia, 1840–1870," in Davis and Haller, eds., *Peoples of Philadelphia,* pp. 97–98.

59. *Life and Adventures of Charles Anderson Chester,* pp. 27–28.

60. See Feldberg, *Philadelphia Riots of 1844,* pp. 125–27; and *P.L.,* Jan. 14 and Feb. 28, 1853.

61. See Laurie, "The Working People of Philadelphia, 1827–53" (Ph.D. diss., University of Pittsburgh, 1971), pp. 177–79.

62. *P.L.,* June 25–29 and July 1–4, 1844.

63. Ibid., Feb. 5, 8, 9, and 16, 1850. See also *D.S.,* Feb. 5, 8, 15, and 23, and March 1–2, 1850.

64. Schell, "Old Philadelphia Volunteer Fire Laddies," ch. 2, p. 10; and Andrew Neilly, "The Violent Volunteers: A History of the Philadelphia

Volunteer Fire Department, 1736–1871" (Ph.D. diss., University of Pennsylvania, 1959), pp. 70–72.

65. *P.L.,* Aug. 13, 1846.

66. *D.S.,* Aug. 29, 1849.

67. Ibid., Jan. 28, 1850.

68. Ibid., April 19–20, 1850.

69. *P.L.,* June 18–19, 1849.

70. *D.S.,* June 18, 1849.

71. Ibid.

72. Ibid., June 19–20, 1849. See also *P.L.,* June 19–20, 1849.

73. *D.S.,* Aug. 20–22, 1849.

74. Ibid., Oct. 10–11, and Nov. 12, 1849. See also *P.L.,* Oct. 10–13, and Nov. 11–12, 1849.

75. *P.L.,* Oct. 10, 1849.

76. Letter signed "P.O.," *D.S.,* Nov. 10, 1849.

77. Theodore Hershberg, "Free Blacks in Antebellum Philadelphia: A Study of Ex-slaves, Freeborn, and Socioeconomic Decline," *Journal of Social History* 5 (Winter, 1971–72): 192.

78. See, for example, *P.L.,* June 23, 1849, for a description of the activities of the Rangers.

79. *D.S.,* Feb. 6, 1851.

80. Ibid., Feb. 10–11, 1851.

81. *C.H.,* March 26, 1846. At least two Catholics were on the Manayunk Ten-hours Committee. Compare the names of the Committee men in *P.L.,* Oct. 15 and 18, 1847, with the list of parishioners in Eugene Murphy, *The Parish of St. John the Baptist, Manayunk: The First One Hundred Years* (Philadelphia: Press of the Church Printing and Envelope Company, 1931).

82. *P.L.,* Feb. 10, 13, 20, 27, and 28, and March 2, 5, 9, and 11, 1846.

83. Stephan Thernstrom, "Urbanization, Migration, and Social Mobility in Late Nineteenth-century America," in Barton J. Bernstein, ed., *Towards a New Past: Dissenting Essays in American History* (New York: Pantheon Books, 1968), pp. 158–75.

Chapter 8

1. *P.L.,* Dec. 13, 1838.

2. Abel Thomas, *A Century of Universalism in Philadelphia and New York: With Sketches of Its History in Reading, Hightstown, Brooklyn, and Elsewhere* (Philadelphia: Collins, 1872), pp. 104–05 and 120–22.

3. First Universalist Church, Minute Book, 1820–1842, Historical Society of Pennsylvania, Philadelphia, Jan. 3, 1842. Forty of the expelled were located in the city directories of 1842 and 1843 and their occupations were:

gentlemen (1), professional (5), manufacturer (2), merchant (4), public official (2), master craftsman (2), journeyman (21), unskilled worker (3).

4. On the tailors see *P. L.,* Aug. 21, 1843, Oct. 1, 1846, and Oct. 5, 1847; on the shoemakers see March 10, 1843, and June 1, 1850.

5. Charlotte Erickson, ed., *Invisible Immigrants: The Adaptation of English and Scottish Immigrants in Nineteenth-century America* (Coral Gables: University of Miami Press, 1972), p. 231; and Mack Walker, *Germany and the Emigration, 1816–1885* (Cambridge: Harvard University Press, 1964), pp. 42–47 and 151–52.

6. United States Census, *Population Schedule, Philadelphia County.*

7. Mack Walker, *German Home Towns: Community, State and General Estate, 1648–1871* (Ithaca: Cornell University Press, 1971), pp. 15–33 and 73–107.

8. Ibid., pp. 185–216 and 307–53. See also Theodore S. Hamerow, *Restoration, Revolution, Reaction: Economics and Politics in Germany, 1815–1871* (Princeton: Princeton University Press, 1958), pp. 3–76; and P. H. Noyes, *Organization and Revolution: Working-class Associations in the German Revolutions of 1848–1849* (Princeton: Princeton University Press, 1966), pp. 15–33.

9. Ibid., pp. 322–47.

10. Hamerow, *Restoration, Revolution, Reaction,* pp. 32–37.

11. See, for example, David McLellan, *Karl Marx: His Life and Thought* (New York: Harper and Row, 1973), pp. 62–136 and 226–89.

12. Carl Wittke, *Refugees of Revolution: The German Forty-eighters in America* (Philadelphia: University of Pennsylvania Press, 1952), pp. 122–46. See also Noyes, *Organization and Revolution,* pp. 34–54.

13. E. P. Thompson, *The Making of the English Working Class* (pbk. ed.; New York: Vintage, 1966), pp. 55–185; and Trygve Tholfsen, *Working-class Radicalism in Mid-victorian Britain* (New York: Columbia University Press, 1977), pp. 25–82.

14. Ray Boston, *British Chartists in America, 1839–1900* (Manchester, England: Manchester University Press, 1971), pp. 21–35. See also ibid., app. A. On the Chartist League see *S. T.,* June 27, 1848. On the Friends of Ireland, a radical organization that included several Chartists, see ibid., Aug. 30, 1848.

15. See Boston, *British Chartists,* pp. 58–62, 66–67, and 90.

16. Ibid. See also John R. Commons, et al., *History of Labour in the United States,* 4 vols. (New York: Macmillan, 1918–35), 1: 516–17.

17. Carl Wittke, *The German-language Press in America* (Lexington: University of Kentucky Press, 1957), pp. 37–38. See also Wittke, *Refugees of Revolution,* pp. 280–99.

18. Wittke, *German-language Press*, pp. 41–44. See also Wittke, *Refugees of Revolution*, pp. 130–31.

19. Wittke, *Refugees of Revolution*, pp. 129–30.

20. See, for example, *P.L.*, Aug. 4, 1849. See also Wittke, *Refugees of Revolution*, pp. 141–42.

21. Wittke, *Refugees of Revolution*, pp. 122–46. See also *D.S.*, Sept. 22–24, 1851. The Universalist minister, John H. Gihon, was a firebrand nativist, but he appears to have been atypical of his sect.

22. Walker, *Germany and the Emigration*, p. 69.

23. Ibid., pp. 158–59.

24. Ibid., p. 155.

25. Erickson, *Invisible Immigrants*, p. 239.

26. Ibid., p. 157. See also pp. 147 and 171.

27. See, for example, ibid., pp. 162–82.

28. Fully one-fifth of the Germans, for example, were shoemakers and tailors. For the occupational distribution of the city's leading immigrant groups in 1840, see Bruce Laurie, et al., "Immigrants and Industry: The Philadelphia Experience, 1850–1880," *Journal of Social History* 9 (Winter, 1975), table 13, pp. 235–38.

29. On the English utopians see Boston, *British Chartists in America*, pp. 58–62 and 66–67. See also John Campbell, *A Theory of Equality: Or, the Way to Make Every Man Act Honestly* (Philadelphia: J. B. Perry, 1848). On the German utopians see Carl Wittke, *The Utopian Communist: A Biography of Wilhelm Weitling, Nineteenth-century Reformer* (Baton Rouge: Louisiana State University Press, 1950); and David Herreshoff, *American Disciples of Marx: From the Age of Jackson to the Progressive Era* (Detroit: Wayne State University Press, 1967), pp. 11–30.

30. See, for example, *D.S.*, March 20, 1845, April 4, 1848, and Oct. 5, 1849. See also John Hancock Lee, *Origin and Progress of the American Party in Politics; Embracing a Complete History of the Philadelphia Riots in May and July of 1844 and a Refutation of the Arguments Founded on the Charges of Religious Proscription and Secret Combinations* (Philadelphia: Elliot and Gihon, 1855).

31. Michael F. Holt, "The Politics of Impatience: The Origins of Know Nothingism," *Journal of American History* 60 (Sept., 1973): 309–32.

32. Eight of the American Republican master craftsmen were traced to the industrial census of 1850 and all but one of them hired less than eight workers. The exception was Philip Dubosq, the son or brother of a large jewelry manufacturer with a labor force of thirty workers.

33. Again, the glaring exception was Dubosq, whose business was well established in the previous decade.

34. The former Trades' Union radicals Joshua Fletcher and Andrew Craig, for example, were members of the John Hancock Temperance Beneficial Society. See *P.L.,* Nov. 29, 1842, and Nov. 21, 1844.

35. See, for example, *D.S.,* March 27, 1847. See also *A.B.,* Jan. 10, 1852.

36. On temperance societies of shoemakers, tailors, and printers see *P.L.,* Jan. 25, 1839, Aug. 14, 1841, and Feb. 21, 1842.

37. See, for example, American Republican Central Executive Committee, *Address of the American Republicans of the City and County to the Native and Naturalized Citizens of the United States* (Philadelphia: n.pub., 1844). See also *P.L.,* Sept. 10, 1847.

38. Order of United American Mechanics, *Journal of the State Council of the Order of United American Mechanics* (Philadelphia: J. H. Jones, 1848–1853), passim. See also Order of United American Mechanics, Fredonia Lodge No. 52, West Philadelphia, Records of the Society, 1850–1857, Historical Society of Pennsylvania, Philadelphia.

39. *A.B.,* Aug. 30, 1851.

40. Letter signed "B.B.," *D.S.,* Feb. 4, 1848. See also *A.B.,* Oct. 1, 1850, and Aug. 30, 1851.

41. *D.S.,* Jan. 10, 1848.

42. *A.B.,* Aug. 30, 1851. See also Aug. 3, 1850.

43. *D.S.,* March 16, 1847. See also June 18, 1846, March 8, 1847, and April 11, 1848.

44. Ibid., April 15, 1848.

45. Ibid. See also March 8, 1847.

46. Ibid., March 27, 1847.

47. Order of United American Mechanics, *Journal,* p. 3.

48. Ibid., p. 22. The occupations of the twenty-two founders were: house carpenter (8), gunsmith (7), cabinetmaker (2), fancy chairmaker (1), shipsmith (1), patternmaker (1) coachmaker (1), and printer (1).

49. On the organizational affiliations of U.A.M. activists see Bruce Laurie, "The Working People of Philadelphia, 1827–1853" (Ph.D. diss., University of Pittsburgh, 1971), app. C.

50. Order of United American Mechanics, *Journal,* p. 91.

51. Ibid., p. 435.

52. Ibid., passim. See also Order of United American Mechanics Fredonia Lodge, No. 52, Records of the Society.

53. *A.B.,* June 1, 1850.

54. See *P.L.,* Nov. 26, 1847. See also *D.S.,* March 27, 1847.

55. Order of United American Mechanics, *Journal,* pp. 254–55.

56. Ibid., p. 3.

57. See Laurie, et al., "Immigrants and Industry," table 8, p. 228.

58. Lee, *Origin and Progress of the American Party in Politics,* pp. 136–61.

59. *D.S.,* July 4, 1846.

60. On the men's shoemakers see *S.T.,* Sept. 4, 1843, and March 16, 1844; and *P.L.,* Aug. 21, and Sept. 20, 1843, March 10, 1845, Feb. 24, and June 23, 1847. On the tailors see *P.L.,* March 4, Aug. 8, and Aug. 23, 1843, April 3 and 14, 1844, Oct. 11, 1845, Feb. 6, Sept. 1, Oct. 1, Nov. 28, and Dec. 12, 1846, March 13, Aug. 14, 18, and 26, 1847.

61. See, for example, *P.L.,* Sept. 2, 1843, and March 10, 1847.

62. Ibid., Aug. 21 and 25, 1843 and Dec. 4–6, 1847.

63. Ibid., Sept. 4, 1847.

64. Ibid., May 4, 1850.

65. Ibid., Sept.13, and Oct. 11, 1845. William F. Green and William Harper, leaders of the Brotherhood, were also members of the U.A.M.

66. Ibid., Dec. 28, 1847.

67. Commons, et al., *History of Labour,* 1: 573–74.

68. *P.L.,* Nov. 15, 1848, Feb. 7 and 27, March 22, and Oct. 3, 1849, and June 17, 1850.

69. Ibid., March 4, 1846.

70. Ibid., May 6, 1848.

71. Ibid., Dec. 28, 1847.

72. *D.S.,* June 15 and 18, 1847.

73. Ibid., June 28 and 29, 1847.

74. Ibid.

75. Ibid., April 25, 1851.

76. Ibid., May 14, 1851.

77. *A.B.,* Sept. 2, 1850.

78. *D.S.,* May 14, 1851.

79. *P.L.,* April 4–6 and May 4, 1847, and April 14 and May 7, 1848.

80. See Laurie, "Working People of Philadelphia," app. C.

81. *D.S.,* Aug. 6, 1850.

82. Ibid. See also *P.L.,* July 27, and Aug. 3, 8, and 22, 1850.

83. *P.L.,* March 5, May 20, June 2 and 9, 1851.

84. *D.S.,* April 25, 1851. See also May 12, 1851.

85. *P.L.,* May 31, June 2 and 16, 1851.

86. *S.T.,* Aug. 10, 1843.

87. See Laurie, "Working People of Philadelphia," app. C.

88. *P.L.,* July 30, 1849.

89. Ibid., July 22 and 29, 1850. See also *D.S.,* July 9, 1850.

90. *P.L.,* Aug. 11, 1851.

91. Ibid., Aug. 21 and 23, 1850. See also *A.B.,* Sept. 21, 1850. See also letter signed "S. H. Johnson, et al.," *A.B.,* Nov. 6, 1850.
92. *P.L.,* Sept. 2, 1850.
93. Letter signed "A Journeyman Printer," *D.S.,* Aug. 27, 1850. See also letter signed "Vindex," Aug. 22, 1850, and letter signed "J," *A.B.,* Nov. 2, 1850.
94. See letter signed "S. H. Johnson, et al.," *D.S.,* Nov. 6, 1850.
95. *P.L.,* Oct. 14 and Nov. 23, 1850.
96. See Laurie, "Working People of Philadelphia," app. C.
97. Wittke, *Utopian Communist,* pp. 197–219. See also Hermann Schlüter, *Die Anfange der deutchen Arbeiterbewegung in Amerika* (Stutgart: J. H. W. Deitz, 1907), pp. 83–85.
98. *P.L.,* Oct. 29, 1850. See also *D.S.,* Oct. 24, 1850.

Chapter 9

1. See, for example, *D.S.,* Oct. 29, 1851. See also *P.L.,* Oct. 24, 1850.
2. The roster of trades included blacksmiths, bookbinders, bricklayers, brushmakers, cabinetmakers, carpenters, carpet weavers, coachmakers, coopers, frame work knitters, hatters, hat finishers, lithographic printers, machinists, plasterers, printers, shipsmiths, shoemakers (ladies' and men's), stone cutters, tailors, tinsmiths, trunkmakers and upholsterers. See *P.L.,* Nov. 1, 7, 8, 16, and 20, 1850. By January 1851, however, the number of affiliated trades fell to under twenty. See *P.L.,* Jan. 2, 1851.
3. Ibid., Dec. 9 and 11, 1850.
4. *N.Y.D.T.,* Aug. 6, 1850.
5. *P.L.,* Nov. 1, 1850.
6. Ibid., Dec. 11, 1850.
7. David Montgomery, *Beyond Equality: Labor and the Radical Republicans, 1862–1872* (New York: Alfred A. Knopf, 1967), p. 219. See also Alan Dawley, *Class and Community: The Industrial Revolution in Lynn* (Cambridge: Harvard University Press, 1976), esp. pp. 188–93.
8. *N.Y.D.T.,* April 12, 19, and 26, 1851. See also *P.L.,* June 18 and July 8, 1851.
9. *N.Y.D.T.,* April 19, 1851.
10. *P.L.,* Aug. 30, 1851. Twenty-tour of the forty-eight delegates were located in the city directory and twenty of them were journeymen.
11. Ibid., Sept. 18, 1851.
12. See, for example, ibid., Aug. 19 and 25, 1851.
13. *D.S.,* Sept. 19, 1851.
14. *P.L.,* Oct. 13, 1851.
15. Ibid., Sept. 19, 1851. See also Oct. 4 and 13, 1851.

16. Ibid. See also *D.S.,* Sept. 18 and 19, 1851.

17. See letters signed "Many Mechanics," "An Old Native," and "Natives," *P.L.,* Oct. 13, 1851.

18. See letter of William J. Mullen, ibid., Oct. 6, 1851.

19. Ibid., Oct. 11, 1851.

20. Ibid., Oct. 6, 1851.

21. See letter signed by A. Martin and T. L. Saunders, ibid., Oct. 6, 1851.

22. Ibid.

23. See letters signed by John Shedden, A. H. Rosenthal, et. al., ibid., Oct. 10 and 13, 1851.

24. *D.S.,* Oct. 18, 1851.

25. See, for example, Edward Pessen, *Most Uncommon Jacksonians: The Radical Leaders of the Early Labor Movement* (Albany: State University of New York Press), pp. 9–13; and Montgomery, *Beyond Equality,* pp. 425–47. The Workingmen of Lynn actually won several elections between 1860 and 1890, but did very little while in office. See Dawley, *Class and Community,* pp. 199–207 and 208–09.

26. See Thernstrom, "Urbanization, Migration, and Social Mobility in Late Nineteenth-century America," in Burton J. Bernstein, ed. *Towards a New Past: Dissenting Essays in American History* (New York: Pantheon, 1968), p. 168. See also Thernstrom, *The Other Bostonians: Poverty and Progress in the American Metropolis, 1880–1970* (Cambridge: Harvard University Press, 1973), pp. 15–44; and Peter R. Knights, *The Plain People of Boston, 1830–1860: A Study in City Growth* (New York: Oxford University Press, 1971).

27. Stuart M. Blumin, "Residential Mobility within the Nineteenth-century City," in Allen F. Davis and Mark H. Haller, eds., *Peoples of Philadelphia: A History of Ethnic Groups and Lower-class Life, 1790–1940* (Philadelphia: Temple University Press, 1973), pp. 37–52.

28. Dawley, *Class and Community,* pp. 230–31.

29. Sam Bass Warner, Jr., *The Private City: Philadelphia in Three Periods of Its Growth* (Philadelphia: University of Pennsylvania Press, 1968), p. 61.

30. Dawley, *Class and Community,* pp. 230–31.

31. Thernstrom, "Urbanization, Migration, and Social Mobility in Late Nineteenth-century America," pp. 171–72.

32. Any number of studies make this point. See, for example, Donald B. Cole, *Immigrant City: Lawrence, Massachusetts, 1845–1921* (Chapel Hill: University of North Carolina Press, 1963); and Victor R. Greene, *The Slavic Community on Strike: Immigrant Labor in Pennsylvania Anthracite* (South Bend: Notre Dame University Press, 1968).

33. This is a major theme of the "new political history," as well. See Paul J. Kleppner, *The Cross of Culture: A Social Analysis of Midwestern Politics, 1850–1900* (New York: Free Press, 1970), pp. 36–37.

34. See Lee Benson, *The Concept of Jacksonian Democracy: New York as a Test Case* (pbk. ed. Princeton: Princeton University Press, 1961), pp. 281–87.

35. In order to avoid competing with mechanized production, they also specialized in fabrics that were not produced on power looms, but this strategy did not always work. In 1842, for example, a Manayunk manufacturer produced by machine the same fabric weaved by the frame tenders of Kensington. The weavers marched into Manayunk intending to burn down the mill, but were intercepted by the sheriff and the mill owner. See Michael Feldberg, *Philadelphia Riots of 1844: A Study of Ethnic Conflict* (Westport, Conn., Greenwood Press, 1975), p. 36.

36. Dawley, *Class and Community,* p. 235. See also Montgomery, *Beyond Equality,* pp. 214–15.

Bibliography

Primary Sources

Manuscript Materials

Adair, Robert. Church Members, Franklin Street Church, 1837–1839. Presbyterian Historical Society. Philadelphia, Pa.
Buchanan, James. Papers. Historical Society of Pennsylvania, Philadelphia.
Cedar Street Presbyterian Church. Records of the Session, 1838–1870. Presbyterian Historical Society. Philadelphia, Pa.
Central Presbyterian Church in Northern Liberties. Minutes of the Session, 1832–1852. Presbyterian Historical Society. Philadelphia, Pa.
First Presbyterian Church in Southwark. Minutes, 1830–1840. Presbyterian Historical Society. Philadelphia, Pa.
First Presbyterian Church in Southwark. Records of Communicants, Baptisms, Marriages, 1827–1831, 1842–1848. Presbyterian Historical Society. Philadelphia, Pa.
First Presbyterian Church of Southwark. Trustees Minutes, 1818–1832. Presbyterian Historical Society. Philadelphia, Pa.
First Presbyterian Congregation of Kensington. Session Books, 1814–1845, 1843–1859. Presbyterian Historical Society. Philadelphia, Pa.
First Universalist Church. Minute Book, 1820–1842. Historical Society of Pennsylvania. Philadelphia.
Halsey, A. O. Papers. Presbyterian Historical Society. Philadelphia, Pa.
Manayunk, Borough of. Council Minutes, 1840–1852, 1852–1854, 2 vols. Historical Society of Pennsylvania, Philadelphia.
Miscellaneous Papers. Presbyterian Historical Society. Philadelphia, Pa.
Mt. Zion Methodist Episcopal Church. Members, Green Lane Methodist Episcopal Church, Manayunk. Philadelphia, Pa.
Niagara Hose Company. Minute Books, 1833–1848, 1848–1864. Historical Society of Pennsylvania, Philadelphia.

Order of United American Mechanics, Fredonia Lodge No. 52, West Philadelphia. Records of the Society, 1850–1857. Historical Society of Pennsylvania. Philadelphia.

Pennsylvania State Archives. Senate File. Harrisburg, Pennsylvania.

Ramsey, William. Diary, 1822–1849. 23 vols. Presbyterian Historical Society. Philadelphia, Pa.

Schell, Frank H. "Old Volunteer Fire Laddies, the Famous, Fast, Faithful, Fistic, Fire Fighters of Bygone Days." In Frank H. Schell Papers, Historical Society of Pennsylvania. Philadelphia.

Second Universalist Church. Minute Book, 1820–1854. Historical Society of Pennsylvania. Philadelphia.

Society of Miscellaneous Collection. Historical Society of Pennsylvania. Philadelphia.

United States Census Office. *Industrial Schedules of the Seventh Census of the United States, 1850: Philadelphia County.* Microfilm. Washington, D.C.: National Archives, 1963.

———. *Population Schedules of the Seventh Census of the United States, 1850: Philadelphia County.* Microfilm. Washington, D.C.: National Archives, 1963.

Published Works

"Account of the Grand Federal Procession in Philadelphia." *American Museum* 4 (July, 1788): 57–75.

Adair, Robert. *Memoir of Rev. James Patterson, Late Pastor of the First Presbyterian Church, Northern Liberties, Philadelphia.* Philadelphia: Henry Perkins, 1840.

An Address to the Workingmen of the City and County of Philadelphia. Philadelphia: Mifflin and Perry, 1839.

Alexander, James W., [Charles Quill,] *The American Mechanic.* Philadelphia: Henry Perkins, 1838.

———. *The Working-man.* Philadelphia: Perkins and Purvis, 1843.

American Protestant Association. *Address of the Board of Managers of the American Protestant Association. Together with a Sketch of the Addresses at the First Anniversary, November 18, 1843.* Philadelphia: n.pub., 1844.

———. *First Annual Report of the American Protestant Association; with the Constitution and Organization of the Association.* Philadelphia: n.pub., 1843.

American Republican Central Executive Committee. *Address of the*

American Republicans of the City and County of Philadelphia to the Native and Naturalized Citizens of the United States. Philadelphia: n.pub., 1844.

American Temperance Union. *Report of the Executive Committee.* Philadelphia: L. Johnson, 1838.

Baird, Robert H. *The American Cotton Spinner, and Manager's and Carder's Guide: A Practical Treatise on Cotton Spinning, Compiled from the Papers of the Late Robert Baird.* Philadelphia: A. Hart, 1851.

Barnes, Albert. *The Connexion of Temperance with Republican Freedom: An Oration Delivered on the 4th of July, 1835, before the Mechanics and Workingmens Temperance Society of the City and County of Philadelphia.* Philadelphia: Boyles and Benedict, 1835.

————. *The Choice of a Profession: An Address Delivered before the Society of Inquiry in Amherst College, August 21, 1838.* Amherst. J. S. and C. Adams, 1838.

————. *The Desire of Reputation: An Address before the Mercantile Library Company of Philadelphia, December 8, 1841.* Philadelphia: Henry Perkins, 1841.

Broom, Jacob. *An Address Pronounced before the Order of the United Sons of America, on the Twenty-second Day of February, A.D., 1850.* Philadelphia: J. H. Jones, 1850.

Campbell, John. *A Theory of Equality: Or, the Way to Make Every Man Act Honestly.* Philadelphia: J. B. Perry, 1848.

Centennial Publishing Committee. *History of Ebenezer Methodist Church, Southwark.* Philadelphia: J. B. Lippincott, 1892.

The Charter, Articles of Faith, Constitution, and By-laws of the First Universalist Church. Philadelphia: Gihon, Fairchild, 1842.

The Charter and By-laws of the Philadelphia Typographical Society, with the Members' Names. Philadelphia: n.pub., 1843.

Cobbett, William. *A Year's Residence in the United States of America.* 1819. Rpt. Carbondale: University of Southern Illinois Press, 1964.

Committee of Boston Mechanics. *Proceedings of the Government and Citizens of Philadelphia, on the Reduction of the Hours of Labor and Increase of Wages.* Boston: Committee of Mechanics, 1835.

Committee of Citizens of Philadelphia. *Paid Fire Department: Letters of the Judge of the Court of Quarter Sessions, and the Marshall of Police and Report of the Board of Trade.* Philadelphia: n.pub., 1853.

Constitution and By-laws of the Association of Journeymen Hatters of the City and County of Philadelphia, Instituted in 1824. Philadelphia: William P. Finn, 1834.

Constitution and By-laws of the Journeymen House Carpenters' Association of the City and County of Philadelphia. Philadelphia: National Labourer, 1837.

Constitution and By-laws of the Union Beneficial Society of Journeymen Cordwainers, on the Ladies' Branch, of the City and County of Philadelphia. Philadelphia: John Thompson, 1834.

The Constitution of the Pennsylvania Society of Journeymen Cabinetmakers of the City of Philadelphia. Philadelphia: Garden and Thompson, 1829.

Desilver's Directory and Stranger's Guide, for 1831. Ed. Robert Desilver. Philadelphia: By the editor, 1831.

Desilver's Directory and Stranger's Guide, for 1833. Ed. Robert Desilver. Maxwell, 1829.

Desilver's Directory and Stranger's Guide, for 1830. Ed. Robert Desilver. Philadelphia: By the editor, 1830.

Desilver's Directory and Stranger's Guide, for 1831. Ed. by Robert Desilver. Philadelphia: By the editor, 1831.

Desilver's Directory and Stranger's Guide, for 1833. Ed. by Robert Desilver. Philadelphia: By the editor, 1833.

Desilver's Directory and Stranger's Guide, for 1835–1836. Philadelphia: Seyfert and Phillips, 1836.

Fisher, Sidney George. *A Philadelphia Perspective: The Diary of Sidney George Fisher, 1834–1871.* Ed. by Nicholas B. Wainwright. Philadelphia: Historical Society of Pennsylvania, 1967.

Freedley, Edwin T. *Philadelphia and Its Manufactures: A Hand-book Exhibiting the Development, Variety, and Statistics of the Manufacturing Industry of Philadelphia in 1857, together with Sketches of Remarkable Manufactories, and a List of Articles Now Made in Philadelphia.* Philadelphia: Edward Young, 1858.

A Full and Accurate Report of the Trial for Riot before the Mayor's Court of Philadelphia, on the 13th of October, 1831, Arising out of a Protestant Procession on the 12th of July, and in which the Contending Parties Were Protestants and Catholics, Including the Indictments, Examination of Witnesses, Speeches of Counsel, Verdict and Sentences. Philadelphia: Jesper Harding, 1831.

Gihon, John H. *A Review of the Sermon against Universal Salvation.* Philadelphia: By the author, 1841.

Gould, Marcus T. C. [recorder]. *Trial of Twenty-four Journeymen Tailors, Charged with a Conspiracy: Before the Mayor's Court of the City of Philadelphia, September Sessions, 1827.* Philadelphia: n.pub., 1827.

Hagner, Charles V. *Early History of the Falls of Schuylkill, Manayunk, Schuylkill and Lehigh Navagation Companies, Fairmount Waterworks, etc.* Philadelphia: Claxton, Remsen, and Haffelfinger, 1869.

[Heighton, William.] *An Address Delivered before the Mechanics and Working Classes Generally, of the City and County of Philadelphia. At the Universalist Church, in Callowhill Street, On Wednesday Evening, November 21, 1827. By the "Unlettered Mechanic."* Philadelphia: Mechanics' Delegation, 1827.

————. *An Address to the Members of Trade Societies, and to the Working Classes Generally: Being an Exposition of the Relative Situation, Condition, and Future Prospects of Working People in the United States of America. Together with a Suggestion and Outlines of a Plan, by which They May Gradually and Indefinitely Improve their Condition. By a Fellow-Labourer.* Philadelphia: Young, 1827.

————. *The Principles of Aristocratic Legislation, Developed in an Address, Delivered to the Working People of the District of Southwark, and Townships of Moyamensing and Passyunk. In the Commissioners' Hall, August 14, 1828.* Philadelphia: J. Coates, Jr., 1828.

Hersey, John. *Advice to Christian Parents.* Baltimore: Armstrong and Perry; n.d.

Hunt, Thomas. *Jesse Jackson and his Times.* Philadelphia: Griffith and Simon, 1845.

————. *Life and Thoughts of Rev. Thomas P. Hunt.* Wilkes-Barre, Pa.: Robert Baur and Son, 1901.

Hunterson, John C. *Echoes of Fifty Years: Memorial Record of Wharton Street Methodist Episcopal Church.* Philadelphia: William H. Pile's Sons, 1892.

Kennady, Rev. J[ohn]. *Sermon Delivered before the Sunday School Teachers' Union of the Methodist Episcopal Church of Philadelphia, September 29, 1839.* Philadelphia: Thomas U. Baker, 1839.

Laws of the General Assembly of the Commonwealth of Pennsylvania. Harrisburg: J. M. G. Lescue, 1848–1849.

Lee, John Hancock. *The Origin and Progress of the American Party in Politics; Embracing a Complete History of the Philadelphia Riots in May and July of 1844 and a Refutation of the Arguments Founded on the Charges of Religious Proscription and Secret Combinations.* Philadelphia: Elliot and Gihon, 1855.

Life and Adventures of Charles Anderson Chester, the Notorious Leader of the Philadelphia "Killers." Philadelphia: Yates and Smith, 1850.

Maguire, John F. *The Irish in America.* 1868. Rpt., New York: Arno Press, 1969.

A. McElroy's Philadelphia Directory, for 1837. Ed. Archibald McElroy. Philadelphia: Rackleff and Jones, 1837.

A. McElroy's Philadelphia Directory, for 1839. Ed. Archibald McElroy. Philadelphia: Isaac Ashmead, 1839.

A. McElroy's Philadelphia Directory, for 1840. Ed. Archibald McElroy. Philadelphia: Isaac Ashmead, 1840.

A. McElroy's Philadelphia Directory, for 1841. Ed. Orrin Rogers. Philadelphia: Isaac Ashmead, 1841.

A. McElroy's Philadelphia Directory, for 1842. Ed. Orrin Rogers. Philadelphia: Isaac Ashmead, 1842.

A. McElroy's Philadelphia Directory, for 1843. Ed. Edward C. Biddle. Philadelphia: Isaac Ashmead, 1843.

A. McElroy's Philadelphia Directory, for 1844. Ed. Edward C. Biddle and John C. Biddle. Philadelphia: Isaac Ashmead, 1844.

A. McElroy's Philadelphia Directory, for 1845. Ed. Edward C. Biddle and John C. Biddle. Philadelphia: Isaac Ashmead, 1845.

A. McElroy's Philadelphia Directory, for 1846. Ed. Edward C. Biddle and John C. Biddle, Philadelphia: Isaac Ashmead, 1846.

A. McElroy's Philadelphia Directory, for 1847. Ed. Edward C. Biddle and John C. Biddle. Philadelphia: Isaac Ashmead, 1847.

A. McElroy's Philadelphia Directory, for 1848. Ed. Edward C. Biddle and John C. Biddle. Philadelphia: Isaac Ashmead, 1848.

A. McElroy's Philadelphia Directory, for 1849. Ed. Edward C. Biddle and John C. Biddle. Philadelphia: Isaac Ashmead, 1849.

A. McElroy's Philadelphia Directory, for 1850. Ed. Edward C. Biddle and John C. Biddle. Philadelphia: Isaac Ashmead, 1850.

A. McElroy's Philadelphia Directory, for 1851. Ed. Edward C. Biddle and John C. Biddle. Philadelphia: Isaac Ashmead, 1851.

Minutes of the General Assembly of the Presbyterian Church, 1821–1835. Philadelphia: By the Stated Clerk of the Assembly, n.d.

Minutes of the General Assembly of the Presbyterian Church, 1836–1841. Philadelphia: By the Stated Clerk of the Assembly, n.d.

Minutes of the General Assembly of the Presbyterian Church, 1842–1847. Philadelphia: By the Stated Clerk of the Assembly, n.d.

Minutes of the General Assembly of the Presbyterian Church, 1848–1849. Philadelphia: By the Stated Clerk of the Assembly, n.d.

Minutes of the General Assembly of the Presbyterian Church in the United States of America from its Organization in A.D. 1798 to A.D. 1820. Philadelphia: Presbyterian Board of Publication, 1847.

Minutes of the General Assembly of the Presbyterian Church in the United States of America (New School), 1838–1851. New York: By the Stated Clerk of the Assembly, n.d.

Minutes of the Philadelphia Conference of the Methodist Episcopal Church, 1833–1846. Philadelphia: n.pub., n.d.

Minutes of the Philadelphia Conference of the Methodist Episcopal Church, 1847–1864. Philadelphia: n.pub., n.d.

Minutes Taken at the Several Annual Conferences of the Methodist Episcopal Church, 1810–1820. Philadelphia: n.pub., n.d.

Minutes Taken at the Several Annual Conferences of the Methodist Episcopal Church, 1821–1829. Philadelphia: n.pub., n.d.

Order of United American Mechanics. *Journal of the State Council of the Order of United American Mechanics.* Philadelphia: J. H. Jones, 1848–1853.

Pennsylvania Senate. *Report of the Select Committee Appointed to Visit the Manufacturing Districts of the Commonwealth, for the Purpose of Investigating the Employment of Children in Manfactories, Mr. Peltz, Chairman.* Harrisburg: Thompson and Clark, 1838.

Pennsylvania Society for Discouraging the Use of Ardent Spirits. *Anniversary Report of the Board of Managers.* Philadelphia: n.pub., 1831.

Philadelphia Directory for 1816. Ed. James Robinson. Philadelphia: n.pub., 1816.

The Philadelphia Directory, for 1817. Ed. Edward Dawes. Philadelphia: n.pub., 1817.

The Philadelphia Directory and Register for 1818. Ed. James E. Paxton. Philadelphia: E. and R. Parker, 1818

The Philadelphia Directory and Register for 1819. Ed. James E. Paxton. Philadelphia: n.pub., 1819.

The Philadelphia Directory for 1820. Ed. Edward Whitely. Philadelphia: McCarty and Davis, 1820.

Philadelphia Directory and Register for 1821. Philadelphia: McCarty and Davis, 1821.

Philadelphia Directory and Register for 1822. Philadelphia: McCarthy and Davis, 1822.

The Philadelphia Directory, and Stranger's Guide for 1825. Ed. Thomas Wilson. Philadelphia: Bioren, 1825.

The Philadelphia Index, or Directory for 1823. Ed. Robert Desilver. Philadelphia: By the editor, 1823.

The Philadelphia Index, or Directory for 1824. Ed. Robert Desilver. Philadelphia: By the editor, 1824.

Porter, James. *Revivals of Religion: Their Theory, Means, Obstructions, Uses, and Importance; with the Duty of Christians in Regard to Them.* 5th ed. New York: Lane and Scott, 1850.

Ramsey, William. *Ebenezer: A Sermon Embracing the History of Cedar Street Presbyterian Church, at the Close of the Year 1844.* Philadelphia: Christian Observer, 1845.

Sewell, Benjamin T. *Sorrow's Circuit, or Five Years' Experience in the Bedford Street Mission, Philadelphia.* Philadelphia: n.pub., 1859.

Smith, Alfred P. *In Memorium: Alfred Oothout Halsey, D.D., 1798–1868:*

First Pastor of Eleventh, Now West-arch Presbyterian Church. Philadelphia: n.pub., 1897.

Society of Friends. *Statistical Inquiry into the Condition of the People of Colour, of the City and Districts of Philadelphia.* Philadelphia: Kite and Walton, 1849.

Statistics of Philadelphia: Comprehending a Concise View of All the Public Institutions and the Fire Engine and Hose Houses of the City and County of Philadelphia, on the First of January, 1842. Philadelphia: n.pub., 1842.

Thomas, Abel C. *A Century of Universalism in Philadelphia and New York: With Sketches of Its History in Reading, Hightstown, Brooklyn, and Elsewhere.* Philadelphia: Collins, 1872.

Thompson, Edward. *Oration Delivered on the Ninety-eight Anniversary of the Birth Day of Thomas Paine, at the Military Hall, Philadelphia, before the Society of Free Enquirers, January 29, 1834.* Philadelphia: Thomas Clark, 1834.

Vansant, Isaac, ed. *Royal Road to Wealth: An Illustrated History of the Successful Business Houses of Philadelphia.* Philadelphia: Samuel Loage, n.d.

Watson, John F. *Annals of Philadelphia.* 3 vols. Philadelphia: Edwin S. Stuart, 1887.

Willson, Shipley W. and Ebenezer Ireson, eds. *The Methodist Preacher: Or, Monthly Sermons from Living Ministers.* Boston: J. Putnam, 1832.

Young Men's Association of the First Presbyterian Church. *Annual Report.* Philadelphia: I. Ashmead, 1839.

Newspapers and Journals

American Banner and National Defender (Philadelphia), 1850–1854.

Catholic Herald (Philadelphia), 1833–1851.

Daily Sun (Philadelphia), 1845–1851.

Daily Tribune (New York), 1848–1851.

Democratic Press (Philadelphia),1828.

Evening Bulletin (Philadelphia), 1847–1855.

Fincher's Trades Review (Philadelphia), 1864–1865.

Fountain (Philadelphia), 1837–1838.

Gazetteer (Philadelphia), 1823–1824.

Germantown Telegraph (Philadelphia), 1833–1851.

Hazard, Samuel, ed. *Register of Pennsylvania.* 16 vols. Philadelphia: William F. Geddes, 1828–1835.

Hunt, Freeman, ed. *Hunt's Merchants' Magazine.* 2 vols. New York: By the editor, 1848–1849.

Liberalist (Philadelphia), 1833–1834.
Manayunk Courier (Philadelphia), 1848.
Manayunk Star (Philadelphia), 1859–1862.
Mechanics' Free Press (Philadelphia), 1828–1831.
Native American (Philadelphia), 1844.
Niles, H., ed. *Niles' Weekly Register.* 4th ser. Vols. 9–12. Baltimore: By the editor, 1833–1836.
Niles, W. Ogden. *Niles' National Register.* 5th ser. Vols. 4–14. Washington, D.C.: By the editor, 1837–1843.
Pennsylvanian (Philadelphia), 1833–1851.
Poulson's Daily Advertiser (Philadelphia), 1828.
Public Ledger (Philadelphia), 1836–1855.
Radical Reformer and Working Man's Advocate (Philadelphia), July 4, 1835.
Spirit of the Times (Philadelphia), 1839–1849.
Temperance Advocate and Literary Repository (Philadelphia), 1841–1843.
Temple of Reason (Philadelphia), 1835–1837.
United States Gazette (Philadelphia), 1834–1840.

Secondary Sources

Books, Articles, and Edited Works

Adams, William F. *Ireland and the Irish Emigration to the New World from 1815 to the Famine.* New Haven: Yale University Press, 1932.
Ahlstrom, Sidney. *A Religious History of the American People.* New Haven: Yale University Press, 1972.
Arky, Lewis H. "The Mechanics' Union of Trade Associations and the Formation of the Philadelphia Working-men's Movement." *Pennsylvania Magazine of History and Biography* 76 (1952): 142–76.
Barnard, James. *Factory Legislation in Pennsylvania: Its History and Administration.* Philadelphia: Publications of the University of Pennsylvania Ser. in Political Economy and Public Law, no. 17, 1907.
Benson, Lee. *The Concept of Jacksonian Democracy: New York as a Test Case.* Pbk. ed., Princeton: Princeton University Press, 1961.
Bernstein, Leonard. "The Working People of Philadelphia from Colonial Times to the General Strike of 1835." *Pennsylvania Magazine of History and Biography* 74 (1950): 322–39.
Bestor, Arthur. *Backwoods Utopias: The Sectarian Origins and the*

Owenite Phase of Communitarian Socialism in America, 1663–1829.
2d ed. Philadelphia: University of Pennsylvania Press, 1970.

Billington, Ray Allen. *The Protestant Crusade, 1800–1860: A Study of the Origins of American Nativism.* New York: Macmillan, 1938.

Blumin, Stuart M. "Residential Mobility within the Nineteenth-century City." In *The People of Philadelphia: A History of Ethnic groups and Lower-class Life, 1790–1940,* ed. Allen F. Davis and Mark H. Haller. Philadelphia: Temple University Press, 1973.

Boston, Ray. *British Chartists in America, 1839–1900.* Manchester: England: Manchester University Press, 1971.

Bridenbaugh, Carl. *The Colonial Craftsman.* Pbk. ed. Chicago: University of Chicago Press, 1966.

Brody, David. "The Old Labor History and the New: In Search of an American Working Class." *Labor History* 20 (1979): 111–26.

Broehl, Wayne G., Jr. *The Molly Maguires.* New York: Vintage, 1964.

Byington, Margaret. *Homestead: The Households of a Mill Town.* 1910. Rpt., Pittsburgh: University of Pittsburgh Press, 1974.

Clark, Dennis. "A Pattern of Urban Growth: Residential Development and Church Location in Philadelphia." *Records of the American Catholic Historical Society* 82 (1971): 159–70.

———. *The Irish in Philadelphia: Ten Generations of Urban Experience.* Philadelphia: Temple University Press, 1973.

Clark, Norman H. *Deliver us from Evil: An Interpretation of American Prohibition.* New York: Norton, 1976.

Cole, Donald B. *Immigrant City: Lawrence, Massachusetts, 1845–1921.* Chapel Hill: University of North Carolina Press, 1963.

Commons, John R. "American Shoemakers, 1648–1895: A Sketch of Industrial Evolution." *Quarterly Journal of Economics* 24 (November 1909): 23–84.

——— et al., eds. *Documentary History of American Industrial Society.* 10 vols., A. H. Clark: Cleveland, 1910–1911. Rpt. Russell and Russell, 1958.

——— et al. *History of Labour in the United States.* 4 vols. New York: Macmillan, 1918–35.

Cott, Nancy F. *The Bonds of Womanhood: "Woman's Sphere" in New England, 1780–1835.* New Haven: Yale University Press, 1977.

Cross, Whitney R. *The Burned-over District: A Social and Intellectual History of Enthusiastic Religion in Western New York, 1800–1850.* Ithaca: Cornell University Press, 1950.

Dawley, Alan. *Class and Community: The Industrial Revolution in Lynn.* Cambridge: Harvard University Press, 1976.

——— and Paul Faler. "Workingclass Culture and Politics in the Industrial Revolution: Sources of Loyalism and Rebellion." *Journal of Social History* 9 (1976): 466–80.

Doherty, Robert W. "Social Basis of the Presbyterian Schism, 1837–1838: The Philadelphia Case." *Journal of Social History* 2 (1968): 69–79.

Erickson, Charlotte, ed. *Invisible Immigrants: The Adaptation of English and Scottish Immigrants in Nineteenth-century America.* Coral Gables: University of Miami Press, 1972.

Faler, Paul. "Cultural Aspects of the Industrial Revolution: Lynn, Massachusetts Shoemakers and Industrial Morality, 1826–1860." *Labor History* 15 (1974): 367–94.

———. "Working-class Historiography." *Radical America* 3 (1969): 56–68.

Feldberg, Michael. *The Philadelphia Riots of 1844: A Study of Ethnic Conflict.* Westport, Conn.: Greenwood Press, 1975.

———. "Urbanization as a Cause of Violence: Philadelphia as a Test Case." In *The Peoples of Philadelphia: A History of Ethnic Groups and Lower-class Life, 1790–1940,* ed. Allen F. Davis and Mark H. Haller. Philadelphia: Temple University Press, 1973.

Ferguson, Charles W. *Organizing to Beat the Devil: Methodists and the Making of America.* Garden City: Doubleday, 1971.

Foner, Eric. *Free Soil, Free Labor, Free Men: The Ideology of the Republican Party before the Civil War.* New York: Oxford University Press, 1970.

———. *Tom Paine and Revolutionary America.* New York: Oxford University Press, 1976.

Formisano, Ronald P. *The Birth of Mass Political Parties: Michigan, 1827–1861.* Princeton: Princeton University Press, 1971.

Geary, Sister M. Theopane. *History of Third Parties in Pennsylvania, 1840–1860.* Washington, D.C.: The Catholic University Press, 1938.

Geffen, Elizabeth M. "Philadelphia Protestantism Reacts to Social Reform Movements before the Civil War." *Pennsylvania History* 30 (1963): 192–212.

———. "Violence in Philadelphia in the 1840s and 1850s." *Pennsylvania History* 36 (1969): 381–410.

Greene, Victor R. *The Slavic Community on Strike: Immigrant Labor in Pennsylvania Anthracite.* South Bend: University of Notre Dame Press, 1968.

Griffin, Clifford S. *Their Brothers' Keepers: Moral Stewardship in the United States, 1800–1865.* New Brunswick: Rutgers University Press, 1960.

————. "Religious Benevolence as Social Control, 1815–1860."*Mississippi Valley Historical Review* 44 (1957): 423–44.

Groneman, Carol. "'She Earns as a Child, She Pays as a Man': Women Workers in a Mid-nineteenth-century New York City Community." In *Class, Sex, and the Woman Worker,* ed. Milton Cantor and Bruce Laurie. Westport, Conn.: Greenwood Press, 1977.

Gusfield, Joseph R. *Symbolic Crusade: Status Politics and the American Temperance Movement.* Urbana: University of Illinois Press, 1963.

Gutman, Herbert G. "Work, Culture, and Society in Industrializing America, 1815–1919." *American Historical Review* 78 (1973): 531–87.

Haller, Mark H. "Recurring Themes." In *The Peoples of Philadelphia: A History of Ethnic Groups and Lower-class Life, 1790–1940,* ed. Allen F. Davis and Mark H. Haller. Philadelphia: Temple University Press, 1973.

Hamerow, Theodore S. *Restoration, Revolution, Reaction: Economics and Politics in Germany, 1815–1871.* Princeton: Princeton University Press, 1858.

Handlin, Oscar. *Boston's Immigrants: A Study in Acculturation.* 2d. ed., rev. and enl. New York: Atheneum, 1968.

Harris, David. *Socialist Origins in the United States: American Forerunners of Marx, 1817–1832.* Assen: Van Gorcum, 1968.

Hartz, Lewis. *Economic Policy and Democratic Thought: Pennsylvania, 1776–1860.* Pbk. ed. Chicago: Quadrangle Books, 1968.

Herreshoff, David. *American Disciples of Marx: From the Age of Jackson to the Progressive Era.* Detroit: Wayne State University Press, 1967.

Hershberg, Theodore. "Free Blacks in Antebellum Philadelphia: A Study of Ex-slaves, Freeborn, and Socioeconomic Decline." *Journal of Social History* 5 (1971–72): 183–209.

Hirsch, Susan E. *Roots of the American Working Class: The Industrialization of the Crafts in Newark, 1800–1860.* Philadelphia: University of Pennsylvania Press, 1978.

Holt, Michael F. *Forging a Majority: The Formation of the Republican Party in Pittsburgh, 1848–1860.* New Haven: Yale University Press, 1969.

————. "The Politics of Impatience: The Origins of Know Nothingism." *Journal of American History* 60 (1973): 309–32.

Hugins, Walter A. *Jacksonian Democracy and the Working Class: A Study of the New York Workingmen's Movement.* Stanford: Stanford University Press, 1966.

Johnson, Allen and Dumas Malone, eds. *Dictionary of American Biography.* 20 vols. New York: Charles Scribner's Sons, 1929–1937.

Johnson, David R. "Crime Patterns in Philadelphia, 1840–1870." In *The Peoples of Philadelphia: A History of Ethnic Groups and Lower-class*

Life, 1790–1940, ed. Allen F. Davis and Mark H. Haller. Philadelphia: Temple University Press, 1973.

Johnson, Paul E. *A Shopkeeper's Millenium: Society and Revivals in Rochester, New York, 1815–1837.* New York: Hill and Wang, 1978.

Katz, Michael B. *The Irony of Early School Reform: Educational Innovation in Mid-nineteenth Century Massachusetts.* Cambridge: Harvard University Press, 1968.

Klebaner, Benjamin J. "The Home Relief Controversy in Philadelphia, 1782–1861." *Pennsylvania Magazine of History and Biography* 76 (1954): 413–23.

Kleinberg, Susan J. "The Systematic Study of Urban Women." *Historical Methods Newsletter* 9 (1975): 14–25.

Kleppner, Paul J. *The Cross of Culture: A Social Analysis of Midwestern Politics, 1850–1900.* New York: Free Press, 1970.

Knights, Peter R. *The Plain People of Boston, 1830–1860: A Study in City Growth.* New York: Oxford University Press, 1971.

Krout, John A. *Origins of Prohibition.* New York: Alfred A. Knopf, 1925.

Krueger, Thomas A. "American Labor Historiography, Old and New: A Review Essay." *Journal of Social History* 4 (1971): 277–85.

Kulik, Gary B. "Pawtucket Village and the Strike of 1824: The Origins of Class Conflict in Rhode Island." *Radical History Review* 17 (1978): 5–38.

Lannie, Vincent P. and Bernard C. Diethorn. "For the Honor and Glory of God: The Philadelphia Bible Riots of 1844." *History of Education Quarterly* 8 (1968): 44–106.

Laurie, Bruce. "Fire Companies and Gangs in Southwark: The 1840s." In *The Peoples of Philadelphia: A History of Ethnic Groups and Lower-class Life, 1790–1940,* ed. Allen F. Davis and Mark H. Haller. Philadelphia: Temple University Press, 1973.

———. "'Nothing on Compulsion': Life Styles of Philadelphia Artisans, 1820–1850." *Labor History* 15 (1974): 337–66.

———, and Mark Schmitz. "Manufacture and Productivity: The Making of an Industrial Base, 1850–1880." In *Towards an Interdisciplinary History of the City: Work, Space, Family, and Group Experience in Nineteenth-century Philadelphia,* ed. Theodore Hershberg. New York: Oxford University Press, forthcoming, 1980.

———, Theodore Hershberg, and George Alter. "Immigrants and Industry: The Philadelphia Experience, 1850–1880." *Journal of Social History* 9 (1975): 219–48.

Lemon, James T. *The Poor Man's Best Country: A Geographical Study of Southeastern Pennsylvania.* Baltimore: The Johns Hopkins University Press, 1972.

Lindstrom, Diane. *Economic Growth in the Philadelphia Region, 1810–1850.* New York: Columbia University Press, 1978.

Macdonagh, Oliver. "The Irish Famine Emigration to the United States." *Perspectives in American History* 10 (1976): 357–448.

Marsden, George M. *The Evangelical Mind and the New School Experience.* New Haven: Yale University Press, 1970.

Mathews, Donald G. *Slavery and Methodism: A Chapter in American Morality, 1780–1845.* Princeton: Princeton University Press, 1965.

———. "The Second Great Awakening as an Organizing Process, 1780–1830: An Hypothesis." *American Quarterly* 21 (1969): 23–43.

McAvoy, T. Thomas. "The Formation of the Catholic Minority in the United States, 1820–1860." *Review of Politics* 10 (1948): 13–34.

McLellan, David. *Karl Marx: His Life and Thought.* New York: Harper and Row, 1973.

Miller, Richard G. "Gentry and Entrepreneurs: A Socioeconomic Analysis of Philadelphia in the 1790s." *Rocky Mountain Social Science Journal* 12 (1975): 71–84.

Miyakawa, T. Scott. *Protestants and Pioneers: Individualism and Conformity on the American Frontier.* Chicago: University of Chicago Press, 1964.

Modell, John. "The Peopling of a Working-class Ward: Reading, Pennsylvania, 1850." *Journal of Social History* 5 (1971): 71–95.

Montgomery, David. *Beyond Equality: Labor and the Radical Republicans, 1862–1872.* New York: Alfred A. Knopf, 1967.

———. "The Shuttle and the Cross: Weavers and Artisans in the Kensington Riots of 1844." *Journal of Social History* 5 (1972): 411–46.

———. "The Working Classes of the Pre-industrial City, 1780–1830." *Labor History* 9 (1968): 3–22.

———. "Workers' Control of Machine Production in the Nineteenth Century." *Labor History* 17 (1976): 485–509.

Murphy, Eugene. *The Parish of St. John the Baptist, Manayunk: The First One Hundred Years.* Philadelphia: Press of the Church Printing and Envelope Company, 1931.

Neale, R. S. *Class and Ideology in the Nineteenth Century.* London: Routledge and Kegan Paul, 1972.

North, Douglass C. *The Economic Growth of the United States, 1790–1860.* Pbk. ed. New York: Norton, 1966.

Noyes, P. H. *Organization and Revolution: Working-class Associations in the German Revolutions of 1848–1849.* Princeton: Princeton University Press, 1966.

Oberholtzer, Ellis P. *Philadelphia: A History of the City and Its People.* 4 vols. Philadelphia: S. J. Clark Publishing Company, 1911.

Osofsky, Gilbert. "Abolitionists, Irish Immigrants, and the Dilemmas of Romantic Nationalism." *American Historical Review* 80 (1975): 889–912.

Pendleton, Othniel O., Jr. "Temperance and the Evangelical Churches." *Journal of the Presbyterian Historical Society* 25 (1947): 14–45.

Pessen, Edward. *Most Uncommon Jacksonians: The Radical Leaders of the Early Labor Movement.* Albany: State University of New York Press, 1967.

———. *Riches, Class, and Power before the Civil War.* Lexington, Mass.: D. C. Heath, 1973.

Pred, Allen R. *Urban Growth and the Circulation of Information: The United States System of Cities, 1790–1840.* Cambridge: Harvard University Press, 1973.

Price, Jacob M. "Economic Function and the Growth of American Port Towns in the Eighteenth Century." *Perspectives in American History* 8 (1974): 123–88.

Richards, Leonard L. *"Gentlemen of Property and Standing": Anti-abolitionist Mobs in Jacksonian America.* New York: Oxford University Press, 1970.

Rosenberg, Charles E. *The Cholera Years: The United States in 1832, 1849, and 1866.* Chicago: University of Chicago Press, 1962.

Runcie, John. "'Hunting the Nigs' in Philadelphia: The Race Riot of 1834." *Pennsylvania History* 39 (1972): 187–218.

Samuel, Raphael. "The Workshop of the World: Steam Power and Hand Technology in Mid-victorian Britain." *History Workshop Journal* 3 (1977): 6–72.

Scharf, J. Thomas and Thompson Westcott. *History of Philadelphia, 1609–1884.* 3 vols. Philadelphia: L. H. Evarts, 1884.

Schlesinger, Arthur M., Jr. *The Age of Jackson.* Boston: Little, Brown, 1945.

Schlüter, Hermann. *Die Anfange der deutchen Arbeiterbewegung in Amerika.* Stuttgart: J. H. W. Dietz, 1907.

Scott, Joan W. *The Glassworkers of Carmaux: French Craftsmen and Political Action in a Nineteenth-century City.* Cambridge: Harvard University Press, 1974.

Sewell, William H., Jr. "The Working Class of Marseille under the Second Republic: Social Structure and Political Behavior." In *Workers in the Industrial Revolution,* ed. Peter N. Stearns and Daniel J. Walkowitz. New Brunswick: Transaction Books, 1974.

Smith, Merritt Roe. *Harpers Ferry Armory and the New Technology: The Challenge of Change.* Ithaca: Cornell University Press, 1977.

Smith-Rosenberg, Carol. *Religion and the Rise of the American City: The New York City Mission Movement, 1812–1870.* Ithaca: Cornell University Press, 1971.

Snyder, Charles M. *The Jacksonian Heritage: Pennsylvania Politics, 1833–1848*. Harrisburg: Pennsylvania Historical and Museum Commission, 1958.

Sullivan, William A. "Did Labor Support Andrew Jackson?" *Political Science Quarterly* 62 (1947): 569–80.

———. *The Industrial Worker in Pennsylvania, 1800–1840*. Harrisburg Pennsylvania Historical and Museum Commission, 1955.

———. "Philadelphia Labor during the Jackson Era." *Pennsylvania History* 15 (1948): 305–20.

Taylor, George R. *The Transportation Revolution, 1815–1860*. 1951. Pbk. edition. New York: Harper and Row, 1968.

Thernstrom, Stephan. *The Other Bostonians: Poverty and Progress in the American Metropolis, 1880–1970*. Cambridge: Harvard University Press, 1973.

———. *Poverty and Progress: Social Mobility in a Nineteenth-century City*. Cambridge: Harvard University Press, 1964.

———. "Urbanization, Migration, and Social Mobility in Late Nineteenth-century America." In *Towards a New Past: Dissenting Essays in American History*, ed. Barton J. Bernstein. New York: Pantheon, 1968.

Tholfsen, Trygve. *Working-class Radicalism in Mid-victorian britain*. New York: Columbia University Press, 1977.

Thompson, E. P. *The Making of the English Working Class*. 1963. Pbk. ed. New York: Vintage, 1966.

———. "Time, Work, Discipline, and Industrial Capitalism." *Past and Present* 38 (1967): 56–97.

Tooker, Elva. *Nathan Trotter, Philadelphia Merchant*, 1956. Rpt. New York: Arno Press, 1972.

Walker, Mack. *German Home Towns: Community, State and General Estate, 1648–1871*. Ithaca: Cornell University Press, 1971.

———. *Germany and the Emigration, 1816–1885*. Cambridge: Harvard University Press, 1964.

Walkowitz, Daniel J. *Worker City, Company Town: Iron and Cotton-Worker Protest in Troy and Cohoes, New York, 1855–1884*. Urbana: University of Illinois Press, 1978.

Wallace, Anthony F. C. *Rockdale: The Growth of an American Village in the Early Industrial Revolution*. New York: Alfred A. Knopf, 1978.

Ware, Norman J. *The Industrial Worker, 1840–1860: The Reaction of American Industrial Society to the Advance of the Industrial Revolution*. Boston and New York: Houghton Mifflin, 1924.

Warner, Sam Bass, Jr. "If all the World Were Philadelphia: A Scaffolding for Urban History, 1774–1930." *American Historical Review* 74 (1968) 26–43.

――――. "Innovation and Industrialization in Philadelphia, 1800–1850." In *The Historian and the City*, ed. John Burchard and Oscar Handlin. Cambridge: MIT Press, 1963.

――――. *The Private City: Philadelphia in Three Periods of Its Growth.* Philadelphia: University of Pennsylvania Press, 1968.

Welter, Barbara. "The Cult of True Womanhood, 1820–1860." *American Quarterly* 18 (1966): 151–74.

――――. "The Feminization of American Religion, 1800–1860." In *Clio's Consciousness Raised: New Perspectives on the History of Women,* ed. Mary Hartman and Lois Banner. New York: Harper and Row, 1974.

Williams, Raymond. *Marxism and Literature.* Oxford: Oxford University Press, 1977.

Wittke, Carl F. *The German-language Press in America.* Lexington, Ky.: University of Kentucky Press, 1957.

――――. *Refugees of Revolution: The German Forty-eighters in America.* Philadelphia: University of Pennsylvania Press, 1952.

――――. *The Utopian Communist: A Biography of Wilhelm Weitling, Nineteenth-century Reformer.* Baton Rouge: Louisiana State University Press, 1950.

Zieger, Robert. "Workers and Scholars: Recent Trends in American Labor Historiography." *Labor History* 13 (1972): 245–66.

Theses, Dissertations, and Other Unpublished Works

Arky, Lewis H. "The Mechanics' Union of Trade Associations and the Formation of the Philadelphia Working-men's Movement." Ph.D. diss., University of Pennsylvania, 1952.

Blumin, Stuart M. "Mobility in a Nineteenth-century City: Philadelphia, 1820–1860." Ph.D. diss., University of Pennsylvania, 1968.

Davis, Edward B. "Albert Barnes, 1798–1870: Exponent of New School Presbyterianism." Ph.D. diss., Princeton Theological Seminary, 1961.

Faler, Paul G. "Workingmen, Mechanics, and Social Change: Lynn, Massachusetts, 1800–1860." Ph.D. diss., University of Wisconsin, 1971.

Fink, Leon. "Workingmen's Democracy: The Knights of Labor in Local Politics, 1886–1896." Ph.D. diss., University of Rochester, 1977.

Greenfield, Richard. "Industrial Location in Philadelphia, 1850–1880." Working paper, Philadelphia Social History Project, University of Pennsylvania, 1979.

Katz, Michael B. "Four Propositions about Family and Social Structure in Pre-industrial Society." Paper delivered at the Comparative Social Mobility Conference, Institute for Advanced Study, Princeton University, July 15–17, 1972.

Laurie, Bruce. "The Working People of Philadelphia, 1827–1853." Ph.D. diss., University of Pittsburgh, 1971.

McLeod, Richard A. "The Philadelphia Artisan, 1828–1850." Ph.D. diss., University of Missouri, 1971.

Modell, John. "A Regional Approach to Urban Growth: The Philadelphia Region in the Early Nineteenth Century." Paper delivered at the Fall Regional Economic History Conference, Eleutherian Mills–Hagley Foundation, Wilmington, Del., 1971.

Neilly, Andrew. "The Violent Volunteers: A History of the Philadelphia Volunteer Fire Department, 1736–1871." Ph.D. diss., University of Pennsylvania, 1959.

Ott, Philip W. "The Mind of Early Methodism, 1800–1840." Ph.D. diss., University of Pennsylvania, 1968.

Pendleton, Othniel O., Jr. "The Influence of Evangelical Churches upon Humanitarian Reform: A Case-Study Giving Particular Attention to Philadelphia, 1790–1840." Ph.D. diss., University of Pennsylvania, 1945.

Quimby, Ian M. G. "Apprenticeship in Colonial Philadelphia." M.A. thesis, University of Delaware, 1963.

Rumbarger, John J. "The Social Origins and Function of the Political Temperance Movement in the Reconstruction of American Society." Ph.D. diss., University of Pennsylvania, 1968.

Weiss, Rona. "The Transition to Industrial Capitalism: Workers and Entrepreneurs in Randolph, Massachusetts, 1800–1870. Seminar paper, University of Massachusetts at Amherst, 1974.

Wilentz, Sean. "Ritual, Republicanism, and the Artisans of Jacksonian New York City." Paper delivered at the Annual Meeting of the Organization of American Historians, New York, April 14, 1978.

Index